The Daoist Monastic Manual

AMERICAN ACADEMY OF RELIGION
TEXTS AND TRANSLATIONS SERIES

SERIES EDITOR
Mark Csikszentmihalyi, University of Wisconsin–Madison

A Publication Series of
The American Academy of Religion
and Oxford University Press

THE SOURCE OF HUMAN GOOD
Henry N. Wieman
With an Introduction by Marvin C. Shaw

RELIGION OF REASON
Out of the Sources of Judaism
Hermann Cohen
Translated, with an Introduction by Simon Kaplan
Introductory essays by Leo Strauss
Introductory essays for the second edition by Steven S. Schwarzchild and Kenneth Seeskin

DURKHEIM ON RELIGION
Émile Durkheim
Edited by W. S. F. Pickering

ON THE *GLAUBENSLEHRE*
Two Letters to Dr. Lücke
Friedrich D. E. Schleiermacher
Translated by James Duke and Francis Fiorenza

HERMENEUTICS
The Handwritten Manuscripts
Friedrich D. E. Schleiermacher
Edited by Heina Kimmerle
Translated by James Duke and Jack Forstman

THE DAOIST MONASTIC MANUAL
A Translation of the Fengdao Kejie
Livia Kohn

AMERICAN ACADEMY OF RELIGION

The Daoist Monastic Manual

A Translation of the Fengdao Kejie

Livia Kohn

UNIVERSITY PRESS

2004

OXFORD

UNIVERSITY PRESS

Auckland Bangkok Buenos Aires Cape Town Chennai
Dar es Salaam Delhi Hong Kong Istanbul Karachi Kolkata
Kuala Lumpur Madrid Melbourne Mexico City Mumbai Nairobi
São Paulo Shanghai Taipei Tokyo Toronto

Published by Oxford University Press, Inc.
198 Madison Avenue, New York, New York 10016

www.oup.com

Oxford is a registered trademark of Oxford University Press

Library of Congress Cataloging-in-Publication Data

Fengdao kejie. English
The Daoist monastic manual : a translation of the Fengdao kejie /
[Edited] Livia Kohn.
p.   cm.—(American Academy of Religion texts and translations series)
Includes bibliographical references and index.
ISBN 0-19-517070-9
1. Monasticism and religious orders, Taoist.   2. Taoism—China.
I. Title: Translation of the Fengdao kejie.   II. Kohn, Livia, 1956–
III. Title.   IV. Series.
BL1941 .F4513 2004
299'.514657—dc21   2003009870

9 8 7 6 5 4 3 2 1
Printed in the United States of America
on acid-free paper

Acknowledgments

This translation of the *Fengdao kejie* grew over the past ten years. I first completed a rough draft in 1993, then worked on the manuscript extensively during a sabbatical leave in Japan in 1996–97, when I also completed a study of the text's date and compilation, which appeared in *Far Eastern History* 13/14 (1997). In the years following, I examined related texts and explored various issues of medieval Daoist monasticism, eventually writing an analytical study, entitled *Monastic Life in Medieval Daoism* (Honolulu: University of Hawaii Press, 2003), which was further followed by an examination of the various Daoist community rules, forthcoming under the title *How to Be a Daoist: Behavioral Guidelines through the Ages* (Cambridge, Mass.: Three Pines Press).

In the course of undertaking this work, I have incurred many debts of gratitude. First and foremost, I am deeply indebted to Boston University for granting me leave of absence twice to work on the text and its related project. I am also grateful to the National Endowment of the Humanities, whose generous funding made the completion of the translation possible. Both in Japan and in the United States, I profited greatly from the extensive libraries and the support of many friends and colleagues, including Yoshikawa Tadao, Tuzuki Masako, Antonino Forte, Hubert Durt, Erik Zürcher, Imre Hamar, Monica Esposito, Robert Sharf, and Harold Roth. In the process of publication, moreover, I benefited much from the insightful comments and suggestions of the two anonymous readers for Oxford University Press. I am very grateful to them all.

The *Fengdao kejie* is a powerful and inspiring document on the concrete situation of medieval Daoist monasteries and priestly ranks. Showing how Daoists organized their institutional life and perceived of it in relation to society and the greater universe, the text grants many fascinating insights that greatly advance our understanding of both Chinese culture and monasticism as an institution. It deserves to be read in its completeness and with all the floweriness and technicalities of its language. This translation is accordingly dedicated to honoring the text. It strives to present a detailed, complete, and accurate rendition of the original source, acknowledging difficulties and including relevant variants and supplementary readings.

The translation proper is preceded by an introduction which consists of three chapters: an outline of the development and nature of Daoist institutions; a discussion of the date and compilation of the text, updated from its original version published in 1997; and a presentation of related medieval sources and the specific terminology used in them, providing insight into the literary environment, worldview, and classification systems of medieval Daoist monasticism. These chapters serve to locate the text in the greater tradition of medieval Daoism. Following the translation, this book contains a glossary of technical terms, bibliography, and index, to make the text as accessible as possible.

Contents

Fragments and Citations

PART I

Introduction

I

The Development and Nature of Daoist Institutions

Daoist monasteries and priestly training seminaries arose in the sixth century and came to flourish greatly under the Tang dynasty (618–907), which saw itself as divinely supported by Lord Lao, the central deity of the Daoist religion and claimed ancestor of the Tang ruling house. They stand at the apex of several centuries of Daoist institutional development, which began in the second century C.E. under the Later Han dynasty (23–220 C.E.), when Zhang Daoling 張道陵 founded the first organized Daoist school, known as Orthodox Unity (Zhengyi 正一) or Celestial Masters (Tianshi 天師). A strictly lay-based communal organization, the Celestial Masters had priestly ranks, communal lodges, formal initiation ceremonies, annual festivals, and sets of moral rules for both leaders and followers.

In their wake and under growing Buddhist influence, Daoists in the fifth century began to establish community centers that also housed celibate practitioners and functioned as separate institutions within larger society rather than as a semiindependent state. Still, the communal ideas and practices of the Celestial Masters continued to play an active role in Chinese society, and the formal institutions of the Tang inherited their practices as much as the monastic arrangements of the Buddhist-inspired community centers. The *Fengdao kejie* 奉道科戒 (Rules and Precepts for Worshiping the Dao, DZ 1125)[1] is a key text of the early Tang dynasty that outlines the ideal organization of medieval Daoist institutions, presenting the fundamental rules and organizational principles involved in their establishment. It is unique in both its scope and the amount of concrete detail it provides, allowing a rare glimpse of the living conditions, physical realities, and ritual practices in medieval Chinese monasteries. Relying strongly on earlier models and sources, it represents a high point in the institutional organization of medieval Daoism.

---

1. Numbers of texts in the Daoist Canon (*Daozang* 道藏, abbreviated DZ) are given according to Schipper 1975; Komjathy 2002.

The Early Celestial Masters

The Celestial Masters arose as one of two major movements of early Daoism, the other being the Way of Great Peace (Taiping dao 太平道; see Hendrischke 2000). They were centered in Sichuan in southwest China, while the Taiping were located mainly in the east, in Shandong. Both groups had very similar backgrounds and ideologies, their respective leaders, Zhang Daoling and Gan Ji 干吉, having received revelations from Lord Lao, the divinized philosopher Laozi who had become increasingly a focus of veneration and sacrality in the Former Han dynasty (206 B.C.E.–6 C.E.; see Kohn 1998b). They both called their leaders "celestial masters," signifying the empowerment they had received from Lord Lao, and they both believed that the world was coming to an end and that their followers were the "seed people" of the new age, anticipating in beliefs and conduct the millennium of the Dao to come.[2] In view of this goal, they created stringent communities and priestly hierarchies, setting the tone for all later Daoist institutions.

The Celestial Masters in particular divided their territory into twenty-four districts matching the twenty-four solar energies of the year, each governed by a priestly officer known as libationer (jijiu 祭酒) who reported directly to the Celestial Master himself. Beneath them were the so-called demon soldiers (guizu 鬼卒), meritorious leaders of households who represented smaller units in the organization. In anticipation of the equality practiced in later monasteries and matching patterns found in millennial organizations worldwide (see Turner 1969), all leadership positions could be filled by either men or women, Han Chinese or ethnic minorities. At the bottom were the common followers, again organized and counted according to households. Each of these had to pay the rice tax or its equivalent in silk, paper, brushes, ceramics, or handicrafts, just as later ordinands had to present material pledges to the Dao upon entry into the order. In addition, each member of the Celestial Masters, from children on up, underwent formal initiations at regular intervals and was equipped with a list of spirit generals for protection against demons—75 for an unmarried person and 150 for a married couple. The list of spirit generals was called a register (lu 籙) and was carried, together with protective talismans, in a piece of silk around the waist, again a practice that continued in later monasteries. Unlike in monasteries, however, where strict celibacy became the rule, initiations in the early communities, at least at the adult level, involved an imitation of the cosmic interaction of yin and yang through the formally choreographed intercourse between selected nonmarried couples. Known as the "harmonization of qi" (heqi 合氣), this was condemned in Confucian and Buddhist sources as "orgiastic" and accordingly is not well documented in the sources.[3]

---

2. The difference here was that the Great Peace movement believed their leader to be the emperor of the new age and, in 184, rose in rebellion against the Han. They were defeated and their organization and documents scattered, but they contributed significantly to the downfall of the house of Han. The Celestial Masters, on the contrary, saw themselves as advisers to the new ruler and restrained their military urges, with the result that they have survived to the present day. See Seidel 1984.

3. Studies of the sexual practices of the Celestial Masters include Stein 1963; Kobayashi 1992; Yan 2001.

Everything a member did or omitted to do was closely monitored by a celestial administration that kept records of life and death and that consisted of the Three Bureaus (*sanguan* 三官) of Heaven, Earth, and Water. These three were celebrated at the major festivals of the year, known as the Three Primes (*sanyuan* 三元), held on the fifteenth day of the first, seventh, and tenth months. These times were also the occasion of general assemblies and tax management: in the first month, the tax was set according to the number of people in the household; in the seventh and tenth months, it was collected as the harvest was brought in. The festivals to the Three Primes and other major community events were celebrated in grand style with lavish banquets known as kitchen-feasts (*chu* 廚). Except for those extraordinary occasions, though, followers lived very frugally and were encouraged to follow a set of three times nine precepts based on Laozi's *Daode jing* 道德經, which they recited on a regular basis. The precepts prohibited killing, stealing, and the creation of social upheaval while encouraging members to develop nonaction, desirelessness, austerity, and discipline (see Bokenkamp 1997; Kohn forthcoming). All these characteristics carried over into the monastic institution. Here, too, practitioners lived very frugally and simply and had hardly any personal property; ritual banquets symbolized the close communion with the deities; and everybody's actions were monitored by celestial bureaucrats arranged according to the the Three Primes who punished sinners by a reduction in life expectancy.

Aside from living morally and harmonizing yin and yang, the early communal Daoists joined popular believers of the time in that they were very concerned with the impact of demons on their lives. Demons were believed to be everywhere and come in every shape, from the lowly rabbit and the dirty rat to all sorts of natural and supernatural creatures. A list of such demons has been excavated from a Han tomb, and several others are found in the earliest surviving texts of the Celestial Masters. To combat them, members had to fortify their houses and bodies with talismans, learn to recognize the demons and call them by their proper names, and visualize themselves as demon-conquering heroes. This would banish the demons forthwith and relieve followers from their harm, especially when accompanied by the ritual formula "Swiftly, swiftly, in accordance with the statutes and ordinances" (*jiji ru lüling* 急急如律令), which concludes all ritual incantations and petitions of the Celestial Masters. The formula remained active in the later religion and is still used today (see Maeda 1989; Miyazawa 1994; Seidel 1987).

If, despite these measures, someone was attacked by a demon, he or she would suffer sickness and disease. Moreover, such an attack could occur only because the person had been careless and had a moral failing. As a result, all healing of the Celestial Masters was undertaken through ritual and magic; acupuncture, herbs, and other medical treatments were expressly prohibited. First the sick person was isolated in a so-called quiet chamber or oratory (*jingshi* 靜室; see Yoshikawa 1987), an adaptation of a Han institution for punishing wayward officials and a forerunner of monastic subtemples used for personal cultivation. There they had to think of their sins going all the way back to their birth to try and find a explanation for the illness.

Once certain sins had been identified, a senior master would come to write them down—in triplicate and together with a formal petition for their eradication from the person's divine record. The three copies would then, in a formal ceremony, be transmitted to Heaven (by burning), Earth (by burying), and Water (by casting into a river), whose officials supposedly set the record straight and restored the person's good health. Additional measures of purification involved the ingestion of "talisman water"—the ashes of a talisman dissolved in water (*fushui* 符水)—gymnastic exercises (*daoyin* 導引), and meditations (*jingsi* 靜思), all practices later undertaken in Daoist monastic institutions. While later monastics did not eschew the healing methods of Chinese medicine, their attitude to suffering remained very similar, and the practice of both sending petitions to the gods and undertaking self-cultivation for purification remained.

The early organization of the Celestial Masters did not survive untroubled for very long. In 215, their leader Zhang Lu 張魯, the grandson of the founder, got involved in the battles at the end of the Han dynasty, and had to submit to the warlord Cao Cao 曹操, who in due course decided not to tolerate a separate organization in his territory. As a result, large numbers of Celestial Masters followers were forcefully evacuated and had to migrate to different parts of the empire, spreading their cult as they went and laying the foundation for the strong Daoist school they later became.

The Buddhist Impact

The second major force that shaped Daoist institutions is Buddhism. Buddhism reached China through merchants, refugees, envoys, hostages, and mendicant monks as early as the Han dynasty (Tsukamoto and Hurvitz 1985, 8; Zürcher 1959, 23). Its presence was officially acknowledged in the first century C.E. with the famous dream of Emperor Ming of a great sage arising in the west and the first shrines erected by Chinese aristocrats, such as Prince Ying of Chu (Tsukamoto and Hurvitz 1985, 43–4, 60–4). The first monasteries are not documented until the late second century C.E. (Zürcher 1959, 28), when also the earliest translations of Buddhist texts appeared. They were for the most part works on doctrine (*abhidharma*) and meditation (*dhyâna*) that originated from both major schools of Buddhism, the ancient mainstream and the newly arising Mahâyâna (Zürcher 1959, 32). The translation style, morever, made heavy use of Sanskrit transliterations, so that terms and concepts remained rather obscure.

This changed in the third and fourth centuries, when a translation form known as "matching the meanings" (*geyi* 格義) arose. This used native Daoist terms and concepts to express Buddhist ideas, so that, for example, *nirvâna* became "nonaction" and *prajnâ* was turned into "nonknowledge" (Zürcher 1959, 16). In addition, at this time, native Chinese first obtained the right to become monks—although traditional Confucians strongly objected to the idea of giving up the family, shaving off one's hair, and living on the donations of others. The first aristocratic monks emerged, and Chinese Buddhist thought began to develop, notably through figures such as Huiyuan 慧遠 (334–417), Daoan 道安 (312–385), and Sengzhao 僧肇 (374–414). Still, monastic institutions were small, scattered, and run individually by abbots according to their versions of the rules.

The big breakthrough came in the fifth century with the northern Toba-Wei rulers who supported the various organized religions of China and made use of their organizations in administering the country (Gernet 1995, 233). They sponsored the Kuchan monk Kumârajîa (350–409) in an extensive translation project, which created a standardized terminology for Buddhist concepts and provided much needed information on worldview and practice. Authoritative translation of the Buddhist monks' rules, the *Vinaya*, appeared together with major doctrinal scriptures such as the *Lotus sûtra*, the *Vimalakirti nirdesa*, and the *Avatamsaka sûtra*.[4] This massive increase of available information in an accessible language that presented Buddhism neither as utterly alien nor as a milder variant of philosophical Daoism created a new religious environment in which both Buddhist and Daoist institutions came to flourish greatly.

Buddhism brought along not only monastic organization and moral rules but also the ideal of the renouncer, the notion of a transcendent community dedicated to personal liberation, and the creation of an ideal organization that stood apart from and opposed to normative society while yet offering rulers new models and support. In terms of worldview, it enhanced the Chinese vision with the doctrines of karma and retribution, which placed the responsibility for all present circumstances and actions on the individual and extended the perspective on human life beyond the present to include past and future forms of existence (see Zürcher 1980).

Adopted universally in Daoism but most strongly in the Lingbao 靈寶 (Numinous Treasure) school, which began shortly before the inception of the Kumârajîa project in the late fourth century (see Yamada 2000), the Daoist understanding of the doctrine of karma and retribution created a new level of Daoist worldview. This involved four major tenets:

1. The belief in rebirth and the retribution of sins or good deeds accumulated during one's own former lives, added to those committed by oneself in this life and to those of one's ancestors

---

4. In addition to the *Pratimoksa*, a list of about 250 transgressions against individual morality and etiquette, which had first been translated in 251, four separate *Vinayas* were translated in the early fifth century:

1. The "Ten Chapter Vinaya" of the Sarvastivâdins (*Shisong lü* 十誦律, T. 1435, 23.1–470), translated under Kumârajîva in 404–409
2. The "Four Part Vinaya" of the Dharmaguptakas (*Sifen lü* 四分律, T. 1428, 22.567–1072), translated by the Kashmirian Buddhayasas in 410–412
3. The "Five Part Vinaya" of the Mahîsâsakas (*Wufen lü* 五分律, T. 1421, 22.1–194), brought to China by Faxian 法顯 and rendered into Chinese by Buddhajîva in 422–23
4. A new version of the "Great Community Vinaya" (*Mohe sengqi lü* 摩訶僧祇律, T. 1425, 22.227–549), imported by Faxian and translated by Buddhabhadra in 416–418 (see Foulk 1991, 9; Hirakawa 1960).

2. The vision of long-term supernatural torture chambers known as "earth prisons" (*diyu* 地獄) or hells, as well as of punishments by being reborn in the body of an animal or hungry ghost

3. The trust in the efficacy of various forms of ritual, such as rites of repentance and the giving of offerings, to alleviate the karmic burden

4. The increasing faith in savior figures, such as bodhisattvas, gods, and the perfected, who would use their unlimited power and compassion to raise people from the worldly mire (see Kohn 1998c)

Daoist monastic institutions, as they slowly emerged in the fifth and sixth centuries, in this context came to be places for the veneration of savior figures, the performance of rituals for ancestors and good fortune, and the expiation of sins of both living and dead family members. As is made clear in the early sections of the *Fengdao kejie*, which discuss the karmic retribution of good and bad deeds, monastics—in both their roles as recluses and priests—became karmically powerful representatives of a divine law that pervaded everything but was most tangible in the recluses' own persons and institutions. They were known as *fashen* 法身 or "holy persons." Literally indicating the "body of the divine law" or, in its Buddhist reading, "dharma body," *fashen* originally referred to an abstract concept indicating the pure form of existence of a buddha (Mochizuki 1936, 4396b–97c). It was adopted in Daoism to indicate the highest gods as embodiments of the pure Dao and also, in its more concrete reading, the "holy persons" of the religious.

In terms of organization, moreover, the Buddhist model led the way both for the inner structure of Daoist monasteries and for their outside relationship with society and the state. On the most elementary physical level, the Buddhist monastery became the model for the Daoist in terms of the layout and names of buildings, the setting up of statues, and the establishment of endowed lands and properties. On the practical plane, it set the tone for the daily ritual schedule, the routine and discipline of monks and nuns, the monthly fast days and annual purgations, as well as the internal ranks and hierarchy of the institution. At the same time, it had little impact on the treatment of women, who were taken much more seriously in Daoism than in Buddhism; on the ritual vestments, formal accessories, and hairstyles, in which Daoists followed traditional Chinese rather than foreign models; and on the contents of the liturgy and the essential structure of Daoist ritual.

The First Centers

By the fifth century, when the Buddhist impact began to be felt, the Celestial Masters had undergone a period of outward expansion (due to their diaspora) and had gradually transformed from a completely separate community into an organized religion that was accessible to any interested citizen. At the same time, their community coherence had declined considerably until it reached the point where members failed to pay their taxes or attend assemblies, libationers were not performing the proper rites, and many returned to the more shamanistic practices of the general population.[5] In the fifth century, then, they were present in two different branches, a northern and a southern branch, which were both eagerly reorganizing and revitalizing the earlier teachings.

In the north, Kou Qianzhi 寇謙之 (365–448), the son of a Celestial Masters family, became a Daoist hermit and visionary on Mount Song 嵩山. In 415 and 423, he received revelations from Lord Lao that appointed him the new Celestial Master and provided him with both longevity methods and community rules. The latter consisted of twenty *juan* (scrolls) and were known as the "New Code," today partially extant in the *Laojun yinsong jiejing* 老君音誦誡經 (Lord Lao's Scripture of Recited Precepts, DZ 785). Taking his new vision and community organization to court, Kou found the support of the prime minister, Cui Hao 崔浩, and became head of a state-sponsored Daoism, the so-called Daoist theocracy, which was geared to bring peace and harmony to the Toba-Wei empire. After establishing Daoist institutions throughout the country, the emperor himself accepted Daoist initiation in 440 and changed his reign title to "Perfect Lord of Great Peace" (Taiping zhenjun 太平真君). Successful for some time, the theocracy declined with Kou's death in 448 and ended with the execution of Cui Hao in 451 (see Mather 1979; Yang 1956). It was later replaced with a Buddhist-run model of imperial administration, known as the sangha-households (see Sargent 1957).

Kou Qianzhi is an important figure in the development of Daoist institutions, not only because his community rules were spread through the entire country but also because he is the first Daoist known to have been actively celibate and a monastic resident. His official headquarters in the Toba capital was an institution called Chongxu si 崇虛寺 (Monastery of Venerating Emptiness), using the Buddhist term for "monastery" (Schipper 1984, 208; Kohn 2003). He and his Daoist followers lived a celibate life bound by a regular schedule and community rules. The priests, on the other hand, who administered the people throughout the country, were more like libationers, that is, married householders with special ritual rank and accomplishment. This dual organization of the clergy remained valid throughout medieval Daoism, joining celibate monastics and married priests in one organization under the protection of the state. Recluses, then, served as the spiritual models and training guides of priests, and larger monasteries functioned also as seminaries for priestly training and as liaisons with the political authorities. As a result, in medieval Daoism—as in medieval Chinese Buddhism and in Zen Buddhism even today—priests and monastics belonged to the same ritual hierarchy and trained in the same institutions, described in detail in the *Fengdao kejie*.

The early monastic Daoists under Kou Qianzhi performed rites for the sake of the empire and engaged in personal longevity and meditational techniques. Kou himself received various "methods of nourishing *qi* [vital energy] and

5. The situation of the Celestial Masters at the time is particularly documented in the *Daomen kelue* 道門科略 (Abridged Codes for the Daoist Community, DZ 1127) by the ritual master Lu Xiujing 陸修靜 (406–477; see Nickerson 1996; 2000).

practicing gymnastics" in his revelations and, following them, gained a physical lightness and radiant complexion like the immortals of old (*Weishu* 魏書 114). His "New Code" of rules, moreover, describes daily, seasonal, and special rites to be observed, often involving formal banquets and community meetings. While the rules were geared toward the libationers who administered the people, it can be assumed that the monastic leaders in the capital followed a similar regimen, anticipating the monastic rules to come (Kohn 2000, 302–3).

After the end of the theocracy, moreover, the northern Celestial Masters had to vacate their quarters in the capital and became freelance Daoists. Many of them congregated in a newly established center in the Zhongnan mountains, about forty miles southwest of the capital. Here Yin Tong 尹通, an alleged descendant of Yin Xi 尹喜, the guardian of the pass and first recipient of Laozi's *Daode jing*, had established his ancestral homestead, which he called Louguan 樓觀 or "Lookout Tower" after Yin Xi's supposed astrological endeavors. He proceeded to create a formal legend surrounding this place, claiming that the transmission of the *Daode jing* did not actually take place at the Hangu Pass 函谷關 where Laozi and Yin Xi met according to traditional sources, but rather at Louguan where Yin Xi took the sage for his greater comfort.

Over time, Louguan grew significantly and rose to prominence; it also became the first established monastery of Daoism, formally initiating the appellation *guan* 觀 for "monastery" which has remained standard ever since. An early code of precepts associated with the Celestial Masters at Louguan, the *Taishang Laojun jiejing* 太上老君戒經 (Precepts of the Highest Lord Lao, DZ 784), has survived in fragments. It presents a Daoist cosmological adaptation of the five central precepts of Buddhism and is typical for the formation of monastic rules and establishments under Buddhist influence (see Jan 1986; Kohn 1994).

At the same time in the south of China, the Celestial Masters were also striving to reorganize and recover some of the organizational and moral integrity of their forebears. To this end, on the basis another set of early Buddhist community rules, the 250 precepts of the *Pratimoksa*, they created an expanded behavioral code, the *Laojun yibai bashi jie* 老君一百八十戒 (The 180 Precepts of Lord Lao, in DZ 786).[6] Its many detailed rules specify the proper behavior in daily living, placing strong emphasis on personal honesty and community life. The text prohibits theft, adultery, killing, abortion, intoxication, destruction of natural resources, and waste of food, and regulates conduct in regard to community members and outsiders. It prohibits fraternization with brigands and soldiers, punishes cruelty to slaves and animals, and insists upon polite distance when encountering outsiders and officials. Its meticulous governance of day-to-day activities and criticism of pettiness, rudeness, and the accumulation of personal wealth are in many ways similar to the codes known from monastic and other religious organizations the world over.

The southern Celestial Masters expanded their sphere of influence further by joining forces with the newly arisen schools of Shangqing 上清 (Highest

---

6. On "The 180 Precepts of Lord Lao," see Schmidt 1985; Penny 1996; Hendrischke and Penny 1996; Schipper 2001; Kohn forthcoming.

Purity), created through a set of revelations in 364–370 (see Robinet 2000), and Numinous Treasure, founded by Ge Chaofu 葛巢甫 in the 390s (see Yamada 2000). In a growing trend to integrate various Daoist teachings, these schools formed new communities and experimented with new organizations. As a result a new type of semimonastic institution arose in south China, known as "abodes" (*guan* 館), a word that describes a hall or a hostel and in Tang official usage denotes an "academy" (Xiong 2000, 86).

Typically sponsored by the emperor, imperial relatives, or aristocrats, such abodes served to house one or several Daoists, permitting them to pursue their spiritual interests and allowing the rulers to keep a close eye on their activities—since they were seen either as potentially subversive or as highly useful to the greater good of the country. Abodes were described as "houses of concentration" (*jingshe* 靜舍), an echo of the early Celestial Masters' oratories, and erected on famous mountains (Bumbacher 2000a, 437, 442). They were not monastic in the strict sense but housed priests and their families and in some cases were passed on from father to son (Bumbacher 2000a, 438–9).

A cluster of abodes located on the southern mountain of Maoshan 茅山 (near Nanjing) came to flourish greatly under the guidance of Tao Hongjing 陶弘景 (456–536), the first formal patriarch of Highest Purity. It had several grottoes for individual practice, a number of lodges for selected hermits, and some larger imperially sponsored insitutions for major activities of worship and cultivation (see Bumbacher 2000b). According to contemporaneous sources, the actual practices undertaken on Maoshan included both Daoist worship and the establishment of Buddhist shrines (see Funayama 1998), ritual ceremonies to the Dao as well as extensive alchemical experiments (see Strickmann 1979). In addition, the record of the calling and ascension of the immortal ascendant Zhou Ziliang 周子良, the *Mingtong ji* 冥通記 (Record of Exploring the Otherworld, DZ 302), notes he did not come to the mountain alone but brought his mother and aunt along, who supported him both physically and spiritually during his sojourn there (see Doub 1971). As Michel Strickmann emphasizes, it would, therefore, be "very wrong to think of [the Daoist community at] Maoshan as a truly 'monastic' centre" (1978, 471) where celibate monks or nuns lived according to a strict rule in a tightly knit religious community.

The transition from abodes to monasteries occurred in the late sixth century with the unification of the empire. At this time the state began to sponsor major religious institutions, and the various Daoist schools—northern and southern, communal and semimonastic—formally integated themselves into one systematic organization, the so-called Three Caverns (*sandong* 三洞). The Celestial Masters and their lay priests came to serve as the foundation, with the various other schools, especially Numinous Treasure and Highest Purity, occupying higher and more monastic levels (Ôfuchi 1979b; 1997, 3–41). The monastic movement came fully into its own as the religion became more integrated and better established in the Chinese polity. The *Fengdao kejie* is the key document showing to just what degree the religion was already integrated at this time and how it envisioned its fully developed institutions.

The Political Arena

In the early Tang dynasty, Daoism became a state-sponsored and state-supporting religion with a newly streamlined organization. Inspired by messianic prophecies that a man named Li 李, a descendant of Laozi, would become the new ruler, Daoists had aided the campaign leading to the establishment of the dynasty (Barrett 1996, 20; Bokenkamp 1994, 60; Hendrischke 1993, 113). Most notable among them were the Louguan monastery in the Zhongnan mountains, whose support assured the confidence of Daoists in the newly rising ruler, and the visions received on Mount Yangjiao 羊角山 (Ramhorn), which granted miraculous predictions of victory (see Bingham 1970, 95–6; Wechsler 1985, 69–70). Both, as well as the appearance at court of the prescient Daoist Wang Yuanzhi 王遠知, helped to legitimize the new dynasty and put Daoism on a positive footing with the new rulers (see Yoshikawa 1990).

This support resulted in the expansion and new foundation of Daoist institutions by the state. Louguan, for example, received lands and grants and in 620 was renamed Zongsheng guan 宗聖觀 (Monastery of the Ancestral Sage). Mount Yangjiao was renamed Longjiao 龍角山 (Dragonhorn), and a new monastery was built there, the Qingtang guan 慶唐觀 (Monastery of Blessings for the Tang; see Kohn 1998a, 47). Similarly, the temple at Laozi's birthplace in Bozhou 亳州, the Taiqing gong 太清宮 (Palace of Great Purity), was expanded and greatly endowed and became the object of many Tang rulers' visits and sacrifices (Barrett 1996, 63–4; Kohn 1998c, 313; Reiter 1998, 4–5). By the mid–eighth century, a total of 1,687 Daoist institutions (including 550 nunneries) were registered in the empire, many of them smaller hermitages (see Benn 1977; Xiong 2000, 246). Located both in the cities and on mountains, they housed individual recluses or small groups of monks or nuns, supported by their native families or by aristocratic sponsors on whose land they erected their huts (Foulk 1993, 164) and in all cases encouraged by the state.

The rulers, however, not only encouraged religious institutions but also strove to control and streamline them. Thus, all monastics, whether Daoist or Buddhist, had to file an official registration with the state and carry their certificate at all times (Gernet 1995, 40). They also had to comply with specific state legislation with regard to their behavior. This legislation is found in two sets of sources, one a special code for the clergy known as the *Daoseng ke* 道僧科 (Rules for Daoists and Buddhists) of the year 637, the other Tang legal codes, such as the *Tang liudian* 唐六典 (Six Departments of the Tang) and the *Tanglü shuyi* 唐律疏義 (Supplementary Interpretations of Tang Laws). The former, unfortunately, is lost but can be recovered partially from its Japanese counterpart, the *Sôni ryô* 僧尼律 (Regulations for Monks and Nuns), written soon after its first conception and representing the same basic outlook (Ch'en 1973, 95).

According to these rules, ordained recluses were not supposed to ride horses, possess military books, form cliques, solicit guests, stay for more than three days among lay families, participate in musical or other entertainments, or behave in any way rudely or abusively to elders or those of higher rank (Ch'en

1973, 102–3). Taking improper foods or liquor was punishable by hard labor; wearing silk clothes or aristocratic colors led to defrocking or hard labor; theft or desecration of sacred objects carried a punishment of prison, hard labor, or exile. Again, monks or nuns engaged in fortune telling and faith healing could be defrocked and, if they still continued their charlatanry, suffer strangulation. In general, all recluses had to be handed over to the secular authorities for any serious crimes, especially robbery and murder (Ch'en 1973, 96–102).

In addition, the civil code, quite consciously, punished offenses more severely than the religious order, whether Buddhist or Daoist. For example, in cases where the *Vinaya* ordered expulsion from the order, the state demanded extradition to secular justice and the death penalty; in situations where the *Vinaya* or comparable Daoist codes demanded confessions, expiations, or rites of repentance, the state imposed imprisonment and hard labor (Ch'en 1973, 97–8). The sources are quite explicit about the fact that the same offense was punished much more harshly in the case of a recluse than in that of a layman. The reason given is that the recluse should know what he was doing and, even worse, was harming or "stealing an object of his own religion" (Ch'en 1973, 100).

Unlike in Indian Buddhism, where recluses were considered "houseless," technically had no property of their own, and depended on charity and begging, the Chinese institution was not permitted to be completely beyond civil society. Even the ordination cermony, a strong breaking of kinship ties in India, was more of an adoption rite in the Chinese system, where recluses would exchange the clan affiliation of their birth with the "family" of the Buddha or the Dao. Prevented from being totally separate from society, religious institions in China depended a great deal more on formal endowments and state support than their Indian counterpart. Begging and charity were strongly discouraged, and instead donations often "took the form of money or farm land given to an individual monk or the sangha" (Tso 1991, 75). This in turn, since monks could control their food source, encouraged the development of a more serious vegetarianism (see Mather 1981). It also led to the growth of monastic riches, expressed with the term "fixed assets" (*changzhu* 常主), used in both Buddhist and Daoist institutions to refer either to the permanent residents and staff of the monastery or to its physical establishments (Soothill and Hodous 1937, 349).

Assets were considered permanent in that they were firmly dedicated to the Triple Gem of Buddhism (buddha, dharma, sangha) or the Three Treasures of the Dao (Dao, scriptures, masters). They included statues, halls, and furnishings of the monastery as well as all the lands and agricultural facilities deeded to it. In its narrow sense, *changzhu* thus indicates "consecrated property;" a wider reading interprets it as all forms of "church property," the entirety of material possessions that made the monastery possible (Gernet 1995, 67; see also Twitchett 1956; 1957). Of this deeded property, agricultural estates and water mills were of the greatest importance. Agricultural estates were small villages whose land and income belonged legally to the monastery. They came with serfs who remained hereditarily attached to the institution and were known as "households held in perpetuity" or "monastery households" (Bumbacher 2000a, 312–13; Gernet 1995, 149).

Water mills were hydraulic facilities used in the milling of various grains. They belonged to the institution and were rented out to lay millers either for a fixed annual income or for a portion of the grain milled. Both agricultural estates and water mills offered lay followers not only employment but also a chance to accumulate merit and gain a good standing in the Dao. They served as a major source of income of the institutions, which had considerable expenses in its art works, regular ceremonies, and feasting of officials (Ch'en 1973, 151–6; Gernet 1995, 143–5).

Supporting riches of the large training monasteries and granting rights to smaller hermitages, the state was a key sponsor of Daoist institutions. It is, therefore, not surprising that Daoist monastics would dedicate much of their ritual efforts to the well-being of the Chinese oikumene. Like Chinese Buddhist institutions, they developed an ideology of serving and supporting the state, believing that their efforts would aid the establishment of Great Peace on earth and cementing the link between successful rulership and a flourishing monastic endeavor. Unlike Buddhists, however, who made several attempts at retaining their independence by refusing to bow to the emperor, Daoists tended to take great pains to express their allegiance and made loyalty a key virtue to be pursued.

The Monastic Establishment

Sponsored and supported by the state, then, Daoist monastic institutions were typically erected on mountainsides or in the suburbs of larger cities and followed the architectural model of traditional Chinese palaces. Usually laid out on a north-south axis, they would be surrounded by a wall and marked first by a major gate. Following a first courtyard, there would be a main sanctuary for worship of the Three Purities (Sanqing 三清), the Heavenly Worthies representing the Three Caverns. This was succeeded by another courtyard and a lecture hall for sermons and scripture recitations. In addition, there sometimes also was a meditation hall located in the back of the lecture hall and/or a shrine to the god of the locality or the mountain.

To the right and left of this central line of essential worship buildings, medieval Chinese monasteries placed various utilities buildings: the bath house, kitchen, and refectory on one, administration, dormitories, and lay quarters on the other side. Which side was chosen depended on the natural terrain, often— as also in the case of palaces—selected according to geomantic or *fengshui* principles (Xiong 2000, 39). And the kitchen and bath houses needed a supply of running water, another essential requirement for Chinese palace and city planning in general (Steinhardt 1990, 10–12, 19–26).

Surrounding this core assembly of buildings were two further levels of monastic habitation: an area that held outhouses, workshops, servants' quarters, guest lodges, and facilities for the sick and dying, as well as subtemples and various hermitages for individual recluses; and a wider territory that provided agricultural services, including sties, granaries, fields, orchards, vegetable gardens, mills, brew houses, fish ponds, pastures, and various other facilities (see Kohn 2000; 2003). Areas further out were increasingly less sacred and housed larger numbers of servants and lay employees. True recluses might not venture further than the middle circle, leaving the management of the farms and gardens to lay brothers and outside tenants.

Recluses lived in cells rather than dormitories, by themselves and "one per bed," as the *Fengdao kejie* specifies. Cells were to be kept empty and clean, simple and stark, and not equipped with heavy curtains, silk fabrics, or screens even if they were drafty or the walls had holes (*Fengdao kejie*, sec. 10). They should be small and humble dwellings, used to rest the body and provide an opportunity for personal practice. They should, moreover, only contain the bare essentials necessary for simple living and worship:

> There may be a slanted bench, a knee-support, a scepter, a broom, an incense burner, an incense holder, a scripture stand, a kerchief, a chest of wood or bamboo, a seat cloth, a rope-bed, a scripture chest, a lamp stand, plates and bowls for food, and a water pitcher. All other objects, especially if nonritual and for pleasure only, must not be kept or used. Failure to comply carries a subtraction of 360 [days of life]. (sec. 10)

Unlike the daily utensils and basic house garb of the monastics, all objects used in the sanctuaries and all ritual vestments were highly ornate and created with much love and expense. The sanctuary, lecture hall, and various oratories all contained statues, scriptures, lecterns, incense burners, bells, chimes, banners, curtains, and so on. They were made from precious substances, metals or fine woods, and usually painted in various colors and decorated with great care. For example, about the execution of the statues of the gods, the text says:

> The Heavenly Worthies should wear capes of nine-colored loose gauze or five-colored cloudy mist over long robes of yellow variegated brocade with mountain-and-river patterns. Their gold or jade headdresses should have tassels and pendants to the right and left and be inlaid in multiple colors.

> Their capes must never be executed in monochrome purple, cinnabar, blue, or turquoise, nor must they be depicted with loose hair, long ears, or a horn. On the other hand, they may wear headdresses showing hibiscus flowers, flying clouds, primordial beginning, or the like. (sec. 5)

The colorful and ornate nature of the sacred implements also applies to the vestments, which were made from fine gauze, heavy brocade, and various types of high-quality silk. Their basic color was often yellow, with women wearing gowns with a light green edge, but many other colors, greens, pinks, and purples were also used. The full set of vestments consisted of a lower garment, described as a "skirt" (*qun* 裙), which was usually a wraparound cloth sewn from three or five panels and tied at the waist; a gown (*he* 褐), which covered most of the body and was tied with a sash; and a cloak or cape (*pei* 帔), a large covering garment of translucent silk with open front and long sleeves that often contained multiple folds and intricate ornamentation. It measured 4.9 feet in width to match the four seasons, and 5.5 feet in length to follow the pattern of the five phases, and was divided into a varying number of folds, both in its main body and its sleeves, depending on the rank of the wearer (*Fengdao kejie*, sec. 9).

Ranks in the medieval Daoist institution indicated the priestly standing of each community member. They followed the basic system of the Three Caverns, originally a bibliographic classification, which arranged all Daoist texts into three main categories and associated them with either a "Cavern" or its "Supplement." Typically, the "Cavern" held revealed scriptures and essential devotional materials, while the "Supplement" contained more technical and hagiographic materials and served as a home for texts of nonmainstream schools. The overall system, still used in the Daoist canon today, is as follows:

Cavern	School	Supplement
Perfection (Dongzhen 洞真)	Shangqing 上清	GreatMystery (Taixuan 太玄)
Mystery (Dongxuan 洞玄)	Lingbao 靈寶	Great Peace (Taiping 太平)
Spirit (Dongshen 洞神)	Sanhuang 三皇	Great Purity (Taiqing 太清)
		OrthodoxUnity (Zhengyi 正一)

In the monastic and priestly organization, the system of the Three Caverns appeared in a formal ordination hierarchy, described first and in great detail in the *Fengdao kejie* (sec. 13). It was a highly complex system, with ranks and sub-ranks, but can be summarized as consisting mainly of seven major levels:

School	Rank
Zhengyi (Celestial Masters)	Register Disciple
Taixuan (Great Mystery)	Disciple of Good Faith
Dongyuan (Cavern Abyss)	Disciple of Cavern Abyss
Laozi (*Daode jing*)	Disciple of Eminent Mystery
Sanhuang (Three Sovereigns)	Disciple of Cavern Spirit
Lingbao (Numinous Treasure)	Preceptor of Highest Mystery
Shangqing (Highest Purity)	Preceptor of Highest Perfection

The first three ranks were those of lay masters, while the last three were monastic, and the middle rank (Disciple of Eminent Mystery) signified a transitional stage that could be held either by a householder or a recluse (see also chapter 3).

Ordinations into these ranks began very early, with children being initiated first into the Celestial Masters level and receiving registers of protective generals. After that, each level required extended periods of training, the guidance of an ordination master, and several sponsors from the community. The most common ordination taken in the Tang was that to Disciple of Pure Faith (*qingxin dizi* 清信弟子; see Kusuyama 1983; Schipper 1985), which involved taking a set of ten precepts, including the five standard prohibitons adopted from Buddhism as well as five more affirmative resolutioons, in a ceremony described in detail in the *Fengdao kejie* (sec. 18). The most elaborate ordination known from the Tang was the elevation of two imperial princesses, sisters of Emperor Xuanzong (r. 712–55), to the rank of Preceptor of Highest Mystery in the year 711 (see Benn 1991).

Once established in their ranks, Daoists could either serve as priests in larger communities, take up residence in a hermitage to pursue self-cultivation, or remain in a monastic institution to perform rituals both in-house and for lay donors, pray for the empire, and continue to strive for greater purity and immortality. The choices were the same for monks and nuns, the latter being fewer in number but equal in rank. Many larger institutions were what medieval Europeans called "double houses," with joint sancturaries and lecture halls, but a separate section for the nuns' cells, kitchens, and cultivation hermitages.

Within these institutions, recluses followed a liturgical schedule divided into six periods of worship, which required chantings and prayers to be performed at cockcrow, dawn, noon, dusk, early evening, and midnight. These six periods were adapted from Buddhism, where they served to schedule hymns chanted to the buddhas (see Pas 1987). The day began with a minor rite at cockcrow to move on to the morning audience at dawn (3–5 a.m.). Breakfast was served afterward, around 6 a.m.; then there was unscheduled time for work or self-cultivation. Around 11 a.m., the main meal, known as the noon purgation (*zhongzhai*中齋) was held, a formal banquet that involved sharing food and merits with the gods and all beings. This was followed by more time for work or meditation. At dusk, the evening audience was held, followed by lesser rites at midevening and midnight.

For each ritual observance, recluses had to don their formal vestments and purify themselves by washing their hands and rinsing their mouths. They could perform lesser rites in their cells but had to assemble in the sanctuary for the morning and evening audiences as well as for the noon purgation. The larger rites in all cases involved taking refuge in the Three Treasures, bowing to the Heavenly Worthies of the ten directions, repenting sins, and chanting various incantations and scriptures. The *Fengdao kejie* describes the procedures for the audience services (sec. 15), the noon purgation (sec. 16) and other assemblies (sec. 17) and also provides details on scripture recitation (sec. 11) and on formal lectures (sec. 12). It is a great resource on the practical circumstances and concrete details of Daoist liturgical and institutional life, providing valuable insights into the lifestyle and aspirations of medieval practicioners.

Placing the Text

The *Fengdao kejie* is the most extensive and most detailed text describing the medieval Daoist institution, presenting its fundamental rules, organizational principles, and concrete establishments. It is today contained in the Daoist canon (DZ 1125) and found in part in several Dunhuang manuscripts. Divided into six *juan*, it contains a total of eighteen sections that discuss the importance of karma and retribution, the physical creation of monastery buildings, sacred statues, and scriptures, the kinds and makes of sacred utensils and ritual wear, and the organization and structure of the ordination hierarchy, as well as a number of essential rituals, from the recitation of the scriptures to the daily devotions and the formalities of ordination.

The *Fengdao kejie* is ascribed to and equipped with a preface by Jin Ming 金明, also known as Qizhenzi 七真子 or Master of the Seven Perfected (stars of the Dipper), a Highest Purity visionary who flourished around 550 C.E. In addition to this ascription, it mentions the *Zhen'gao* 真誥 (Declarations of the Perfected, DZ 1016) and the *Dengzhen yinjue* 登真隱訣 (Secret Instructions on the Ascent to the Perfected, DZ 421) by Tao Hongjing 陶弘景 (456–536) and was therefore written no earlier than the latter's lifetime. The text itself, moreover, is referred to in a fragment of the *Quhuo lun* 袪惑論 (To Remove Doubts) by the Louguan master Yin Wencao 尹文操 (622–688)[7] and cited with several clearly identified passages in the *Miaomen youqi* 妙門由起 (Entrance to the Gate of all Wonders, DZ 1123). While the former is part of a Buddhist-Daoist debate in the mid–seventh century, the latter is Zhang Wanfu's 張萬福 postface to a collection of glosses on the *Daode jing* that was sponsored by Emperor Xuanzong and completed in 713. From these references and citations, we know that the *Fengdao kejie* was present in the mid–seventh and well known in the early eighth century.

Within this period of roughly 150 years (from 536 to 688), then, scholars date the work to either about 550, accepting the ascription to Jin Ming as authentic, or to the early Tang, around the year 630, arguing on both philological and historical grounds for a compilation after unification. The main difference between the two dates in terms of the history of Daoism is the exact placement of Daoist doctrinal integration and flourishing of formal institutions. Did it already occur under the Six Dynasties and while the country was still divided? Or was it a function of overall political and cultural integration and only took place under the Sui and Tang? Studying the date and compilation of the *Fengdao kejie* helps to find answers to these important questions.

About 60 percent or nine sections of the *Fengdao kejie* are also found in manuscripts from Dunhuang, with remnants of an additional five sections recovered from further manuscripts and citations in Tang works. Textual variants between the *Daozang* and Dunhuang editions are not substantial, in that entire paragraphs or sentences would be missing from one or the other, but tend to be technical and limited to the use of alternative characters or writing styles, with an occasional difference in nomenclature or syntax.[8] *Juan* numbers, on the other hand, vary considerably, giving rise to speculations about a process of early expansion and later condensation as well as partial loss of the text.

---

7. This fragment is found in the *Chuxue ji* 初學記 (Record of Initial Learning) 23.552. See Barrett 1996, 34; 1997, 539. For details on Yin Wencao, his biography and role in the Louguan school or the northern Celestial Masters, see Kohn 1997b.

8. The *juan* numbers and contents in their various version have been studied especially by Yoshioka (1955, 301–40). See also Liu 1986; Yoshioka 1963; repr. Yoshioka 1976, 75–219.

The Text Today

The *Fengdao kejie* as it is contained in the Daoist canon today consists of eighteen sections in six *juan*. The first ten sections in three *juan* describe the conceptual framework and concrete conditions of Daoist institutional practice, while the last eight sections, in three more *juan*, deal with specific rituals.

It begins, after a preface that deplores the lack of unity in Daoist practice and expresses serious anxiety about the loss of proper modes of worship, with a discussion of karma and retribution in three sections:

1. Retribution of Sins 罪緣品 (1.2a–8b)
2. Retribution of Good Deeds 善緣品 (1.8b–12a)
3. Comprehensive Structures 總列品 (1.12ab)

The first two of these contain lists of karmic punishments and rewards, presenting an abbreviated version of sections 2 and 3 of the *Yinyuan jing* 因緣經 (Scripture of Karmic Retribution, DZ 336, 2.1a–10a).[9] The latter is a work in twenty-seven sections and ten *juan* that reports on the dialogue between the Perfected of Universal Rescue (Puji zhenren 普濟真人) and the Highest Lord of the Dao (Taishang daojun 太上道君) in front of a great celestial assembly located in the Heaven of Blissful Virtue. Answering the query of the Perfected, the Lord of the Dao details the gory fate of people who harm the sacred objects or persons of the Dao and the never-ending bliss that awaits those of a more supportive disposition. The text represents the standard Buddhist visions about retribution in this and future lives.

The third section of the *Fengdao kejie*, not based on the *Yinyuan jing*, consists of one short paragraph that specifies the method of karmic calculation, detailing units of lifetime that the heavenly administration subtracts for offenses and adds for virtuous conduct. The entire part on karma and retribution in these first three sections of the text serves to establish the overall conceptual and judicial framework of Daoist institutions and monasticism. Following this overall outline, the text time and again appends notes to its rules that specify just how many days of one's life are being subtracted for disobedience or "failure to comply."

The next three sections of the text deal with the physical establishment of Daoist institutions:

4. Setting up Monasteries 置觀品 (1.12b–19b)
5. Making Sacred Images 造像品 (2.1a–5b)
6. Copying Scriptures 寫經品 (2.5b–7a)

A Daoist monastery, pattered on its Buddhist counterpart, is not complete without a sanctuary to the highest deities, a hall for lecturing on the scriptures, and a series of special buildings for meditation, ecstatic excursions, memorial services, and the like. It also needs cells for the recluses and residences for

---

9. A detailed comparison with the *Fengdao kejie* is found in Yoshioka 1976, 117–33.

the masters, as well as the more practical facilities of daily life, such as a refectory, kitchen, bath house, stable, and vegetable garden. All these are described in some detail, giving recommendations on their functional structures and adornments.

The same holds true for the making of sacred images and the preparation of the scriptures, without either of which a monastery cannot function properly. Images in particular are described for the entire pantheon, from the Heavenly Worthies (*tianzun* 天尊) through the many sages, perfected, and immortals, down to the jade lads and numinous guardian animals. Suitable materials, appropriate sizes, acceptable adornments, and numbers of statues are outlined, giving an indication of the rich artistic industry in the environment of medieval religious institutions. In a similar way, the text deals with the production and preservation of the sacred scriptures, specifying materials and scripts to be used as well as providing various options of copying and storage arrangement.

Section 7, "Conditions for Ordination" 度人品 (2.7a–15a), switches back from the physical setup to karmic concerns with the right kind of people to join the Daoist community. Consisting of ten lists of up to thirty items each, the section details what to look for (longstanding devotion, compassionate behavior) and who to avoid (fired officials, adulterers) in selecting future monks and nuns.

Having thus established the physical basis and suitable inhabitants of the ideal Daoist institution, the *Fengdao kejie* in the next three sections presents further physical details:

8. Ritual Implements 法具品 (3.1a–6a)
9. Ritual Vestments 法服品 (3.6a–8b)
10. Residences 居處品 (3.8b–10a)

Bells and gongs, banners and canopies, incense burners and scripture cases are discussed as much as robes and capes, headdresses and kerchiefs, hairpins and shoes. The simple cell of a Daoist, moreover, should contain only a bench and a bed, a clothes chest and a scripture case, a lamp and a water pitcher, and be located conveniently close to the well, bath house, and privy. Monks and nuns are allowed to own two complete sets of eating utensils, one for outside use, the other only for the pure dining hall of the Dao. All utensils as well as ritual implements and vestments must be kept scrupulously clean at all times and remain simple and without overdue luxury.

Following this set of concrete instructions on institutional establishment, the second half of the *Fengdao kejie* divides into eight sections on ritual "observances" (*yi*):

11. Reciting the Scriptures 誦經儀 (4.1a–3a)
12. Lecturing on the Scriptures 講經儀 (4.3a–4b)
13. The Ritual Order 法次儀 (4.4b–5.4a)
14. Illustrations of Ritual Vestments 法服圖儀 (5.4a–8a)
15. Daily Services 常朝儀 (6.1a–4a)
16. The Noon Purgation 中齋儀 (6.4a–7a)

17. Major Assemblies 中會儀 (6.7a–9b)
18. Formal Ordinations 度人儀 (6.9b–12a)

Most of these, except sections 13 and 14, describe the performance of specific ceremonies together with the necessary hymns and incantations. Section 13, in addition, contains a detailed outline of the medieval Daoist ordination system and has as such served variously as the basis for its description in scholarly studies (Benn 1991, 72–98; Ren 1990, 340–90; Yoshioka 1961). Section 14, moreover, describes the formal robes worn by the masters of the various ranks together with suitable illustrations and instructions on their proper care.

Altogether, the *Fengdao kejie* presents a detailed and inclusive picture of medieval Daoist organization and monastic practice, lacking only a detailed discussion of administrative structures and the specific roles played by the various Daoist masters within the institution. Unlike later materials on the monastic organization of Quanzhen 全真 (Complete Perfection) Daoism, which arose in the twelfth century, medieval sources only mention offices twice. First, the *Fengdao kejie* briefly alludes to "office-holders," listing "masters at the presentation of offerings, senior monks of high virtue, artisans who work on the ornamentation of scriptures and sacred images, and officers in the monastery administration" (3.7a); second, there is a mention of ritual officers necessary for the performance of purgation rites for lay followers: they include a ritual master, a cantor, a purgation overseer, an incense attendant, and a lamp attendant (*Yaoxiu keyi* [DZ 463] 8.7a–14a). The brevity with which ranks and duties are treated may have to do with the fact that they were taken for granted; or they may possibly be implied in the general organizational setup and ritual ranking order described in the text. Still, the *Fengdao kejie* captures the life of the Daoist institution in bright and vivid colors, allowing the Daoists of medieval China to come to life even after a millennium of history.

2

Authorship and Textual History

The *Fengdao kejie* contains a preface ascribed to a personage named Jin Ming 金明.[1] Also known as Qizhenzi 七真子 or "Master of the Seven Perfected," a term that refers to the seven stars of the Dipper, he was a powerful visionary in south China, who received various revelations from Highest Purity deities.[2] The first of these is dated to the year 543, when he was given the Numinous Register of Highest Prime by the Highest Lord of Jade Dawn, the central deity of Highest Purity. Then, eight years later, after, as he says, he "used the precious register to concentrate my spirit and *qi*, never allowing the sacred text to be defiled or despoiled" (*Sanbai liushiwu bu yuanlu*, 1a), he had another divine encounter. This is documented fully in the *Sanbai liushiwu bu yuanlu* 三百六十五部元籙 (Primordial Register of the 365 Division [Generals], DZ 1388). Here we have:

> Then, this year, the fifth year of the era Great Purity, with the year star in *xinwei* [551], at noon of the first day of the fifth month, I was again visited by the Most Eminent Jade Emperor of Heavenly Treasure, who descended to the jasper palace on the Dai peak to transmit to me the Mysterious Register of Perfect Numen of the Highest Prime of the Nine Heavens. Through this, I was confirmed in the rank and title of an official general [of heaven]. (1a; Yoshioka 1976, 103)

---

1. This chapter is an adaptation of an earlier discussion, first published in Kohn 1997a.

2. Jin Ming's agnomen is explained in *Sanbai liushiwu bu yuanlu* 24a (see Yoshioka 1976, 103). A detailed study examining the three key texts surrounding Jin Ming was undertaken by Liu Ts'un-yan. He concludes that nothing of solid historical value is known about the personage and speculates that the name may even indicate more than one person (1986, 513). He also concludes that the "seven perfected" may or may not refer to the stars of the Dipper, possibly indicating a group of major Daoist deities (528). He accepts Jin Ming as a figure of the 550s (512) but does not comment on the date of the *Fengdao kejie*.

The reference to the year by the era "Great Purity," the last reign title of Emperor Wu of the Liang, indicates that Jin Ming was writing under that dynasty in the south of China. In addition, it shows that he was either so far removed from political events that he was unaware of the emperor's death in the third year of that period,[3] or that, as Yoshioka suggests, he wrote after Emperor Yuan had ascended the throne in 552 and rewritten history to the exclusion of the intervening Emperor Jianwen (Yoshioka 1976, 104).

In addition to this evidence of a southern origin of the text, the revealing deities mentioned are clearly of Highest Purity provenance, thus placing Jin Ming in the environment of southern Daoism after the death of Tao Hongjing. The register he received, on the other hand, has a distinctly Celestial Masters flavor. It contains the names and competencies of the 365 division leaders or brigadier generals who serve under the thirty-six perfected emperors (zhenhuang真皇) of heaven and control 100,000 troops each. Created from the "pure qi of Highest Prime," the top section of the celestial realm, and born from "the numinous and wondrous qi in perfect accordance with spontaneity," they obtained the physical form of vajras or diamond gods and appeared thirty thousand feet tall and clad in five-colored robes of pure celestial power. Their number of 365 matches, of course, the number of days in the year but also corresponds to the cycles of heaven and the planetary movements (Sanbai liushiwu bu yuanlu 1b).

Their might is tremendous: above, they control the right qi of heaven and earth in its various movements; in the middle, they aid the celestial emperors to order the universe; and below, they make the divine law of perfection available to all suffering beings in the Three Worlds (of Desire, Form, and Formlessness). They are agents of salvation and rescue from pain, they prevent disasters and eliminate dangers, they preserve good fortune and heal diseases. "Their merit has nothing it does not encompass; they help all beings, human and celestial" (Sanbai liushiwu bu yuanlu 2ab).

Receiving this register with a list of the generals' names and powers as well as instructions for the necessary rites to activate them, Jin Ming himself became a powerful official of heaven who was the master of the seven stars of the Dipper and could rescue and save people with his might. The revelation also made him into the founder of a new lineage of practice that focused specifically on the invocation and activation of the 365 generals, and it was to this end that he compiled the text, outlining the revelation and supplementing it with details of procedures and rules (Sanbai liushiwu bu yuanlu 24a).

Already established as a powerful visionary, Jin Ming had yet another revelation in the following year (552, referred to only by cyclical characters), when on the full moon day of the tenth month, around 3 a.m., the Jade Emperor Lord of the Nonultimate Great Dao descended to the layered palace of Mount Kunlun and transmitted to him the "Numinous Register for the Protection of

---

3. A contemporary example for the political unconsciousness of recluses is mentioned in Bill Porter's work on hermits in mainland China, where he came across one old man who, when asked how he felt about communist rule under Mao Tse-tung, asked "Mao who?" See Porter 1993.

Residences," today contained in a text of the same title, *Zhenzhai linglu* 鎮宅靈籙 (DZ 674, 1a; Yoshioka 1976, 105).[4] The work, which also has a two-page author's postface on the wonders of the Dao, records the encounter between the two, with Jin Ming knocking his head and asking humble questions and the god enfeoffing him with the seal of the Three Primes and teaching him the register's powers (1a; Yoshioka 1976, 107). This register, like that of the 365 generals, is a major device for the exorcism of evil and protection of life that helps the right *qi* of heaven and earth in its various movements and establishes peace and harmony among the people. It, too, centers on the figures of divine generals, in this case three major military leaders of Upper Prime who control 360,000 troops each (*Zhenzai linglu* 4a), plus one leader each of Middle and Lower Prime with again large numbers of soldiers at their disposal (5b–7a). Each group is represented by a talisman that contains their numinous essence (5a, 6b, 8a).

In addition, the text has a list of forty rules, in this case called "statutes of the orthodox divine law" (*zhengfa lü* 正法律), which specify behavioral patterns that disciples of Jin Ming's lineage should or should not engage in (11b–21b). The statutes are varied in nature and do not appear in any particular order. Some contain categorical statements, such as "All officials and rulers who wish to create a peaceful country should worship this register" or "All officials in heaven who wish to secure celestial order should worship this register" (11b). Then there are warnings about the abuse of the master-disciple relationship with dire underworld consequences attached to them. For example, "If a master receives an annual stipend in rice from a disciple and uses it for himself and his own family only, never improving the disciple's fate with it, the punishing officers of the Nine Capitals will enter his name into the three ledgers of punishment where it will remain for the duration of five kalpas" (12a). Or "A master who on the day of the Three Primes does not establish merit on behalf of his disciple will be executed in this life and after death will have his name entered in the three ledgers of punishment" (12b).

The statutes also specify that a possessor of the Numinous Register must activate it ritually as soon as he learns of a disaster in his area or of a case of sickness in a disciple's family (*Zhenzai linglu* 12b–13a). At the same time, he must not worship gods outside of the register, must not engage in religious misconduct, such as dancing, singing, and other forms of entertainment, must not betray his teacher but always support and aid him while regularly observing the festivals of the Three Primes and performing the proper rites for the register (13b–15b). He must not steal from or otherwise harm people or treat the sacred text with contempt; he must protect all people and expel bad *qi*, and never reveal the text to outsiders or those not eligible for it; he must strive to continually visualize the generals and other relevant deities in his mind; he must not barter with the goods he receives from his disciples or other faithful followers; and so on (16b–18a).

4. A completely different text of a very similar title, *Zhenzhai lingfu* 鎮宅靈符 (Numinous Talisman for the Protection of Residences), which deals with geomantic ways of building and securing houses, has been found at Dunhuang (S. 6094) and appears variously in Song dynasty materials in the Daoist canon. For a discussion, see Yûsa 1981.

These statutes as given in the *Zhenzhai linglu* are of a rather vague and unco-ordinated nature, vacillating between rules concerning the relationship of master and disciple, behavioral guidelines in regard to larger society, and the right ways of treating the sacred text. In addition, they are strictly limited to the use and proper treatment of one particular register and the divine generals it controls, and as such address householders or followers who, if not entirely lay, yet still maintain an active relationship to their families. The statutes of the "Numinous Register" are therefore significantly different in nature, outlook, and organization to anything contained in the *Fengdao kejie*. Even the mode of underworld retribution differs—here an entry of the culprit's name in the "ledger of punishment" for so-and-so many kalpas, there a subtraction of a specific number of days in this life and the threat of unfavorable rebirth later.

While Jin Ming was therefore undoubtedly a powerful visionary of the mid–sixth century whose teaching, based on Highest Purity revelations and activating Celestial Masters–type registers, became quite prominent, he was, at least according to the materials that have survived from him directly, not the kind of integrative and systematic organizer who might have compiled the *Fengdao kejie*. More than that, his concern was limited to the proper treatment of specific registers and did not include the practice of all the teachings contained in the Three Caverns. And his disciples were not primarily monks or otherwise ordained followers but householders with concerns for family security and political peace.

Jin Ming as Divinity

Not the author of the *Fengdao kejie* himself, Jin Ming's high status in the celestial hierarchy, enfeoffed in 551 as an official general of heaven, and the fact that he laid down rules for his disciples in the form of "statutes" (a word, incidentally, that has a distinct Celestial Masters ring to it and does not occur once in the *Fengdao kejie*) made him a highly suitable candidate for a later attribution of authorship. In fact, even as early as the late sixth century, he was described as one of the "Three Worthies" of Highest Purity and worshiped as a major heavenly figure.

This is first documented in the *Shangqing sanzun pulu* 上清三尊譜錄 (Genealogical Record of the Three Worthies of Highest Purity, DZ 164), by the Perfected of Emptiness and Nonbeing (Xuwu zhenren 虛無真人), a disciple of Jin Ming who wrote the account on orders of his master (1a). The text consists of twelve pages and describes three major Highest Purity "ordination masters" (*dushi* 度師): the Perfected and Radiant Lord of the Dao of Highest Mystery, identified in a note as the Highest Worthy of Primordial Beginning (Yuanshi tianzun 元始天尊), the senior lord of Numinous Treasure and increasingly of integrated Daoism (1a–2a); the All-Highest Mysterious Elder, identified as the high king of the Nine Heavens (2a–3a); and Jin Ming Qizhen, the patriarch of this particular lineage. The latter is described as follows:

The third master of salvation is known by his ritual name "Great King," by his posthumous ritual name "Great Absorption," and by his appellation "Great Radiance."[5]

His body is eighteen feet tall and radiates with a metal sheen, a precious brightness that equally illuminates all the ten directions. Above his head a halo of the seven treasures is suspended; on his head he wears a jade headdress of golden radiance and flying essence that transforms a hundredfold. His body is clad in a robe of cloudy brocade, spontaneous and emitting a flowing radiance. He is covered with a precious cape of spontaneous great radiance that is studded with pearls of the flying forest.

On his belt he carries a shining pendant that matches the brightness of the sun and the moon together with a jade ribbon of flowing gold and fast lightning. Above he is covered by a precious canopy of nine-colored radiance, while his feet step on the threefold efflorescence of the flying mist of the jade-perfected Three Heavens.

He sits on a high seat of cloudy brocade and dragon-curling smoke. To his right and left, front and back, jade lads and jade maidens stand, together with thirty thousand perfected. They continuously burn the hundred kinds of numinous incense that creates harmony and renews life; they constantly scatter blossoms that shine in nine colors and are like flying clouds. Waiting on his path, on all four sides, the utterly perfected of the ten directions are arranged in rank and file, a crowd truly without limits. They also wear robes of the flying celestials and, like him, sit on high seats of numinous flowers and renewing life.

The true body of Jin Ming resides always among the jade perfected of Highest Purity. He is in the Jade Country of Golden Appearance and Copper Radiance in the Most Eminent Nine Heavens, more specifically in the village of Highest Luminescence and the Golden Wheel, in the county of Ninefold Perfection, in the divine prefecture of Unfolding Purity, and the highest region on Cinnabar Numen. (*Shangqing sanzun pulu* 3ab)

This describes Jin Ming as much more than a mere visionary who had established a position among the celestials. Here he is a true god of highest divine proportions, with a huge body of metal radiance, heavenly features and vestments, and a large company of celestial retainers and guards. A divine personage, residing in a specific celestial village and prefecture, he has the power of a true master of salvation, only slightly less in rank than the great lords of the Dao themselves.[6]

---

5. These "names" of the god consist of several words put together and written as a single character.

6. His divine stature is also emphasized in the *Zhuzhen shengbi* 諸眞聖秘 (Sage Secrets of the Various Perfected, DZ 446, an account of the gods of Highest Purity, dated to the mid-Tang. See Ren and Zhong 1991, 330–1. Here (7.11a) we find the information that Jin Ming was a resident of the celestial realm as described above, where he served specifically in the position of a minister of the rank of the ninth perfected.

As such Jin Ming had great powers of salvation and support. The text
continues:

> After you have visualized the perfected [Jin Ming] in this way, devote
> your heart in prayer and chant the following incantation:

I pray:

> May the Three Worthies open salvation for me, so-and-so,
> So that my millions of forebears and thousands of ancestors
> All through history
> May forever ascend to the world of bliss,
> Their bodies receiving a radiant appearance,
> They themselves living eternally from kalpa to kalpa!
> May all those living in mountainous seclusion,
> All my fellow disciples who pursue perfection,
> Together with me attain the perfection of the Dao!
> May a cloudy chariot with green awnings
> Speedily descend to me, so-and-so.
> And on the day that I attain the Dao,
> Take us all to ascend and enter the formless realm!
> (*Shangqing sanzun pulu* 4a)

Here Jin Ming is a superior divinity who, together with the other two
worthies, can grant salvation to the disciple, exonerate him from the sins of his
ancestors by transferring them into the heavens of the immortals, and allowing
him, in the company of his fellows, to ascend bodily into heaven. Jin Ming, the
visionary and leader of a small community, has thus become a divine personage
of high celestial standing, who, once Daoism was integrated and the Three
Caverns organized into one system, could easily be seen as the divine sponsor of
a synthesis that joined the teachings and practices of the different schools into
one harmonious whole. The choice of Jin Ming as alleged author of the *Fengdao
kejie* is thus meaningful and intelligent, given his visionary career, outline of
statutes, and impressive divinization. The materials that survive from him as
a living person, on the other hand, do not warrant the conclusion that he had
anything to do with the compilation of the text in historical fact.

Materials Cited in the Text

Daoist texts cited in the *Fengdao kejie* divide into three groups: texts listed as part
of the description of the ordination hierarchy in the section entitled "Ritual
Ranks"; passages cited from ritual and precepts texts in the last several sections
of the work; and texts cited by title in the first three sections. Although there
are some materials that can be clearly dated to the sixth century, the cited texts

only confirm that the *Fengdao kejie* could not have been compiled before Tao Hongjing's lifetime but do not necessary place it later.

As regards the first group, the *Fengdao kejie* lists a total of 253 texts, including scriptures, registers, talismans, tallies, and "transmission tablets," under a heading of twenty-five ranks that reach from male and female followers to the preceptors of the Highest Three Caverns (*Fengdao kejie* 4.5a–5.2b). The scriptures listed for the highest ranks coincide in both titles and order with those found in standard catalogs and described in academic studies;[7] scriptures for the other ranks, too, match what is known about the preferences and canons of the various schools. Most of the texts listed date from the fifth century, with only a few exceptions that can be placed in the sixth. Among them are, most prominently, Tao Hongjing's *Zhen'gao* and his *Dengzhen yinjue*, written in the early decades of the sixth century. In addition, there are the *Shengxuan jing* 昇玄經 (Scripture of Ascension to the Mystery) and the *Guanling neizhuan* 關令內傳 (Esoteric Biography of the Guardian of the Pass), both compiled in the first half of the sixth century and cited in Zhen Luan's 甄鸞 anti-Daoist polemic *Xiaodao lun* 笑道論 (Laughing at the Dao) of the year 570.[8] Whereas this overall tendency to list early scriptures may be interpreted to imply a sixth-century date of the *Fengdao kejie* itself, its list yet represents the standard ordination pattern of the high Tang as indicated in the various works of Zhang Wanfu. Unlike texts revealed or compiled in the fifth and sixth centuries, materials from the early Tang never made it to quite the same status of orthodoxy and did not become part of formal ordinations. On the other hand, this particular integration of schools, joining both northern and southern traditions into one organized system, is hard to envision before unification. Still, this is not proof, and the texts and ordination steps listed in the section entitled "The Ritual Order" do not offer a conclusive solution to the problem of the text's date.

The second group of materials cited includes passages from ritual and precepts texts in the last several sections. Two examples stand out here. First, the second chant in the section on "Daily Services," which introduces the scripture recitation and is otherwise known as the "Ode to the Scriptures," is taken from the *Benyuan dajie* 本願大誡 (Great Precepts and Original Vows, DZ 344), one among the old Numinous Treasure scriptures of the early fifth century that is also found in Dunhuang manuscripts.[9] The same text reappears as the introductory verse of the northern Celestial Masters work on the five basic

7. On early catalogs of the Numinous Treasure and Highest Purity scriptures, see Ôfuchi 1974; Bokenkamp 1983; Robinet 1984; Yamada 2000.

8. The *Shengxuan jing* has survived in a number of Dunhuang manuscripts, reprinted in Ôfuchi 1979b, 151–90; Yamada 1992. The *Guanling neizhuan* is identical with the *Wenshi neizhuan* and is found in scattered fragments and citations, the longest of which is contained in chapter 9 of the seventh-century encyclopedia *Sandong zhunang* 三洞珠囊 (A Bag of Pearls from the Three Caverns, DZ 1139). For more on the text, see Kohn 1997b. The *Xiaodao lun* is found in the Buddhist canon, T. 2103, 52.143c–52c. It is translated and discussed in Kohn 1995.

9. *Fengdao kejie* 6.2b–3a; *Benyuan dajie* 7b–8a. For details on the Lingbao scripture, see Bokenkamp 1983, 484. The text also remains among Dunhuang manuscripts; see Ôfuchi 1979b, 77–85. For more on the text, see also Kusuyama 1982; Ren and Zhong 1991, 260–1.

precepts, the *Taishang Laojun jiejing*. The very same chant is, moreover, still actively used in Daoist services today.[10] It therefore appears to have been a standard chant that was commonly used in daily services at Daoist institutions, from the early Numinous Treasure communities to the center of Louguan and fully established monasteries.

The other text cited is the *Shijie jing* 十戒經 (The Ten Precepts, DZ 459), a short text that contains a speech of the Heavenly Worthy to encourage new ordinands together with ten basic precepts and fourteen so-called principles of self-control. The bulk of the text, all except the fourteen principles, is cited verbatim in the *Fengdao kejie* section on "Formal Ordinations." In its entirety it appears several times in Dunhuang manuscripts, showing its popularity in the Tang, when it is also cited in the *Yaoxiu keyi* 要修科儀 (Essential Rules and Observances, DZ 463).[11] In terms of origin, the ten precepts that form the center of the text appear first in the *Zhihui dingzhi jing* 智慧定志經 (Scripture on Wisdom and the Fixation of the Will, DZ 325), another of the early Numinous Treasure texts that is also found in Dunhuang.[12] They, like the "Ode to the Scriptures" discussed earlier, seem to have been of widespread use in basic Daoist ritual and given a standard of behavior to initial ordinands, those achieving the rank of "disciple of pure faith." They reconfirm the nature of the *Fengdao kejie* as an elementary and highly standardizing text but do not help in its dating.

The third group of materials cited in the text consists of three works cited in the first three sections that deal with karma and retribution and the rules for subtracting days from the lifespan for offenses committed. They are the *Yinyuan jing*, the *Xuandu lüwen* 玄都律文 (Statutes of Mystery Metropolis, DZ 188), and the *Zhengyi fawen* 正一法文 (Code of Orthodox Unity, lost). All three are dated somewhere in the sixth century, with only the first having possibly a Sui dating and thus indicating a postunification date of the *Fengdao kejie*.

To begin with the last, the *Zhengyi fawen* was a long and extensive collection of the rules and rites of the Celestial Masters that was probably begun under the Liu-Song in the fifth century and continued well into the sixth. In its heyday consisting of a total of sixty *juan*, it was later divided into separate documents and for the most part lost. Fragments remain today in the Daoist canon, with no traces recovered from Dunhuang.[13] Citations begin with the *Wushang biyao* 無上秘要 (Esoteric Essentials of the Most High, DZ 1138) of the year 574 and continue into the early Song, but are not very numerous.[14] One of the remaining texts, the *Zhengyi fawen jing* 正一法文經 (Scripture of the Code of Orthodox Unity, DZ

---

10. See Lagerwey 1987, 137–9, 141–2. The *Taishang laojun jiejing* is discussed and translated in Kohn 1994.

11. *Yaoxiu keyi* 4.9ab. The manuscripts are S. 6454, 2347, 2350, 3770, 3417; reprinted in Ōfuchi 1979b, 191–201. For more on the *Shijie jing*, see also Fukui 1952, 197; Kusuyama 1982; Ren and Zhong 1991, 341. The *Yaoxiu keyi* dates from the early eighth century. For details, see Ren and Zhong 1991, 344; Zhu 1992, 111.

12. *Dingzhi jing* 7b. On the text, see Bokenkamp 1983, 481. Among Dunhuang texts, it appears in 5563, 3022, reprinted in Ōfuchi 1979b, 53–5. The text is also cited in *Wushang biyao* 13.9, 34.9, 46.7. For more, see Kusuyama 1982; Ren and Zhong 1991, 243.

13. The Harvard-Yenching index lists a total of twenty-five texts beginning with the title "Zhengyi fawen," nine of which are extant. See Weng 1935, 67. On the history of the text, see Kobayashi 1990, 328–56.

14. For a study of the *Wushang biyao*, see Lagerwey 1981. In the early Song, the text is cited in the encyclopedias *Yunji qiqian* and *Taiping yulan*. For a complete list of citations, see Ōfuchi and Ishii 1988, 592.

1204), has the Highest Lord recommend that people pursue devotional activities, such as performing rites of repentance, burning of incense, giving of charity, sponsoring of institutions, making of sacred images, and so on (1b–2a). While this sounds like the *Fengdao kejie* in general phrasing and outlook, neither this text nor other fragments or citations of the *Zhengyi fawen* contain the specific information on the subtraction of days from the lifespan that is attributed to the text in the *Fengdao kejie*.

The second work cited in the same context, the *Xuandu lüwen*, like the *Zhengyi fawen*, is addressed to the priesthood of the Celestial Masters. It contains six sets of statutes governing concrete Daoist behavior, the fifth of which specifies, as indicated in the *Fengdao kejie*, subtractions of periods (*ji* 紀) from the lifespan for various improper actions. The latter include not following the inheritance procedures when taking over the teaching from one's father, squabbling over the transmission after the death of a master, failure to attend assemblies or pay the right amount of tax, seeking fast promotion, making mistakes in setting out banquets, creating disturbances during the Three Assemblies, failure to worship properly or at the right times or worshiping in a state of uncleanliness, and so on. All these are punishable by a subtraction of anywhere from two hundred days to three periods from the life span.

While the offenses listed here clearly describe problems that would occur in a communal, nonmonastic organization, they yet have an obvious impact on the system of the *Fengdao kejie*, which frequently details exact numbers of days to be deducted for specific offenses. Still, the text with its rules is commonly dated to the late fifth or early sixth centuries,[15] so that, although it may illuminate the development of Daoist institutional life from rules originally written for lay priests, it does not help with the date of its first organized rules.

The *Yinyuan jing*, finally, is a long text in ten *juan* on the laws of karma and retribution, the second and third sections of which, as noted earlier, are cited at great length in the *Fengdao kejie*. Besides outlining the karmic results of good and bad deeds, the *Yinyuan jing*, which primarily addresses lay followers, urges its readers to attend rites of repentance, receive and honor the precepts, hold purgations, chant the scriptures, and sponsor or perform rites to the Dao. They are to develop a cheerful attitude and give amply in charity, so that specialized practitioners in the monasteries can do their best to improve the karma of the world. Nurturing compassionate attitudes, all should worship the Ten Worthies Who Save from Suffering (Jiuku tianzun 救苦天尊).

The date of the *Yinyuan jing* has usually be determined in connection with that of the *Fengdao kejie*, scholars agreeing that the two texts go back to the same lineage of compilers and are about twenty years apart, with the *Yinyuan jing* being earlier.[16] Agreement also exists on its *terminus post quem non*, which is the

---

15. On the text and its date, see Kobayashi 1990, 206–7; Ren and Zhong 1991, 137; Robinet 1984, 2:280; Noguchi Sukade, Fukui, and Yamada 1994, 132.

16. The two texts share much information and many technical expressions. See Akizuki 1965, 57, 61–62. For discussions of the text and its date, see Nakajima 1984; Kohn 1998. Short notes on the text are also found in Kobayashi 1990, 236, 240; Ren and Zhong 1991, 254–5; Noguchi et al. 1994, 177.

Sui dynasty. This dating is reached on the basis of a citation of the text in a fragment of the *Xuanmen dayi* 玄門大義 (Great Meaning of the Gate of the Mystery, DZ 1124), with which it also shares a section on purgation ceremonies.[17] Because the *Xuanmen dayi* was compiled in the Sui, the *Yinyuan jing* must have been available then. Scholars moreover are certain of the importance of the text in the Tang dynasty, which is documented by its large number of Dunhuang manuscripts recovered.[18]

Within this framework, the *Yinyuan jing*, just as the *Fengdao kejie*, is placed either in the Liang or after unification. There is no mention of historical facts or citation of materials that would ascertain either dating. However, there are a number of doctrinal features that are mentioned in the *Yinyuan jing* but only become prominent in the Tang and are therefore not likely to have been around in the early sixth century. Among them are the use of a bodhisattva-like figure as the main interlocutor of the deity, a feature typically found in Daoist texts of the Tang; the belief in the Ten Worthies Who Save from Suffering, which is documented only in the Tang and developed most fully in the Song; and the practice of the so-called ten days of uprightness (*shizhi* 十直), monthly days of purgation adopted from a similar Buddhist practice, that does not take off until the Tang.[19] These, of course, constitute only circumstantial evidence; there is no firm way of dating the *Yinyuan jing* to either period.

All the various materials cited in the *Fengdao kejie* thus reveal it as a highly standardizing and integrating work that reflects Daoist practice as it was commonly undertaken in the early Tang dynasty but may nevertheless go back to an earlier period. There is no firm evidence found in the cited texts that would date the *Fengdao kejie* either to the mid–sixth or early seventh century. In terms of its compilation, too, the materials only show a highly developed state of integration, of joining both southern and northern traditions, but do not pinpoint one or the other area, tradition, or compiler.

The Text in Dunhuang Manuscripts

Among the eighteen sections of the *Fengdao kejie* as it stands today the last eight are the best documented. Not only mentioned in the preface as the "eight sections on observances," they are also completely preserved in a Dunhuang manuscript (P. 2337),[20] where, however, they appear in a single *juan* instead of three. More than that, this *juan* is numbered "five" both in the beginning and the end of the manuscript, conflicting both with the preserved *Daozang* edition,

---

17. Section 7 of the *Yinyuan jing* matches 4b–15b of the *Xuanmen dayi*.
18. See Yoshioka 1976, 133. The Dunhuang manuscripts are reprinted in Ōfuchi 1979b, 147–73.
19. On the Ten Worthies and their cult, see Yūsa 1989. A discussion of the ten days is found in Soymié 1977, 3.
20. *Fengdao kejie* 1.1b. The manuscript named "P." after its finder, Raul Pelliot, is reproduced in Ōfuchi 1979b, 223–42; a reprinted and punctuated edition appears in Yoshioka 1955, 311–40, together with textual notes comparing it with the *Daozang* edition. The manuscript also names Jin Ming as its author. See Liu 1986.

where the material is in *juan* 4 to 6, and with the preface, which states that the entire text consisted of only three *juan*.

Yoshioka assumes that this "five" is a copying error for "three" and that the eight sections on observances constituted the last third of the original text. From this he concludes that the present *Daozang* edition is a truncated version of the old text, which consisted of three rather longer *juan* of about thirty Chinese pages each. This compares with today's *juan* length of 19, 15, 10, 10, 8, and 12 pages, respectively. The total text should therefore have consisted of about 90 pages, as opposed to the 74 pages remaining in the *Daozang*, counting about one sixth of the text as lost (Yoshioka 1976, 307).

While Yoshioka's estimate of the amount of loss may or may not be correct, his suggestion of a copying error is certainly wrong. Not only is the word "five" clearly legible both at the beginning and the end of the manuscript, but another Dunhuang source (P. 3682),[21] of which he was as yet unaware, contains the last portion and concluding note of *juan* 3—presenting, however, two sections of the text that are not found in the *Daozang* version. One of them is fragmentary but connects to a citation of the *Fengdao kejie* contained in the *Miaomen youqi*. The other is complete and entitled "Compassionate Assistance."[22] To complicate matters further, it is numbered "24," indicating that at least six sections of the total are missing or, if we place *juan* 3 where it is today, that the first ten sections are either a minor remnant of what used to be there before or that they were subdivided into about twice as many shorter sections as we have today. Aside from the problem of numbering, the manuscript is consistent in style and content with the established text of the *Fengdao kejie*, giving precise instructions on how to deal with ordinary people and what kind of mental attitude to develop in the religious life. It says, for example:

> The *Rules* say: All Daoists, whether male or female, whenever they have ordinary people coming to pay respect and obeisance to them, should join their palms [at chest level] and return the bow with respect, invoking the Three Treasures that they dissolve all [the ordinary folk's] immeasurable sins and give them good fortune without measure. Under no circumstances must they be arrogant or boastful. Failure to comply carries a subtraction of 120 [days of life].

or:

> The *Rules* say: All Daoists, whether male or female, whenever in conditions of severe heat, should always be mindful and develop the good intention that they should set up free juice [stands] everywhere to give freely to all [beings], allowing them to avoid the disaster of [dying

---

21. The text is reproduced in Ōfuchi 1979b, 219–21. A punctuated reprint is found in Tonkô kôza 1983, 174–6.

22. This title is identical with that of section 14 of the *Yinyuan jing* (6.1a–3a), which however contains anecdotes and not lists of rules about compassionate behavior.

from] thirst. May they all attain good fortune without measure! This attitude carries an addition of 220 [days of life]. (Ôfuchi 1979b, 220)

The major difference of this latter section to the *Daozang* text is that it speaks of mental attitudes rather than physical organization and that here alone, among all the many rules, numerical values are given for rewards, that is, days added to the life span, rather than punishments or subtractions of life.

It is my contention that this manuscript, as well as the various other extant passages not contained in today's text, are part of a high-Tang expansion of the work that succeeded the creation of the *Fengdao kejie* and its various precursors in the sixth and seventh centuries. This probably vast compendium was later reedited into a shorter and more concise version, from which the present *Daozang* text derives. The particular sections found in this manuscript on interaction with ordinary people and compassionate attitudes were taken out because of their differences from the main body of the text, which overall shows a remarkable coherence and consistency in structure, diction, and outlook.

The notion of an expansion and later condensation of the text is further borne out by the various titles by which it is referred to. First, there is the basic title *Sandong* 三洞 *fengdao kejie*, which I have used, with slight abbreviation, in my discussion; it is found in the preface and probably refers to a basic version that we no longer have (*Fengdao kejie* 1.1b). Then there is the title *Sandong fengdao kejie jing* 經, found in both Dunhuang manuscripts that contain the end of a *juan*, adding the word "Scripture"; this indicates the text as it existed in the high Tang, a goodly portion of which has survived in the Daoist canon. Next there is the addition *yifan* 儀範 or "Observances" in the title of the long manuscript on the eight observances. It appears at the beginning but not the end of the work, indicating that the sections on the eight observances were considered a significantly separate portion of the whole work. It may well be suspected that other *juan* had similar additions in their initial titles to show at a glance which particular rules and precepts were being discussed. The *Daozang* version, finally, is called *Dongxuan lingbao sandong fengdao kejie yingshi* 營始 or "Practical Introduction to the Rules and Precepts . . . of the Mystery Cavern of Numinous Treasure." This shows not only that the text was placed in the Numinous Treasure section of the canon but also that the editors were conscious of having a shorter and more elementary version on their hands, something that gives an indication of, but is not identical with, the full "Scripture" with its longer *juan* and more separate sections.

Another indication of the vagaries of the text's development is the fact that the preface speaks of "520 entries" (*tiao* 條), which are impossible to identify. If one counts items introduced with "The *Rules* say" (*ke yue* 科曰), as suggested by P. 3682, which mentions in a note that section 24 consisted of "19 entries," there are only about 120 in the *Daozang* text, with an additional 35 found in manuscripts and citations. If one adds the "Scripture" items on karmic retribution in the first two sections, the number rises to about 250, which is more than doubled when one counts every single entry that is itemized and could thus be considered a *tiao*. In no case does one get close to 520, having either not enough or too many, leaving open the riddle of to what exactly the preface refers.[23]

There are two further Dunhuang manuscripts that were probably part of the extensive "Scripture" of the Tang. First, there is S. 3863, which contains a portion of the second half of section 4, "Setting up Monasteries," describing the concrete establishment of various buildings, from terraces over gates, carriage houses, and guest quarters to corridors.[24] The text is close to the *Daozang* version, containing character variants, such as *heng* 恆 (constant) for *ding* 定 (fixed), and a few differences in names or terms, such as, for example, using the expression "female officer" (*nüguan* 女官) instead of "female hat" (*nüguan* 女冠)—so designated because the only way a female Daoist's attire differed from that of her male counterpart was in the headdress—and calling the "ascension building" (*shengxia yuan* 昇霞院) the "immortality transformation building" (*xianhua yuan* 仙化院). Only in one case does it give an alternative syntax, describing the gate of the monastery as being "comparable to the mouth in the human body, to the eyes in the human face" and thus clarifying the meaning of the *Daozang* version, which does not have the words "compared to the mouth" and thus lacks the clear parallelism.

The other manuscript is S. 809,[25] which seems a supplement to section 18, "Formal Ordinations," as it specifies details of the transmission procedure. It speaks of the kinds of rituals to be used for the different ordinations and of the immense efforts needed to attain "the one encounter when, once in ten thousand kalpas [of successive lives], a master or perfected transmits the Dao." It also specifies the necessary purgations and good omens, and warns seriously against caving in to the pressures of scheduling so that, when the scriptures are not yet ready, "ordinands receive some blank sheets of paper or a roll of plain silk." This, the text scolds, "is an insult to the sacred scriptures and a major fraud, a faked ascent to the altar!" In addition, after the event, the text insists, ordinands must

> choose an appropriate time and prepare an offering purgation as a
> present to the great sages, masters, and worthies of the various
> heavens. This is to thank them for their enfolding grace without which
> the transmission could not have taken place. Failure to comply carries
> a subtraction of 2,800 [days of life]. (Ôfuchi 1979b, 222)

This text, in diction and content, is well suited to the rest of the *Fengdao kejie* and was probably part of it in the mid-Tang.

---

23. A discussion of the 520 entries, including the various ways of counting them, is found in Tonkô kôza 1983, 169–70.

24. The text matches *Fengdao kejie* 1.16b7–18a6. It is reprinted in Ôfuchi 1979b, 219.

25. The manuscript is named "S." after its discoverer, Sir Aurel Stein. Its text is found in Ôfuchi 1979b, 222, as well as, in a punctuated version, in Tonkô kôza 1983, 176.

Tang and Song Citations

Four texts contain citations of the *Fengdao kejie* (Ôfuchi and Ishii 1988, 550). First, there is the *Miaomen youqi* by the great ritual master Zhang Wanfu, who not only cited the text in his work but also wrote a treatise to supplement its information on ritual dates and summarized it in his discussion of the ordination hierarchy, notably in his *Chuanshou lueshuo* 傳授略説 (Synopsis of Transmission, DZ 1241) and his *Sanshi wen* 三師文 (Text on the Three Masters, DZ 445).[26]

Zhang's *Miaomen youqi* is the work of a man who knew the *Fengdao kejie* well and used it frequently. Dated to the year 713, it has three passages of citation: one corresponding to the beginning of section 4, "Setting up Monasteries"; another that matches the central part of section 16, "Illustration of Ritual Vestments"; and a third that is not found in the *Daozang* edition but connects with the manuscript P. 3682; it describes different kinds and levels of Daoists.[27]

While the first two passages show character variants, such as *li* 理 (control) for *zhi* 治 (govern), but no changes in syntax or meaning, the third passage is different in content from the rest of the *Fengdao kejie* in that it presents a division of Daoists into six types, from heavenly perfected through spirit immortals, mountain recluses, ordained monks, and devout householders to libationers, including both ordained and lay practitioners and in each case specifying their respective merits and preoccupations. For example:

> 3. Mountain recluses rest in nonaction and no-desires, guarding the Dao and preserving their essence. Their *qi* is crowned by the hazy empyrean, while their minds are concentrated in utter serenity. They are comparable to Xu You and Chaofu. (*Miaomen youqi* 18a)

Each of the six types is described in a similar fashion, including two concrete examples, the interesting feature about which is the selection of Louguan patriarchs for both the spirit immortals and the ordained monks. This indicates a certain closeness of the text to the northern Celestial Masters with their center at Louguan, which rose to national importance after Laozi was recognized as the ancestor of the Tang ruling house and became the divine sponsor of the new dynasty (see Kohn 1997b), thus indicating an early Tang date of at least this citation.

Another citation from the *Fengdao kejie*, not matching anything in the *Daozang* edition, occurs in the *Zhaijie lu* 齋戒錄 (Record of Purgations and Precepts, DZ 464) and again in the *Zhiyan zong* 至言總 (Comprehensive Perfect

---

26. On these works by Zhang Wanfu, see Benn 1991, 2; Yoshioka 1976, 91–4; Schipper 1985, 129.

27. The three passages are found in *Miaomen youqi* 14ab (= *Fengdao kejie* 1.12b–13a); 19b–20a (= 5.4a–6a); and 17b–18b. They are reprinted with punctuation in Yoshioka 1976, 95–7. The third passage is partially translated and discussed in ôzaki 1984, 100–103.

Words, DZ 1033).[28] As Yoshioka has shown, these two texts are closely related, the latter being about a century later and making heavy use of the former.[29]

The passage from the *Fengdao kejie* details *zhai* 齋 or purgation ceremonies to be held throughout the year. For example:

> On the eighth day of the fourth month, one holds the purgation
> ceremony to announce summer. On the fifth day of the fifth month,
> one holds the purgation ceremony for continued life. On the sixth day
> of the sixth month, one holds the purgation ceremony for clear heat.
> (*Zhaijie lu* 9a)

It also describes necessary attitudes of sincerity and humility, indicates taboos and prohibitions, such as the avoidance of "filial sons in deep mourning and women after parturition or during menstruation," and forbids unruly behavior, such as "climbing to the sacred hall in an irregular manner" in order to obtain one's pardon as quickly as possible.

The citation does fit into the *Fengdao kejie* only insofar as its outline of the annual purgation schedule appears also, with some variation, in the *Yinyuan jing* (4.11a). On the other hand, it probably did not appear in the seventh-century version of the text, because Zhang Wanfu specifically mentions that he compiled his *Ze rili* 擇日曆 (Selecting Proper Days, DZ 1240),[30] a ritual calendar of suitable days for the transmission of Daoist scriptures and precepts, as a supplement to the *Fengdao kejie*, which does not deal with proper days or the ritual schedule at all. In his own words:

> As the Daoist rules of Jin Ming deal mostly with ritual utensils [and
> procedures] and do not clarify the selection of proper days for
> purgation ceremonies and announcements to the gods, I have here
> concentrated on the latter. (*Ze rili* 8b; Yoshioka 1976, 93)

Zhang Wanfu mentions specifically that the *Fengdao kejie* did not deal with dates, either for ordinations or purgation ceremonies, which is precisely what the *Zhaijie lu* citation does. It is therefore quite possible that the passage was not actually part of the *Fengdao kejie* even in the early eighth century but either appeared in a later expansion or originated with the *Zhaijie lu*, which chose the *Fengdao kejie* as a prestigious source of attribution.

A third citation of the *Fengdao kejie*, not found in the *Daozang* edition, appears in the *Xuanmen shishi weiyi* 玄門十事威儀 (Ten Items of Dignified

---

28. *Zhaijie lu* 9a and *Zhiyan zong* 1.4b–5b. The passage is also found in the *Yunji qiqian* (DZ 1032, 37.10ab). For a punctuated reprint and a discussion of its variants, see Yoshioka 1976, 97–9. A study of the *Zhaijie lu* is found in Malek 1985.

29. Yoshioka (1967) dates the *Zhaijie lu* to the first half of the eighth century because it cites the *Xuanmen dayi* and the *Daomen dalun* 道門大論 (Great Treatise on the Gate of the Dao, which were lost under Xuanzong and recovered only in parts (DZ 1124). The *Zhiyang zong* he places into the ninth century with the help of the list of karmic rewards and punishments contained in *juan* 5. It is later than the *Yaoxiu keyi* of the early eighth and comes before Du Guangting's 杜光庭 *Yongcheng jixian lu* 墉城集仙錄 (Record of the Assembled Immortals in the Heavenly Walled City, DZ 783), written about the year 900. From this he concludes a ninth-century date for the *Zhiyan zong*.

30. On this text, see Ren and Zhong 1991, 981–2; Benn 1991, 84.

Observances of the Gate to the Mystery, DZ 791), a text on ritual instruction transmitted by Lord Lao to the Perfected of No-Thought (Wuxiang zhenren 無想真人) and divided into ten sections. It, too, like Zhang Wanfu's Ze rili, is a supplement to the Fengdao kejie, covering similar ground but focusing on the concrete activities of Daoists rather than their material surroundings. For example, the Shishi weiyi has a detailed section on the performance of obeisances (sec. 2), describing exactly how far, with what body parts, and how many times to bow or knock the head in what situation, a feature taken entirely for granted in the Fengdao kejie.

In two places, moreover, the text refers to the Fengdao kejie for the text of an incantation that is part of the rite it describes and does not spell the incantation out in full.[31] The one citation it has from the text is in its last section on "Protecting and Guarding":

1. In general, scriptures and sacred images are of the same kind and [treated] without distinction. As the "Precepts for Worshiping the Dao" says:

Wherever scriptures and sacred images are housed, the place must be well protected and sparkling clean. They should be surrounded and properly separated by bamboo railings. If you leave them even for a short time, always take a clean cloth to cover them.

At those times when practitioners study and read the scriptures, they must not unroll them more than three times in a row. Once they are done, they should use the handy hand to roll the scripture back up. If the juan has not been read completely, never leave it unrolled even for an instant. Should there be an urgent affair [to interrupt the reading], then start again later from the beginning while uttering the proper expressions of repentance. (Shishi weiyi 14a)

This citation, which might well fit into section 6, "Copying the Scriptures," together with the two references as well as the entire tone of the text show that the compiler of the Shishi weiyi was aware of the Fengdao kejie and viewed his work as a supplement to it, relying on the information already in the text and focusing largely on the behavioral details it left out. The two texts thus stood in close mutual relation, with the Fengdao kejie the earlier and more fundamental compilation. Yoshioka places them in the sixth century, with the Shishi weiyi of Sui origin (Yoshioka 1976, 99–100). However, the text's title and structure, notably the link between the number 10 and the term xuanmen, indicate a later date, especially also because the latter plays a prominent role in seventh-century Buddhism, where it occurs in the Huayan school and is found as the "Ten Gates to the Mystery" in Fazang's 法藏 (643–712) Jin shizi zhang 金獅子章 (Treatise on the Golden Lion).[32] The Shishi weiyi, therefore, appears to have been a technical

---

31. Shishi weiyi 10a, 11a. In addition, a series of chants appear equally in the Shishi weiyi (10a–11b) and the Fengdao kejie (6.6a–7a).

32. The text is found in T. 1880, 45.663–67. For a translation and comment on the term, see Chan 1963, 411.

supplement to the *Fengdao kejie*, written in the late seventh or early eighth century, almost contemporaneous with the work of Zhang Wanfu.

The last, and rather brief, citation of the *Fengdao kejie*, which is not found in the *Daozang* edition either, is from the eleventh-century encyclopedia *Yunji qiqian*:

> The "Rules for Worshiping the Dao According to the Three Caverns" says:
>
> Before combing the hair, first wash your hands and your face, and only then comb it. Under no circumstances let this be observed by anyone else. This activity carries an addition of 820 days of life. (*Yunji qiqian* 47.2a; see Yoshioka 1976, 99)

The passage continues with further instructions on how to dispose of hair and nails (bury them but don't put them into water or fire) and describes various exorcistic rituals and visualizations to aid their proper disposal. Yoshioka doubts that this is still part of the citation (Yoshioka 1976, 99), and indeed both format and contents are rather untypical of the *Fengdao kejie*.

Even the short first citation does not entirely fit the text, as it speaks of the act of combing rather than the forms and materials of which combs might be made. Placing it in the present text is thus rather hard: it could be part of section 9, "Ritual Vestments," which mentions hairpins but describes their make and not their application; or it could be located in section 14, "Illustration of Ritual Vestments," which has a more practical tone and mentions that one should, for instance, place shoes on racks rather than directly on the floor (*Fengdao kejie* 3.7b, 5.8a). Still, this section does not contain taboos about personal hygiene, either, and there is certainly no place where the *Fengdao kejie* describes exorcistic rituals for the disposal of bodily waste.

Then again, the passage specifies a reward for the activity in terms of an increased life expectancy rather than using the more typical formula that outlines punishments for "failure to comply." It was, therefore, probably not contained in the *Fengdao kejie* as it existed in the early Tang but appeared as part of a later expansion.

The various Dunhuang manuscripts and citations of the *Fengdao kejie* thus show a text that was a great deal longer and more complex in the high Tang than either before or after. Highly prominent in the early eighth century, it invited various supplements, and probably also an expansion, so that the basic compendium on institutions and observances seems surrounded by a forest of related materials. The work, then known as the "Scripture of Rules and Precepts for Worshiping the Dao," was a long text of at least five *juan*, the last of which contained all the observances today in *juan* 4 to 6. Its first three *juan*, moreover, consisted of altogether twenty-four sections of rules regarding Daoist organization and proper behavior, only ten of which are still present in the first three *juan* today, but which probably also included the section on "Levels of Daoists" recovered from the *Miaomen youqi*. We know nothing about the old *juan* 4, but a sixth *juan*, possibly created in the eighth century and not yet available to Zhang

Wanfu, might have contained the passage cited in the *Zhaijie lu* and the section partially found in S. 809, since they both seem supplementary to the observances described toward the end of the text (secs. 17 and 18). This long and complex work, then, of which the *Daozang* text is a reliable remnant, reflects the practice of institutional Daoism under the Tang.

Arguments about the Date

This conclusion, reached through the detailed examination of the text, its citations and fragments, and Jin Ming's works and hagiography, is the exact opposite of what Yoshioka Yoshitoyo proposes in his discussion of the *Fengdao kejie*. He clearly accepts Jin Ming as the historical author of the work and places its date between the death of Tao Hongjing (536) and the end of the reign of Emperor Yuan (554), after the revelations to Jin Ming (Yoshioka 1976, 148). This is not his first conclusion, however, but a development from his initial position, which was that the work played an active role in the integration of the Daoist teaching around the time of unification and could thus be placed in the Sui dynasty. Jin Ming, a divinity of some standing at the time, only served as a prestigious attribution (Yoshioka 1955, 303).

This first reading of Yoshioka, not yet referring to any of the materials surrounding Jin Ming as a historical person but based entirely on an evaluation of the text and a detailed comparison with the Dunhuang version of the last three *juan*, was readily accepted by the Japanese scholarly community (see Akizuki 1960; Fukui 1960; Ôfuchi 1959). Then, however, Yoshioka discovered the works of Jin Ming and changed his mind, considering him the original author of the *Fengdao kejie* and placing the text in the mid–sixth century. He presented his new dating at the thirty-seventh annual meeting of the Japanese Society for Daoistic Research (Dôkyô gakkai) at Ôtani University in Kyoto. It unleashed a stream of protest and arguments for a Sui/Tang date of the text.

The two main protagonists of this were Akizuki Kan'ei and Ôfuchi Ninji (Akizuki 1964; 1965, 55–65; Ôfuchi 1964, 254–8). They both adduced the fact that the *Fengdao kejie* was not reliably cited before the early eighth century, that the *Yinyuan jing*, to which it is closely related, did not date from the early sixth century, that Jin Ming was divinized so quickly that he supplied a suitable character for attribution, and that the political terms used for administrative units in the text, such as "county" and "prefecture," reflected a usage only established after unification and the Sui reform of government in 593.

In addition, Ôfuchi emphasized the lack of citations of the *Fengdao kejie* and of the *Yinyuan jing* in the sixth-century encyclopedia *Wushang biyao*, and the rather vague appearance of the former in the *Sandong zhunang* and the *Shangqing daolei shixiang* 上清道類事相 (Daoist Affairs of Highest Purity, DZ 1132) of the seventh century (Ôfuchi 1964, 255). Akizuki, moreover, supplied three arguments:

(1) The festivals held at the days of the Three Bureaus in the first, seventh, and tenth months, although part of Celestial Masters practice from an early

time, were not called festivals of the Three Primes until the late sixth century, but appear as such in the *Fengdao kejie* (Akizuki 1965, 437–42).[33]

(2) Private estates and water-powered stone mills, although occasionally mentioned in the texts, were not common usage before the Sui but appear as a standard feature of Daoist institutions in the *Fengdao kejie*, thus placing the text after the year 600 (Akizuki 1964, 31–3; 1965, 445–8).[34]

(3) The widespread production and formal worship of Daoist statues did not take off before the Tang; although individual pieces existed earlier, they were primarily located in north China and did not depict, nor their inscriptions describe, the Highest Worthy of Primordial Beginning as the first god of the Three Caverns (Akizuki 1965, 449–52).[35]

Yoshioka's long discussion of the *Fengdao kejie* constitutes a detailed summary and refutation of these arguments (Yoshioka 1976, 75–159). In addition to reading the documents by Jin Ming as indicative not of a visionary and worshiper of registers but of a strong tendency for leadership and a will to order in the Daoist community, he argues that none of the items presented could be dated as definitely as Akizuki and Ôfuchi might believe and that they could all be found before the Sui (Yoshioka 1976, 140–5).

He also presents various additional Daoist texts that refer, in one way or the other, to something like "Rules and Precepts for Worshiping the Dao." One example of this is the *Shishi weiyi* and its citation, already mentioned, which he dates to the Sui, thus claiming an earlier date for the *Fengdao kejie*. Another is the *Zhengyi xiuzhen lueyi* 正一修真略儀 (Summary of Orthodox Unity Observances for the Cultivation of Perfection, DZ 1239), an outline of the major ranks of integrated Daoism as it began to emerge in the late Six Dynasties or Sui (Ren and Zhong 1991, 980). Focusing largely on the Celestial Masters practice of registers, the text presents a total of sixty ranks with one or more registers each. Among the sixty, the first twenty-four belong to Orthodox Unity or the Celestial Masters, then come six each of Spirit Cavern (Three Sovereigns) and Mystery Cavern (Numinous Treasure), to culminate in twenty-four ranks of Perfection Cavern (Highest Purity).

The Orthodox Unity list contains a total of twenty-nine texts, eight of which are also mentioned in the *Fengdao kejie*, but in a completely different order and linked with different ritual ranks. In its Spirit Cavern section, unlike the *Fengdao kejie*, which clearly associates this section with the schools of the Three Sovereigns, the list presents further materials of Celestial Masters background, including scriptures and works on observances (*Zhengyi xiuzhen lueyi* 11a).

---

33. Yoshioka first responded to this in a festschrift article, which places the festivals with their specific dates and nomenclature in the Liang dynasty, again basing his dating on the *Fengdao kejie* and the *Yinyuan jing*. See Yoshioka 1964. For more on the festival of the Middle Prime as influenced by the Buddhist observance of Ullambana, see Teiser 1988, 35–40.

34. For details on the private property and tax situation of Buddhist institutions and clergy, see Twitchett 1956; 1957; Ch'en 1973, 127–35; Gernet 1995. For the use of stone mills in the Tang and in Buddhist institutions, see Ch'en 1973, 151–6.

35. For more on Daoist statues of the middle ages, see Kamitsuka 1993; 1998; Pontynen 1983.

Three out of six are also listed in the *Fengdao kejie*. The Mystery Cavern section has ten texts, of which six are also in the *Fengdao kejie* and four are part of the ancient Numinous Treasure canon (11b–12a).[36] Again, they are not listed in the same order, nor do they even represent texts of the same ritual category. Only the section of Highest Purity with its twenty-four texts is fairly close to what is found in the *Fengdao kejie*, with twenty works being the same (17b–18a; *Fengdao kejie* 5.1a–6.2b). However, once again, the order is entirely different, and the *Zhengyi xiuzhen lueyi* places a much higher emphasis on registers than on scriptures or observances.

At one point, after listing the works of Mystery Cavern, the text says that they "belong to the highest ritual and follow the list of rules for worshiping the Dao of the Three Caverns"; Yoshioka reads this to indicate the title of the *Fengdao kejie* and concludes a pre-Sui date for the text (*Zhengyi xiuzhen lueyi* 12a; Yoshioka 1976, 88). My own contention is that this phrase constitutes a generic reference to rudimentary rules of the Three Caverns that must have circulated at the time.

A similar situation applies to the single semireference to the *Fengdao kejie* in the *Sandong zhunang*:

> According to the "Precepts of the Three Caverns," section 11, "Setting up Quiet [Chambers], Monasteries, Palaces, and Halls," a common [follower's] house [of worship] is called a quiet [chamber], while a master's house [of worship] is called a governing [lodge]. It then cites the "Statutes," which have:

> A quiet [chamber] has to be erected in [the direction of] heavenly virtue. Heavenly virtue includes all places of [the cyclical signs] *jia*, *yi*, *bing*, and *ding*. It should be eighteen feet long and sixteen feet wide. To be at peace [and practice properly] in either a quiet [chamber] or a governing [lodge], always wear your immortal talismans and registers [when entering]. (6.13b)[37]

As Ôfuchi points out, this must refer to a separate work on precepts circulating at the time, one in which section 11 was a comprehensive discussion of all kinds of buildings, both residential and devotional. It is unlike the *Fengdao kejie*, which treats monasteries in section 4 and residences in section 10, and even there concentrates entirely on the monastic situation and does not refer to lay followers' places in any way (1964, 255). The outlook as well as the phrasing of the two texts is thus significantly different, making it impossible to regard this citation as proof for the existence of the *Fengdao kejie* before unification, not even considering the fact that the *Sandong zhunang* was only compiled in the latter half of the seventh century.

Overall, therefore, Yoshioka with elaborate and detailed research makes an argument for an early, Liang-dynasty date of the *Fengdao kejie*, which has been

---

36. The Numinous Treasure texts are those numbered LB 1, 10, 26, and LBX 1. See Yamada 2000, 234.

37. The same citation, with minor variants, is also found in the *Shangqing daolei shixiang* (1.1a). See Reiter 1990, 105.

severely debated in the scholarly community right from its inception. Many of the materials he adduces do indeed add to our information and understanding of the text, but they are themselves not securely enough dated to warrant a mid-sixth-century compilation of the *Fengdao kejie*. In addition, historical arguments about the overall development and social situation of Daoist institutions tend to tilt the scales toward a postunification dating.

Current Views of the Text

As a result, most scholars today opt for an early Tang origin of the text, with only a few serious voices still placing it in the Liang dynasty. Underlying this remaining division, however, there is strong overall agreement on three points:

(1) The *Fengdao kejie* is of central importance for our understanding of medieval Daoism, because it is the first, oldest, and most concrete text to detail the organization of Daoist institutions, their material and moral culture, and the ordination hierarchy of the religion. The date of the work therefore has a tremendous value as evidence on where and how exactly the integration of Daoist teachings and monastic organization took place.

(2) The text is closely related to the *Yinyuan jing* and was probably written by the same compiler or lineage of compilers within twenty years of the latter. Since the *Yinyuan jing*, being cited in fragments of the *Xuanmen dayi*, which is clearly dated to the Sui, existed in Sui times, the date of both texts is limited to either the Sui/early Tang or the Liang.

(3) There are three major editions of the *Fengdao kejie*, an early version in three *juan* (as described in the preface), a Dunhuang version, and the text contained today in the *Daozang*. The *Daozang* edition is a truncated and fragmentary version of that found in Dunhuang, but how close the Dunhuang edition and the earliest text are, or even whether they identical, is open to debate.

The strongest proponent of a Liang date of the text is of course Yoshioka, whose key evidence lies in the biographical sources found about Jin Ming and the early citations of *Sandong ke* in various Sui dynasty texts. His followers are the Dunhuang lecture group (Tonkô kôza), Kobayashi Masayoshi, Michel Strickmann, and Charles Benn.

The Dunhuang group examines the various manuscripts related to the text and reaches the following conclusions: P. 2337, which is called *juan* 5 in the manuscript and contains the text of *juan* 4–6 of the *Daozang* edition, retains the original third *juan* of Jin Ming's text; P. 3682, which has the end of *juan* 3, corresponds to the end of Jin Ming's second *juan*, of which a great deal was lost; S. 809, on transmission details, represents a lost part of the *Daozang* section 3, "Comprehensive Structures," contained in the first *juan* in all editions but again truncated in the *Daozang* version (Tonkô kôza 1983, 169–70).

Kobayashi supports Yoshioka not only in an unpublished article that especially examines the *Yinyuan jing* (1990, 99) but also by adding the following argument to the dating of the *Fengdao kejie*. In the catalog of Numinous Treasure scriptures compiled by Lu Xiujing in 437 and discovered at Dunhuang (Yamada

2000, 232–3), fifteen *juan* of texts are marked "not yet revealed." These texts appear as extant in catalogs compiled in the mid–sixth century, which are now lost but referred to in the anti-Daoist polemic *Xiaodao lun* of the year 570 (Kohn 1995, 136). As the *Fengdao kejie*, however, still uses the old Numinous Treasure list, disregarding the newly available texts, it must therefore have been written before 570 (Kobayashi 1990, 97–100).[38]

Aside from the fact that Kobayashi has since reconsidered his understanding,[39] two lines of argument can be presented against his reasoning: If the various newly emerging Numinous Treasure texts had become standard after 570, they should have been supplemented by Zhang Wanfu in his version of the ordination system. However, whereas he has three tallies and scriptures not contained in the *Fengdao kejie*, the number of *juan* he supplies is identical to the those in the latter (Benn 1991, 95). Also, the newly emerging texts were seriously criticized as forgeries in the *Xiaodao lun* and it is quite possible that they were never fully accepted as canonical, in the same way as various older Numinous Treasure works were purged of overly Buddhist terms and concepts.[40]

Michel Strickmann, third, accepts Yoshioka's arguments and writes that "there can be no doubt that the four texts just listed [the works of Jin Ming and the *Fengdao kejie*] are all of one piece" (Strickmann 1978, 472 n. 20). At the same time, he emphasizes that it would be "very wrong to think of [the Daoist community at] Mao Shan as a truly 'monastic' centre" and points out that under Emperor Wu of the Liang, many originally celibate Daoists were forced to return to lay status, and that "the years from 517 to 549 are exceedingly meagre in regard to datable Daoist texts" (Strickmann 1978, 471–2). With Daoist organization in such a haphazard state, he further says, new revelations, such as those experienced by Jin Ming, were needed to reestablish a strong Daoist presence in the country. Strickmann's findings about the state of the religion under the Liang flatly contradict his assertion of an early date of the *Fengdao kejie*. Following his very own arguments, it seems rather difficult, if not outright impossible, for the religion in such a state of recuperation from persecution to have anything near the complex institutional organization and estates described in the *Fengdao kejie*.

Charles Benn, finally, describes the text as a work of codification by Jin Ming around 550 C.E. and uses it as the master source for his description of the Daoist ordination hierarchy as it was active under the Tang. He accordingly notes that "although changes occurred again in the intervening period, the state of the priesthood was basically the same in A.D. 711, it had been in 550" (Benn 1991, 73).

---

38. Kobayashi further details the argument by identifying one juan of Numinous Treasure texts that appeared in the sixth century as the *Tiandi yundu jing* 天地運度經 (Scripture on the Revolutions of Heaven and Earth, DZ 322) because it is mentioned in certain catalogs and lists of the time, while others claim that only fourteen juan of Numinous Treasure scriptures are still in the heavens (1990, 99). The issue is complicated, however, by Christine Mollier's identification of the same text as of Jiangnan origin and a date of about 430. According to her, it is not a Numinous Treasure text at all but a work detailing preapocalyptic signs that is related to the *Shenzhou jing* 神咒經 (Scripture of Divine Incantations, DZ 335). See Mollier 1990, 23.

39. Personal communication, December 15, 1996.

40. For a study of the reediting process, see Maeda 1994.

This assumption of an early integration of the Daoist religion and of its system's continuity, despite cataclysmic political and social changes, forms precisely the key argument of those who prefer an early Tang date of the text. Here we have first of all Yoshioka's major contenders Akizuki Kan'ei and Ôfuchi Ninji, who, as described earlier, present both philological and philosophical arguments for a Sui/Tang date. In more recent scholarship, Ren Jiyu and Zhong Zhaopeng cite Yoshioka but do not follow him, instead placing the text around the time of unification and no later than the early Tang, in other words, between 590 and 630 (Ren and Zhong 1991, 872–4; see also Zhang 1994, 571). The same policy is followed by the compilers of the Japanese encyclopedia of Daoism, in which both Yamada Toshiaki on the *Fengdao kejie* and Nakajima Ryûzô on the *Yinyuan jing* opt for a date around unification (Noguchi, Sakade, Fukui, and Yamada 1994, 217, 177).[41] Ôzaki Masaharu similarly locates the text in the reign of the Tang emperor Taizong, that is, between 626 and 649, without, however, explaining the reasons for his selection (1984, 100).

Among Western scholars, Florian Reiter follows Ôfuchi's arguments and dates the text to the early Tang, while emphasizing its incomplete nature yet accepting the *Sandong zhunang* reference as accurate (Barrett 1997, 538; Reiter 1988, 58; 1998). Kristofer Schipper, finally, dates the *Fengdao kejie* clearly to the Tang and provides several sound arguments for this dating. First, in discussing the establishment of the Four Supplements to the Three Caverns, he writes that "the most remarkable feature of this evolution is the fundamental position rendered, in the beginning of the Tang period, to the liturgy of the Heavenly [Celestial] Masters. The latter is henceforward integrated into the unified Daoist system, of which it forms the basis and also the first step" (1984, 212). As the seven parts are very prominent in the *Fengdao kejie*, a date before the Tang is out of the question. And in a discussion of the development of Daoist monasticism, Schipper finds that the Daoist monastic institution did not develop until the second half of the sixth century and only under the Tang was sponsored with imperial seriousness. Like various scriptures typical of the same period, the institution was strongly influenced by Buddhism and in a way distorted the originally communal inclination of the Daoist religion. As a result, the *Fengdao kejie*, with its detailed descriptions of physical layout and behavioral rules, was created in response to a situation that was characteristic for the Tang (Schipper 1984, 212–3).

To conclude, my own contention follows the latter arguments and adds the strong conviction that in the sixth century, all Daoist texts were still largely determined by sectarian divisions. They might refer to the "Three Caverns" but would in all cases still place primary emphasis on the doctrines and practices of specific schools. Even the *Wushang biyao*, a monumental effort of integration of the teachings, which truly accomplished a highly unified picture, had its sectarian prejudices in that it ignored the figure of Laozi, the conversion of the barbarians, the texts relating to the *Daode jing*, and other trappings related to northern

---

41. In Nakajima's case, this represents a revision of an earlier position, which used the Yoshioka dating of the *Fengdao kejie* to place the *Yinyuan jing* in the early sixth century (1984, 335).

Celestial Masters' teachings. The reason for this is that the *Wushang biyao* was compiled upon imperial orders of Emperor Wu of the Northern Zhou after, in 570, his vision of a Daoist-inspired state orthodoxy with Laozi and northern Celestial Masters doctrines at the center had been thoroughly criticized in the *Xiaodao lun* (see Kohn 1995, 32). Thus, even the most consciously integrative of works still gave way to a basically sectarian attitude.

Although a certain sectarian awareness continued even after unification, it was increasingly subsumed under a strong striving for real integration. The latter was especially pushed by the Tang rulers who wished to put the Daoist teaching, claimed to originate with the ancestor of their clan, to political uses and had little patience for sectarian discrepancies. Also, the late sixth century was a period of great Buddhist expansion and philosophical growth, with the strong emergence of the Tiantai school under Huisi (517–77) and Zhiyi (538–98), the new adaptation of Mâdhyamika philosophy by Jizang (549–623) in his two-truths theory, and the beginnings of the Huayan school with Dushun (557–640). Here, as much as in Daoism, the political unification of the country went hand in hand with the doctrinal and organizational synthesis of the religions.[42]

These various developments increased the urgency for integration and systematization of the Daoist teaching, giving rise to several types of new Daoist scriptures typical of the period after unification. Among these are Buddhist-style sûtras with bodhisattva-like figures at the center (e.g., the *Haikong jing* 海空經, *Yuqing jing* 玉清經), to which also the *Yinyuan jing* belongs; philosophical scriptures that integrate Mâdhyamika-style argumentation (*Benxiang jing* 本相經, *Benji jing* 本際經, commentaries to the *Daode jing*); and encyclopedias that present a coherent and systematic overview over Daoist doctrines and practices (*Xuanmen dayi, Sandong zhunang, Daojiao yishu* 道教義樞). The *Fengdao kejie*, in my view, belongs to the third group and represents a type of text that is truly encyclopedic in outlook and attempts to present an integrated structure and logical sequence on a specific topic, in this case monastic organization.

As a result of this conviction and taking into account all the various materials presented by Yoshioka and found at Dunhuang, I conclude that the *Fengdao kejie* underwent a seven-stage development from the 550s to the compilation of the Daoist canon in 1445, as follows.[43]

(1) First, there was a collection of statutes on the proper behavior of Daoists who owned certain powerful registers, dated to the year 552. It was revealed to and compiled by Jin Ming, a Highest Purity visionary, who was soon divinized as a master of salvation and became the inspiration for a later collection of rules of the "Three Caverns."

(2) After unification and responding to the more active integration of the Daoist teaching, there appeared a rudimentary collection, already encyclopedic but not yet quite as well organized, of *Sandong ke* or "Precepts According to the

---

42. On the role of the unification in Chinese Buddhism, see Strickmann 1996, 132.

43. A tendency toward seeing the development of the *Fengdao kejie* in terms of a gradual expansion and later reduction is also found in Barrett 1997, 539–40.

Three Caverns." This was referred to in several seventh-century works, such as the *Zhengyi xiuzhen lueyi* and the *Sandong zhunang*.

(3) Next, in the early Tang, these rudimentary rules were expanded and developed not only to accommodate the increasingly complex Daoist organization and ordination hierarchy but also to follow the overall trend toward greater systematization; they reflected the standard of actual Tang practice. The first text known as *Fengdao kejie*, this consisted of three *juan* as indicated in the preface.

(4) By the mid to late seventh century, as the Dunhuang manuscripts document, this work had grown to at least five *juan* and was known as the *Fengdao kejie jing* or "Scripture of Rules and Precepts." It was the key manual for institutional Daoist practice and as such was referred to by Yin Wencao as well as both cited and supplemented by Zhang Wanfu and others of his time.

(5) In the eighth century, the text continued to grow to include a possible sixth *juan* that included supplementary materials on the practice of purgation ceremonies that remain, however fragmentary, in citations of Tang texts, such as the *Zhaijie lu*, and in the Dunhuang manuscripts P. 3682 and S. 809.

(6) By the Song there was a revised, and possibly already reduced, edition that again consisted of three *juan* and was listed in the *Chongwen zongmu* 崇文總目 (Comprehensive Catalog of Venerated Texts) of the year 1144 (Loon, 1984, 85).

(7) In the early Ming this was rearranged and complemented by other, similar materials into the six-*juan* edition that we have in Daoist canon today under the title "Practical Introduction to the Rules and Precepts . . ."; this happened in a process of editing that can be observed variously (see Ôzaki 1996).

The *Fengdao kejie* we still have today is thus a text of central importance, which is not complete but does in fact reflect the ideal envisioned for Daoist institutional organization and practice in the early to high Tang. Not only complemented by manuscripts and citations but also surrounded by a number of supplementary texts that specify details it does not contain, it provides a vivid and detailed picture of the life in medieval Daoist monasteries.

3

Related Texts and
Relevant Terminology

However central and important in medieval Daoism, the *Fengdao kejie* did not stand alone. Rather, it was surrounded by various other texts that reinforce, supplement, and expand the information contained in the text. These surrounding works include behavioral manuals that add to the organizational and ritual information contained in the *Fengdao kejie*; collections of rules, often haphazard, that are both behavioral and organizational and to a large extent cover the same ground; technical works on ordination ranks, procedures, and vestments, mostly associated with the eighth-century ritual master Zhang Wanfu; and one other extensive ritual collection of the eighth century that discusses organizational structures and practices relevant to both lay priests and monastic institutions (see table). All these texts provide supplementary data and are used variously in the footnotes of the translation.

Aside from covering a highly similar ground, these various texts on medieval Daoist institutions also have a particular vocabulary in common that is highly specific to them and often cannot be found in dictionaries. Terms cover notions of worldview, an extensive hierarchy of people and priests, monastic buildings and institutions, rules of different form and dimensions, and ritual procedures, as well as specific physical and mental actions to be undertaken in proper veneration of the Dao. This chapter, after presenting the main supplementary sources to the *Fengdao kejie*, will outline the major terms used in the text, providing an overview of the worldview and organization through the specific vocabulary employed.

Texts Relating to the *Fengdao Kejie*

---

1. Behavioral manuals

Xuanmen shishi weiyi 玄門十事威儀   Ten Items of Dignified Observances of the Gate to the Mystery
DZ 792

Daoxue keyi 道學科儀   Rules and Observances for Students of the Dao
DZ 1126

2. Collections of rules

Qianzhen ke 千真科   Rules for the Thousand Perfected
DZ 1410

Zhengyi weiyi jing 正一威儀經   Scripture of Dignified Observances of Orthodox Unity
DZ 791

3. Technical works

Chuanshou lueshuo 傳授略説   Synopsis of Transmission
DZ 1241

Fafu kejie wen 法服科戒文   Rules and Precepts Regarding Ritual Vestments
DZ 788

4. Ritual collection

Yaoxiu keyi 要秀科儀   Essential Rules and Observances
DZ 463

Behavioral Manuals and Collections of Rules

The most important supplementary work to the *Fengdao kejie*, which actually refers to the text in several instances, is the *Xuanmen shishi weiyi* 玄門十事威儀 (Ten Items of Dignified Observances of the Gate to the Mystery, DZ 792; tr. Kohn forthcoming). Consisting of one *juan* and seventeen pages, it can be dated to the mid–seventh century on the basis of its citation of the *Fengdao kejie* as well as its title. The latter contains both the number 10 and the term *xuanmen* 玄門 (gate to the mystery), which also appears in late seventh-century Buddhism. Here it plays a prominent role in the Huayan school and is found as a section as "Ten Gates to the Mystery" in Fazang's *Jin shizi zhang* (Chan 1963, 411).[1]

The *Shishi weiyi* in its ten sections presents 144 behavioral rules for Daoists that were allegedly transmitted by the Highest Lord Lao to the Perfected of No-Thought (Wuxiang zhenren 無想真人). It focuses on the concrete, physical activities and behavior of Daoists, where the *Fengdao kejie* concentrates more on their overall organization and material surroundings. To give an example, the *Shishi weiyi* has a detailed section on the personal hygiene of monastics, the way to wash the face and brush the teeth—a feature taken entirely for granted in the *Fengdao kejie*.

As pointed out earlier, moreover, the work refers to the *Fengdao kejie* twice, noting that the specific text of certain incantations can be found there (10a, 11a). Overall it appears that the compiler of the *Shishi weiyi* was well aware of the *Fengdao kejie* and viewed his work as an addition to it, relying on the information

---

1. For more on the text, see Ren and Zhong 1991, 570–1; Yoshioka 1976, 99–100; Kohn 2001.

already in the text and focusing largely on the behavioral details it left out. It is, therefore, an important supplement to the knowledge expressed in the longer manual.

Another supplementary work is the *Daoxue keyi* 道學科儀 (Rules and Observances for Students of the Dao, DZ 1126). It consists of two *juan* of about twenty pages each and was allegedly transmitted by the sage Taiji taixu zhenren 太極太虛真人 (Perfected of Ultimate Great Emptiness). It, too, can be dated to the seventh century (Ren and Zhong 1991, 874–5). Containing a well-organized and highly systematic presentation of guidelines for Daoist behavior, mostly for ordained monks or nuns, it is, in style and outlook, very close to the *Fengdao kejie*—after which it is also placed in the Daoist canon.

Like the *Fengdao kejie*, the *Daoxue keyi* in its thirty-five sections emphasizes the concrete circumstances and organizational patterns of medieval Daoist monastic life. Unlike it, the text presents numerous details on the actual behavior to be observed. For example, in the discussion of headwear, the text echoes the *Fengdao kejie* in emphasizing that all Daoists have to wear kerchiefs or headdresses, such as the kerchief of the two forces, the headdress of primordial beginning, and the like. In addition to this information, however, it also notes that Daoists must always keep their heads covered even when resting or relaxing, because otherwise the gods on the top of the head—Niwan 泥丸 and Xuanhua 玄華—will be exposed and tempted to leave. One may only expose them briefly in the morning when combing the hair, but certainly not in the presence of others (1.6b–7a). Keeping a proper headdress on at all times, moreover, according to the *Daoxue keyi*, has five benefits:

1. One is treated with veneration and taken seriously
2. One avoids sins in contact with outsiders
3. One attains communication with the gods and perfected
4. One enhances one's inner good spirits
5. One increases the fields of blessedness all around (1.7a)

Not taking the headgear seriously, on the other hand, will lead to the loss of these five benefits and the overall increase of sins (1.7b).

A similar case in point is the treatment of bells. The *Fengdao kejie* describes the various materials that bells can be made of and outlines their overall importance. The *Daoxue keyi* echoes this and even cites the same scriptural passage on the use of bells in the highest heavens. Then, however, it goes on to describe the times when bells are rung and how to ring them: first, strike gradually and loudly eight times; then burn incense and wait; next strike gradually and softly twelve times, then very subtly twelve times, and once more gradually and loudly twelve times. This sequence allows the recluses to cease their activities, change into ritual vestments, and make their way to the sanctuary in good time (1.16b). The *Daoxue keyi*, therefore, has a strong tendency to summarize the concrete conditions of any particular item, then go beyond these conditions both in terms of actual usage and the wider implications of social standing and worldview.

Another collection of rules that contains many similar data is the *Qianzhen ke* 千真科 (Rules for the Thousand Perfected, DZ 1410), in one *juan* and thirty pages (Ren and Zhong 1991, 119–20). It begins with a revelation story describing the descent of Lord Lao to appear before Ge Xuan 葛玄, the immortal patriarch of the Numinous Treasure canon, allegedly in 240 C.E. Accompanied by a host of perfected, the deity takes a seat on a formal platform and graciously answers Ge's questions about rules in Daoist institutions. The text then consists of 109 rules, each introduced with "The Rules say." They appear in no particular order or system, but can be divided into five general categories: interaction with outsiders, etiquette within the community, treatment of food and resources, prohibitions of disruptive behaviors, and the proper mental attitudes to be developed. The text echoes materials contained in the *Fengdao kejie* and can be seen as supplemental to it, focusing predominantly on human interaction patterns rather than formal organization and liturgy. To give one example, it addresses problems aspirants to the Dao may have:

> The *Rules* say: Among a group of famous masters of great virtue living together in one place there may also be some disciples who are crafty and cunning and have trouble finding refuge [in the Dao]. Some may be unable to let go of their sensuality; some may think themselves above the others and avoid their duties, not sticking to their proper rank but attempting to be more; others again may command everybody around them as if they were their servants.
>
> Then again, some disciples may beguile others with flowery words; some may constantly go off by themselves to sit in oblivion; others may feel rejected and tend to wander about in far-off places. Yet others may open the scripture and treasures and teach them indiscriminately to outsiders, allowing them to perform rites and precepts for exorcistic purposes. Others again may deign themselves venerable and majestic and get outsiders to honor and entertain them.
>
> If these various forms of misbehavior do not change over a period of time and there is no visible effort toward goodness in the training of such disciples, it is best to consider them detrimental to the community of the Dao and to separate oneself firmly from them. (2a)

Another text of a very similar nature is also found in the *Zhengyi weiyi jing* 正一威儀經 (Scripture of Dignified Observances of Orthodox Unity, DZ 791), in one *juan* and twenty pages (Ren and Zhong 1991, 570). It contains 132 entries under a total of thirty headings, formulating concrete instructions for priests and renunciants of the Celestial Masters and probably dating from the late sixth century, the early Sui dynasty. In a concluding note (19b–20a), the text claims that it originated with the Heavenly Worthy of Primordial Beginning (Yuanshi tianzun 元始天尊) and was transmitted to the Highest Lord (Taishang 太上), who in turn passed it on to the first Celestial Master Zhang Daoling.

In content the *Zhengyi weiyi jing* deals with procedures of ordination and daily religions behavior. It is to a large extent compatible and even identical with instructions given in the *Fengdao kejie*. However, the rules here are less well organized and do not appear in a structured setting of systematic explanation. And they are limited in sectarian context by their close link to Zhang Daoling, who was particularly venerated among the southern Celestial Masters. The work, which can be dated to the time of unification, is thus a precursor of the *Fengdao kejie*. It provides an idea of how much of the institutional organization was directly inherited from the lay priesthood of the Celestial Masters.

Technical Works and Ritual Collections

In the eighth century, further specialized texts describe specific items also discussed in the *Fengdao kejie*. Among them are notably the works by Zhang Wanfu, the great ritual master and compiler of manuals. One work he wrote is the *Fafu kejie wen* 法服科戒文 (Rules and Precepts Regarding Ritual Vestments, DZ 788), a short treatise of ten pages that can be dated to the year 712 (Benn 1991, 143–4; Kohn 1993, 335–43). It divides into two parts, a dialog between the Highest Lord and the Celestial Master (1a–7a) and a list of rules on the treatment of vestments given by the Celestial Master (7b–10b).

The first part contains a detailed description of the flowing robes of pure transformation worn by the celestials in heaven, dividing them into nine distinct ranks and categories. Next, in close imitation of the *Fengdao kejie*, it discusses the vestments of the seven major ritual ranks on earth and explains the symbolism of major garments. Going beyond the discussion in the former, the *Fafu kejie wen* also explains the appellation of the various vestments with the help of relevant homophone characters—the inner skirt *qun* 裙 with the word *qun* 群 for "multitude," indicating that Daoists have cut off the multitude of errors; the middle gown *he* 褐 with the word *e* 遏, "restraint," symbolizing utter control over passions and desires; and the outer cape *pei* 帔 with the word *pei* 披, "to open," referring to the Daoists' opening to purity. Its first section concludes with the Highest Lord recounting the various robes he wore throughout his divine career.

The second part is attributed to the Celestial Master. It consists of forty-six rules regarding ritual vestments, followed by a list of ten groups of beings, both earthly and celestial, that will despise a Daoist who does not treat his or her vestments properly.[2] It ends with two injunctions against wearing the vestments at improper times and using them for improper purposes, each linked with a specific deduction of days from the life span. To give an example of the kinds of rules included, the text insists that all vestments had to be consecrated by being offered to the deities before they could be first worn. During active ownership, the Daoist had to treat them with special care, keeping them safe in a special clothes chest located in his or her cell and regularly washed and purified. They should not be placed anywhere lightly or allowed to come into contact with defiling objects, such as dirty hands, unclean dishes, soiled beds and mats, dusty carriages, outsiders, and animals. Worn during all ritual activities, formal meals,

---

2. The forty-six rules of the Celestial Master appear also in the *Chuzhen jie* (Precepts of Initial Perfection) of the Complete Perfection school. See Kohn forthcoming.

and visits with outsiders, vestments had to be taken off when sleeping or resting, bathing, using the outhouse, or moving about in mud and rain. They were, moreover, not fit to be used as bedspreads or seat cushions and must never be mixed with commoners' garb or lent out to others. If worn out and torn, moreover, they could not be discarded or made into rags—as comparable Buddhist robes—but had to be "transformed by burning" in a sacred spot and unobserved by outsiders (7b–8b).

Similarly detailed and concrete is Zhang Wanfu's presentation of ordination ceremonies and ritual ranks, which are both also outlined in the *Fengdao kejie*. Specifically his *Chuanshou lueshuo* 傳授略說 (Synopsis of Transmission, DZ 1241), in two juan of twenty pages each, presents a thorough description of the major ordination ranks of the Daoist hierarchy. Dated to 713, this text also contains a minute account of the ordination of two Tang princesses into the rank of Numinous Treasure in 711, the most detailed and concrete description of a Daoist ordination rite surviving from the Middle Ages.[3]

Its more technical part outlines the different ranks of the ordination hierarchy, specifying the numerous scriptures, registers, and talismans necessary in each case. This is closely patterned on the *Fengdao kejie*, both texts representing the standard Tang system of religious ranks.

A more general work, also of the early eighth century, which recoups much material contained in the *Fengdao kejie*, is the *Yaoxiu keyi* 要修科儀 (Essential Rules and Observances DZ 463).[4] A long collection of sixteen juan that range in length from nine to twenty-four pages, this was compiled by Zhu Junxu 朱君緒, better known by his *zi* as Zhu Faman 朱法滿, a monk of the Yuqing guan 玉清觀 (Monastery of Jade Purity), one of the major institutions of the capital.

The text is encyclopedic in scope and provides both original descriptions of practices and citations of earlier materials. The latter include works related to the *Fengdao kejie*, such as the *Qianzhen ke*, *Xuandu lüwen*, and *Yinyuan jing*, as well as other early Tang works that are no longer extant, such as the *Benji jing* 本際經 (Scripture of Original Juncture; see Wu 1960), the *Benxiang jing* 本相經 (Scripture of Original Phenomena; see Yamada 1995), and the *Louguan benji* 樓觀本紀 (Original Record of Louguan; see Kohn 1997a).

In content the *Yaoxiu keyi* can be divided into ten parts:

1. Scriptures: transmission, recitation, lectures (j. 1–2)
2. Relationship of master and disciple (j. 3)
3. Precepts of various schools and types (j. 4–6)
4. Retribution of sins (j. 7)
5. Purgation rites (j. 8)
6. Vestments and discipline (j. 9)
7. Ceremonial space and proper memorials (j. 10–11).
8. Daoist acts and their karmic consequences (j. 12)
9. Miscellaneous rules and behavioral guidelines (j. 13–14)
10. Rites for sickness and death (j. 15–16)

3. 2.18a–21a; see Benn 1991. The text is also described in Ren and Zhong 1991, 982; Benn 2000, 322–3.
4. On the text, see Ren and Zhong 1991, 344–5; Zhu 1992, 111; Ōfuchi and Ishii 1988, 188–99.

These ten are further subdivided into distinct sections. For example, part 1, on the scriptures, has nine sections, dealing with classification, transmission, presentation, copying, recitation, lecture, reception, and maintenance of the scriptures. Similarly, part 5, on purgation rites, begins by detailing the proper months, days, and hours for their performance, then moves on to describe the roles of the various officiants, including masters and preceptors, cantors, purgation overseers, incense attendants, and lamp managers.

Materials in the *Fengdao kejie* and *Shishi weiyi* are most closely echoed in part 6, where the *Yaoxiu keyi* discusses vestments, obeisances, sitting and rising, overseeing purgation rites, and food taboos. Part 7 focuses more on communal organization and community rites, but the last three return again to the monastic setting. Part 8 in many ways echoes the *Yinyuan jing*, when it details the karmic consequences of various deeds, including

Feeding the Religious (12.1a)
Building Halls and Sanctuaries (2b)
Remembering the Dao in Chanting (3a)
Sickness and Impurity (5a)
Stealing and Being Greedy (7a)
Faults and Transgressions (9b)
Good Deeds and Merits (11b)
Ordination as a Recluse (14a)

This is followed by a set of Miscellaneous Rules regarding the relations among fellow disciples and the proper procedures to be followed in setting up an altar and a prayer or commemorative stele. General rules, moreover, describe the spiritual effects of drinking wine, abstaining from grain and taking medicines, reciting incantations, and sleeping in the proper manner. The final part of the text contains more details on the lives of medieval Daoists, focusing on "Rites for Sickness and Death," including offices to be performed immediately after death, during encoffining, while preparing the shroud, and burying the body, as well as for resting the soul, the return of the disciples, and when taking off mourning garb.

On the whole, the *Yaoxiu keyi* is a rich resource for the concrete life and practices of Daoists in medieval China, both communal and monastic. It provides ample citations of earlier sources, many no longer extant, and gives a comprehensive overview over the religious Daoist life. It shows not only how Daoists were supposed to behave but also how closely the different religious paths—lay and monastic—were integrated in the medieval mind. As do the other texts described here, it provides detailed behavioral instructions and concrete rules, thus recounting and supplementing information found in the *Fengdao kejie*.

The Worldview

The underlying worldview that made this organization, hierarchy, and ritual activity possible focused on the idea of the Dao as the essential power of the universe that arranged everything in its best possible way. This Dao in the texts is often called *zhendao* 真道 or Dao of perfection, and is also referred to as *zhengzhen* 正真, right perfection. The term *zheng* 正, also apparent in the classification of the Celestial Masters as *Zhengyi* 正一, means "right," "true," "proper," or "orthodox." It refers to the best way things can be, the way they are meant to be by the Dao, the natural, smoothly flowing, straightforward way of being. The word is used in Buddhism to refer to *sât*, which also means "right" and indicates the correct way of doing things in order to alleviate the burden of karma and attain liberation (see Nakamura 1975, 697). In Daoism, it also occurs in conjunction with *dao* to form the compound *zhengdao* 正道 or "orthodox Dao," "right Dao."

This Dao, then, on earth manifests through *qi* 氣 or vital energy, a complex concept that denotes the material and manifest yet subtle and utterly fluid presence of the Dao. More important in medieval literature, the Dao is actively represented by *fa* 法, the "divine law," a term used in ancient China for "law" or "standard," and in Buddhism for "dharma." In Daoism, *fa* indicates the way the Dao works in the world, especially in the holy system and organization of the religion. As an adjective, the term accordingly also means "holy," as in *fashen* 法身 ("holy person"), or "ritually proper," as in *feifa* 非法 ("nonritual"). Other terms similar to *fa* itself—and similarly used in Buddhism for "dharma"—are *jingfa* 經法 (the divine law of the scriptures), *zhengfa* 正法 (the right divine law), and *jingjiao* 經教 (the teaching of the scriptures). Living in accordance with this law will bring one closer to the Dao and the universe to greater harmony; going against it will create unfortunate conditions for oneself and calamities on a cosmic scale.

The way to go with or against the divine law, moreover, is described in terms of karmic retribution (*yinyuan* 因緣), a concept adopted from Buddhism (see Zürcher 1980) that yet also echoes the traditional Chinese concept of *ganying* (impulse and response). By committing either good (*shan* 善) or evil (*wu* 惡) deeds, one creates cosmic reverberations or karmic conditions (*ye* 業) that result in either good fortune (*fu* 福) or sin (*zui* 罪). Especially the term *zui* indicates both the initial crime and the punishment or karmic suffering one undergoes for it, thus implying the notion of retribution of evil as already planted in the bad deed itself (see Eberhard 1967). In retribution literature it is often paired with *fu* into the compound "suffering and good fortune." Karmic punishment, moreover, is expressed as suffering (*ku* 苦) and hardship (*nan* 難), subtraction from the life span (*jiansuan* 減算), receiving the three bad rebirths (*sanku* 三苦), or falling into hell (*rudiyu* 入地獄).

The hells, then, come either in a group of eighteen or are described as nine realms of darkness. The eighteen hells (*shiba diyu* 十八地獄) go back to Buddhist origins; they are dark places where people are being tortured for their past sins with swords, knives, fiery carriages, boiling cauldrons, iron beds, freezing lakes, and so on. There are eight hot and ten cold hells, as described in the *Shiba diyu jing* 十八地獄經 (Sûtra on the Eighteen Hells, T. 731, 17.528b–30a), ascribed to An Shigao 安士高 of the Later Han but most certainly a Chinese apocryphon (Mochizuki 1936, 3574c; Ôno 1980, 5.198c–99b). The nine realms of darkness (*jiuyou* 九幽) are an ancient Chinese abode of the dead, at the deep springs of the nine rivers and also known as the "nine springs" (*jiuquan* 九泉), not unlike the better known Yellow Springs (*huangquan* 黃泉) at the source of the Yellow River (see Sawada 1968).

Good fortune, on the other hand, is envisioned as the tilling and planting of fields, the so-called fields of blessedness (*futian* 福田), imagined to match the physical fields that farmers plow and cultivate in ordinary life (see Cole 1998). They are areas where practitioners can establish the good fortune that will lead to the good karma necessary for enlightenment and liberation. A Buddhist concept, these "fields" refer to the acquisition of virtues, such as charity, kindness, and goodness toward all beings (Nakamura 1975, 1187). More specifically, as described in the *Da zhidu lun* 大智度論 or "Greater Wisdom Sutra" (*Mahâprajnâpâramitâ-sâstra*, T. 1509, 25.57–756), they indicate the development of five virtues, such as leaving the common world, giving up egoistic tendencies in favor of the dharma, cutting off emotional relationships, giving up worldly fate and ambition, and pursuing the Greater Vehicle by developing the wish to save all beings (Mochizuki 1936, 4396b–97c). In Daoism, as described in the beginning of the *Yinyuan jing*, they indicate the activities and wishes to create good living conditions for all beings, from the emperor and the state on down to the poor and orphaned (1.1a–9b). Throughout, medieval texts never tire of encouraging practitioners to "widely establish fields of blessedness" (*guangjian futian* 廣建福田).

There are various ways of doing this, depending on one's status in the Daoist hierarchy. As a lay follower, the best way, aside from observing the precepts and periods of temporary renunciation, is to give donations (*shi* 施, *shibu* 施布) to feed, clothe, and house the monks and nuns. The merit gained from such donations is unlimited and stands in no relation to the effort made, coming back time and again to grant good fortune to one's family, estate, and future rebirths.

As a religious of lower standing, a key activity for planting good fortune is the development of the right attitude of mind, expressed as the creation of good intentions, positive resolutions, and vows in one's heart. The key term here is *yuan* 願, literally "wish," "resolve." In Buddhism, the term renders *pranidhâna* and expresses the vow, commonly undertaken by bodhisattvas, to be firm and resolute in seeking liberation and do everything in one's power to assist all beings in their effort toward it (Nakamura 1975, 200). It first appears in Daoism in the early Numinous Treasure texts, meaning "vow" or "resolution" (see Bokenkamp 1989). In institutional manuals, it is used either to encourage practitioners to develop the good intentions (sec. 24) or to introduce a communal chant or prayer on behalf of all beings (sec. 15–18). In the latter sense, the term may also express a formal ritual action and appear in the compound *qiyuan* 啟願, "announcement and prayer." It is still used in this sense today (see Lagerwey 1987, 146). In the translation hereafter, *yuan* is most commonly rendered with the word "pray."

As a more advanced practitioner, one can go beyond mere mental prayers and good wishes and begin to actively "assist and save" (*jidu* 濟度) all beings, preferably by encouraging them to observe the precepts, give ample donations, and participate in activities of the Dao. Eventually one may go on to actually save people (*duren* 度人), a term used first in Numinous Treasure scriptures with reference to "universal salvation" (e.g., *Durenjing* 度人經; see Bokenkamp 1997). In both Buddhist and Daoist texts, the term indicates "ordination," the ritual by which the practitioner is already considered part of the Dao and thereby "saved." Attaining this salvation, the devout Daoist will eventually ascend to the higher realms of heaven, where he is protected by martial deities such as the vajras (*jingang* 金鋼) and vîras (*lishi* 力士), assisted by jade lads (*yutong* 玉童) and jade maidens (*yunü* 玉女), and joins the ranks of the sages, perfected, and immortals (*sheng zhen xian* 聖真仙) in the entourage of the Heavenly Worthies (*tianzun* 天尊). A life of ease and celestial splendor is the result, happiness never ending for eternities to come.

Rules and Formalities

Before this desired state is reached, however, there is much hard work to be done, and both body and mind have to be thoroughly disciplined. To do so, practitioners submit to a large variety of rules and formalities. The texts have a highly specific terminology for these practices and use ten different terms for "rules" alone, each providing a slightly different slant on the issue of regulating and organizing human behavior.

The most general among them is *ke* 科, which means "rules" in the widest sense and can refer to anything from a moral injunction to a specific behavioral guideline. The term is combined with several other characters to form compounds, such as *kemu* 科目, "standardized rules," "code"; *zunke* 遵科, "rules and regulations"; and *kejie* 科戒, "rules and precepts." *Jie* 戒, "precepts," is a term used specifically for proscriptive and prescriptive sets of attitude guidelines, as for example in the ten precepts, contained also in the *Fengdao kejie*, which include "Do not steal or receive unrighteous wealth!" and "When I see someone unfortunate, I will support him to recover good fortune!" (sec. 18). The term commonly occurs also in two compounds: *jingjie* 經戒, indicating the "scriptural precepts," moral rules based on the teachings of the scriptures, or the "scriptures and precepts," two of the four items (plus ritual methods and registers) transmitted at ordination; and *zhaijie* 齋戒, describing the devotional practice undertaken by lay followers to observe a set of basic precepts and certain periods of intensified purgation practice.[5]

More strictly prohibitive are two further terms for rules, *jin* 禁, "prohibition," and *ji* 忌, "avoidance," "taboo." They are used to express radical rules against certain types of behavior or infringement that will cause major karmic fatalities. More prescriptive rules, moreover, are expressed as either *lü* 律, "statutes," or *ling* 令, "ordinances," words that also occur in combination, as in the famous Celestial Master formula, "Swiftly, swiftly, in accordance with the

---

5. Most prominent among these are the ten days of uprightness (*shizhi* 十直), adopted from Buddhist practice. See Soymié 1977.

statutes and ordinances."[6] They refer to the idea that the celestials set up specific codes that have to be followed at all times and can be invoked to prevent or limit unwarranted interference.

Then again, there are more specific, concrete terms, such as *yi* 儀, "observances," which refers to the concrete activities to be undertaken in a ritual or formal monastic context and often appears in the compound *weiyi* 威儀, "dignified observances." Numerous texts have this term in the title when their content includes prescriptions of practical daily behavior. Other concrete terms are *ze* 側, "regulations," which appears in the context of lesser details, such as the size of certain statues, buildings, and the like; and *gui* 軌, "organization" or "pattern," used to describe the overall system or structure of regulations. Last but not least, there is *gangji* 綱紀, "guidelines," which is used in the *Fengdao kejie* specifically in relation to setting up standards for the behavior of newly ordained monks and nuns. Following these standards of devotion, honesty, virtue, and goodness, they can become strongly established in the Dao and attain higher ranks; otherwise they have to return to the laity (sec. 7).

While violation of the rules is most commonly expressed with words like "go against" or "fail to comply with" (*wei* 違), "neglect" (*sun* 損), or "violate" (*fan* 反), obedience to them is expressed with terms like "honor" (*feng* 奉—also used to express "worship" in relation to the Dao), "uphold" (*chi* 持—commonly used in the compound *fengdao chijie* 奉道持戒), and "observe" (*xing* 行). Usually obedience also involves the feeling of respect (*jing* 敬) or "cinnabar sincerity" (*dancheng* 丹誠), which is often described as essential or keen (*jing* 精).

Physically this obedience manifests in frequent bows (*bai* 拜) or obeisances (*li* 禮), prostrations (*jishou* 稽首), and kowtows (*ketou* 磕頭). Bows usually involve a standing posture and the joining of the palms (*hezhang* 合掌), the folding of hands over the chest (*gong* 拱), or their positioning in a specific sacred gesture (*shoujue* 手訣), an adaptation of Buddhist mudras (see Mitamura 2002). Prostrations commonly are described as "opening the hands and placing the head between them on the floor" (*jikai* 稽開). Obeisances of any form can also be paid mentally (*xinli* 心禮) (*Shishi weiyi*, sec. 2). They are an essential part of all rituals, involving activities such as circumambulating (*rao* 繞) a sacred image, offering incense (*shangxiang* 上香), or reciting (*song* 誦), chanting (*yong* 詠), or intoning (*chang* 唱) an incantation (*zhou* 咒) or scripture (*jing* 經) (*Fengdao kejie*, sec. 11).

Ritual activities in general are described as performing rites to the Dao (*xingdao* 行道)—not to be confused with *daoxing* 道行, which is a generic term for Daoist practice—and commonly involve the presentation of offerings (*gongyang* 供養), a term also used to express the Buddhist practice of *pûjâ*. Rites could be audiences with the gods (*chao* 朝), ceremonies of repentance (*xieguo* 謝過, *chanhui* 懺悔), including formal confessions (*shouyan* 首言; see Tsuchiya 2002), or purgations (*zhai* 齋). The latter is a most complicated term, which can refer to four different forms of ritual. First, as documented in ancient sources it has the

6. For a discussion of this formula in Han funerary documents and the early Celestial Masters, see Seidel 1987. On its role in later Daoism and Japanese Shugendô, see Maeda 1989; Miyazawa 1994.

original meaning of "purification." In this sense, *zhai* refers to the preparatory purification before rituals through baths, fasting, sexual abstention, and the avoidance of death, blood, and other forms of defilement. Second, under the influence of Buddhism and following the Hindu practice of *pûjâ*, *zhai* also came to mean "vegetarian feast," the offering of food to the deities and the sharing of food among humans and gods, lay donors and recluses; in this sense it is used to refer to the ceremonial noon meal of monastics, with compounds including *zhaifu* 齋服, "consecrated food," *zhaichu* 齋廚, "kitchen," *zhaiqi* 齋器, "ceremonial dishes," *zhaishi* 齋食, "ceremonial meal," and *zhaitang* 齋堂, "refectory."

Third, the term indicates "temporary renunciation," an occasion when members of the laity took eight precepts instead of five and participated in the monastic routine on certain specific days (see Soymié 1977); it is in this sense that *zhai* most commonly occurs in the compound *zhaijie* 齋戒. And fourth, *zhai* means "rite of purgation," "festival," or "levee," a major ritual event dedicated to the expiation of sins or the blessing of ancestors and the emperor, held at regular intervals throughout the year (see Benn 2000; Kohn 2001; 2003; Malek 1985; Yamada 1999). Commonly, *zhai* activities involved the participation of lay followers, called, according to their roles in the festivities, purgation head (*zhaizhu* 齋主) or purgation leader (*zhaiguan* 齋官), both expressions for "donor" or "sponsor";[7] and purgation participant (*zhairen*), anyone joining the festivities and participating in the accompanying banquet.[8]

Simple regular rites did not involve such complex activities but usually consisted of taking refuge (*gui* 皈、歸) in the Three Treasures (*sanbao* 三寶), the Dao, the scriptures, and the masters (*dao jing shi* 道經師)—a concept adopted from Buddhism, where the Triple Gem (*sanbao* 三寶) included Buddha, dharma, and sangha (*fo jing seng* 佛經僧). Refuge usually meant to surrender one's life (*ming* 命), body (*shen* 身), and heart (*xin* 心) or spirit (*shen* 神) to the Dao. Following this, incense was offered and incantations sung, and hymns (*song* 頌) or praises (*zan* 贊) were offered. Requests (*qing* 請) or prayers (*yuan* 願) might follow, and more rarely a formal communication to the gods, such as a memorial (*biao* 表, *zou* 奏), petition (*zhang* 章), announcement (*gao* 告), or invocation (*qi* 啟).[9]

Regular rites were held at the six periods (*liushi* 六時) every day—midnight, cockcrow, dawn, noon, dusk, and midevening—a schedule also followed in Buddhism (see Pas 1987). Ceremonies at dawn and dusk were slightly more extensive and known as regular audience services (*changchao* 常朝) (*Fengdao kejie*, sec. 15). The activities at noon included the ceremonial meal and were known as the noon purgation (*zhongzhai* 中齋) (*Fengdao kejie*, sec. 16). The other three occasions are described simply as rites to the Dao (*xingdao* 行道).

---

7. These lay participants are still active today and still called *zhaizhu*. For a picture of one holding an incense burner during a modern *jiao*, see Lagerwey 1987, 309.

8. Earlier forms of banquets involved so-called kitchen feasts (*chu* 廚) and a rite known as "rice for the wise" (*fanxian* 飯賢). See Stein 1971; Mollier 2000. For details on ritual meals in medieval Daoism, see Kohn 2001.

9. This sequence of ritual events still holds true today. See Lagerwey 1987.

Even when not engaged in formal ritual activities, Daoists were encouraged to keep their minds focused on the Dao at all times, a practice described as *niandao* 念道 (being mindful of the Dao) or *nianjing* 念經 (remembering the scriptures). A similar idea is also expressed in the injunction to maintain continuous awareness of the deities residing in the body, keeping their image and essence present at all times.[10] This continuity of awareness is also emphasized in Buddhism, which describes it as the development of mindfulness (*smrti*), a state in Chinese expressed with the term *nian* 念 or, if one is to remain mindful of the Buddha, as *nianfo* 念佛. The practice can be purely mental or find expression in the vocalization of chant reciting the Buddha's name (see Kiyota 1978).

The Physical Setting

All this activity and observation of rules, moreover, took place in a complex monastic compound known as *guan* 觀. This term originally means "to observe," and as such was used in words describing observation places, such as *louguan* 樓觀 or "observation tower." Louguan is also the name of the major Daoist institution of fifth- and sixth-century north China and its first known major monastery. It is assumed that the expression *guan* for monastery derives from this location (see Kohn 2001; 2003; Schipper 1984). Before the prominence of Louguan, the term used for Daoist institutions was *guan* 館, a word meaning "hostel," "lodge," "abode." It referred to small institutions, often single buildings, given to renowned recluses by emperors or local aristocrats, partly to honor their spiritual powers, partly in an effort to control unregulated and potentially upsetting members of the populace (see Bumbacher 2000a; 2000b). The recluses living in these "abodes" could be celibate hermits or groups of devotees, married and with children. The word *guan* 館, then, does not refer to monastic institutions proper but indicates their forerunner, especially in south China.

   Guan 觀, the standard term for monasteries, from the late sixth century onward, has a much more precise organizational definition and involves celibacy, sets of rules, regular rituals, and so on. The term is also translated "belvedere" in reference to its original meaning of "lookout" (see Reiter 1983; 1998; Schafer 1978); sometimes the English term "abbey" is used, because many *guan* had communal functions and were locations of great festivals and other lay engagements (see Kohn and Kirkland 2000). In the mid-Tang, when Emperor Xuanzong relocated the administration of Daoist priests into the Bureau of the Imperial Family—since they all, as the Tang rulers, claimed descent from Lord Lao—many *guan* were renamed *gong* 宮, "palace," in acknowledgment of the Daoists' imperial status (see Hahn 2000). Another more technical term sometimes used instead of *guan* is *daochang* 道場, the "sacred space of the Dao," or the

---

10. Meditation manuals often emphasize the need to maintain constant awareness of the deities. Among gods so remembered are especially the Great One (Taiyi 太一)—as in the practice of *shouyi* 守一 (guarding the One)—and the Three Ones (Sanyi 三一). See Kohn 1989; Andersen 1980.

"Daoist ritual center." This term is also used for ordinary spaces dedicated temporarily for ritual purposes through formal consecration. It is still applied today, signifying the "Land of the Way," the high point of the three-day *jiao* 醮 ceremony (Lagerwey 1987, 106).

A typical medieval Daoist institution, then, was considered a holy location of the Dao, an auspicious place (*fudi* 福地) for cosmos and community. It typically consisted of three concentric circles: an inner circle of worship, meditation, and daily necessity; a second circle of support activities, including servants' quarters, guest houses, and separate buildings for spiritual work; and a third circle of economic necessity, with fields, orchards, stables, and mills.

As outlined in section 4 of the *Fengdao kejie*, the key facility in the inner circle was the Sanctuary of the Heavenly Worthies (Tianzun dian 天尊殿), a holy audience hall built in an imposing size of many *jian* 簡 (bays) and ornamented with gold and jade carvings, painted with murals using cinnabar and green colors, and covered with a tiled or thatched roof. Immediately in front of it, a flat area remained open for the erection of an altar platform (*tan* 壇). Often called *lingguan xuantan* 靈觀玄壇, the "holy altar in a numinous monastery," it was set up for special ceremonies and ordinations. Built on a foundation of tamped earth, layered bricks, or piled stones, it consisted of a wooden scaffold that usually rose three or five layers up. It symbolized the division of the cosmos in heaven, earth, and humanity, and forms a central axis of communication with the divine (Lagerwey 1987, 25–48).

Behind the sanctuary, moreover, there was the scriptural lecture hall (*jiangjing tang* 講經堂), accessible also to the laity, plus a lesser hall of teaching reserved for the recluses, the law explanation building (*shuofa yuan* 説法院). In addition, next to the sanctuary were the scripture tower (*jinglou* 經樓) and the bell pavilion (*zhongge* 鍾閣), which imitated the holy storage spaces and announcement centers of the celestials above. To the right and left of this central axis were buildings of practical necessity. On one side, usually the one that had running water, there were the kitchen (*zhaichu* 齋廚), the refectory (*zhaitang* 齋堂), the bath house (*yutang* 浴堂), and the scriptorium (*xiejing fang* 寫經坊). On the other side were masters' chambers (*shifang* 師房) and residences of the monks (*juchu* 居處), plus their center of personal practice, the meditation building (*jingsi yuan* 靜思院).

The second circle had buildings of two types: one of a more utilitarian nature that included the servants' quarters (*jingren fang* 淨人坊—adopting the Buddhist term "pure people" for servants), the main gate house (*menlou* 門樓), the stables (*leima fang* 驟馬坊) and carriage houses (*che'niu fang* 車牛坊), and workshops for fashioning and repairing statues, as well as quarters for both lay (*suke fang* 俗客坊) and ordained visitors (*shifang ke fang* 十方客坊). Another set of buildings was of a more spiritual nature, important for spiritual worship and cultivation. Here we have the ascension building (*shengxia yuan* 昇遐院) for the dying, also called the "building for transforming into an immortal" (*xianhua yuan* 仙化院), ideally placed in the northwest corner of the compound and containing an altar with an image of a deity. After successful transformation, the spirits of Daoists were further honored in another hall of the same type, the incense building (*shaoxiang yuan* 燒香院), where memorial services would be held at regular intervals.

In addition, the second circle contained a number of special terraces, pavilions, and towers (*tai* 臺, *ge* 閣, *lou* 樓), built in continuation of the immortals' hermitage of immortals and the oratory of the Celestial Masters. The latter was a smaller, detached building, ten to twenty square meters in size, covered by a thatched roof, surrounded by running water, and protected by a wall. Kept extremely simple, it could contain only a wooden bench, an incense burner, incense lamp, table for petitions, and writing knife. Devotees had to enter it very circumspectly and only after undergoing extensive purification. All actions in the oratory were to be accompanied by ritual formality and conscious awareness of the spirits).[11]

The terraces, pavilions, and towers of the medieval monastery were, as was the compound as a whole, build in imitation of similar structures in the heavens above. There terraces were raised edifices that provided room for celestial audiences and always had divine music chiming about them; pavilions housed gods and immortals, sporting vermilion corners and jade turrets; and towers were multistoried structures used for keeping the life records in jade ledgers and the originals of the sacred scriptures in golden tablets (*Shangqing daolei shixiang* 2.3a). Examples of edifices used on earth include Terraces to Search Perfection, to Refine *Qi*, and to Wait for the Immortals; Pavilions of the Wandering Immortals, of Striding on the Clouds, and of Meeting the Wind; and Towers of the Nine Immortals, of Free and Easy Wandering, and of Tranquil Mindfulness. They were dedicated to the ecstatic excursions of the Daoists and to the reception of the immortals should they decide to descend; in some cases they might even house alchemical laboratories and be "elixir chambers" (*danfang* 丹房).

The terminology for the various types of buildings is distinct and clearly defined. As the *Fengdao kejie* says, "'sanctuary' [*dian* 殿] is what we call a residence of the sages, while 'hall' [*tang* 堂] refers to a place lived in and used by people" (1.14a). Both terms come from ancestor worship and are equally used in the mainstream, Confucian tradition, the former denoting an audience hall in Tang official usage (Xiong 2000, 61). *Yuan* 院, on the other hand, is more of a garden in civil use and has acquired the sense of "hermitage" in a Buddhist context. The word is translated by the neutral term "building" because it designates various separate structures for specific purposes, some of which are more secluded than others. The translation "cloister" for *yuan*, sometimes used in Buddhist studies (e.g., Foulk 1993, 164), is only of limited value because the facility intended is a separate building often far away from any courtyard. *Fang* 房, next, means "chamber" and indicates the masters' residences; to be distinguished from *fang* 坊, "quarters" or "workshop," used for the dormitories of servants and practical work stations.

The third circle of the monastic compound, finally, included more mundane facilities. It housed the herb garden (*yaopu* 藥圃), orchard (*guoyuan*

---

11. For details on the oratory, see Yoshikawa 1987; Bumbacher 2000a, 481–2; Chen 1975, 330–51; Stein 1963, 38.

果園), and vegetable plots (*zaitian* 菜田), as well as agricultural estates (*zhuangt-ian* 莊田) and water mills (*nianwei* 碾磑). The *Fengdao kejie* emphasizes that all fruits and flowers to be presented in offerings as well as all vegetables used in meals, excluding the five strong-smelling vegetables (*wuxin* 五辛, garlic, ginger, scallions, leeks, and onions), should be grown locally in the sacred compound. Commonly large religious institutions also owned property that they rented out for income. Most prominent among these were the agricultural estates and water mills, an important part of the institution's "fixed assets" (*changzhu* 常主), a term used both to indicate the communal monastic property and the per-manent residents of the monastery (Gernet 1995, 67; see also Twitchett 1956; 1957).

All these various buildings and facilities, then, were where Daoists activated their ritual practice and followed their detailed rules of life. Instructions on their organization and construction usually involve technical details and measure-ments, such as *jian* (bay), the space between pillars, usually about five meters. Others include the following.

LENGTH:

> mu 畝, acre = 450–600 square meters
> li 里, mile = about 500 meters
> zhang 丈, ten feet = about 30 meters
> bu 步, step = 1.50 meters
> chi 尺, foot = about 30 cm
> cun 寸, inch = about 3 cm

WEIGHT:

> dan 石, picul = 72 kilos (120 *jin*)
> jin 斤, catty = 597 grams (16 *liang*)
> liang 兩, ounce = 37 grams

LIQUIDS:

> dou 斗, peck = about 7 liters
> sheng 升, pint = about 0.7 liters

People and Ranks

Within this environment of sacred space and ritual activity, people played a number of different roles and were designated by many different terms. The most fundamental division was made between ordinary people (*suren* 俗人), people of the Dao (*daomin* 道民), and ordained monks or nuns (*chujia* 出家). People of the Dao were generally also known as good men and women (*shan nan-*

ren 善男人, *shan nüren* 善女人), believers (*xinshi* 信士), Daoist followers (*daomen* 道門), or followers of the divine law (*famen* 法門, *fatu* 法徒). Those among them in good standing, moreover, were known as elders (*shangren* 上人, *huchang* 戶長); those giving amply to the institution were benefactors (*shizhu* 施主); and those sponsoring purgation rites on behalf of their family and country were donors or sponsors (*zhaizhu* 齋主, *zhaiguan* 齋官)

Ordained monks and nuns in the texts are often specifically referred to as *daoshi nüguan* 道士女冠. Reiter refers to them as "Daoist priests or nuns" (1998, 51) conflating two different types of religious specialists that are less separate in the East than in the West. Typically in Western religions, priests are trained to handle the sacraments, while monks and nuns are dedicating their lives to worship and prayer. Historically only a fraction of Christian monastics were also priests (see Dudley 1991). In contrast, in Eastern traditions, monks— unless they pursued the isolated life of hermits—typically were also priests, and monastic institutions functioned as priestly seminaries. As a result, female practitioners could just as easily be described as priestesses, or priests as monks; they were all empowered to perform services matching their respective rank of ordination.

The phrase *daoshi nüguan* is used pervasively throughout medieval literature. This indicates that both men and women joined the Dao as recluses and were treated equally in all respects—in fact, the *Fengdao kejie* makes a strong point emphasizing that the only way women Daoists were different is in their headgear, their headdress being larger and more elaborate than that of their male counterpart. The appellation *nüguan* 女冠 or "female hat," derives from this feature, replacing the term *nüguan* 女官, female officer, commonly used earlier.[12] Daoists referring to themselves, moreover, often speak of "poor Daoists" (*pindao* 貧道), while when treated by outsiders they are "holy persons" (*fashen* 法身), inviolate and of supernatural standing.

Altogether the crowd of the faithful and the ordained monks and nuns are known as the "four ranks" (*sibei* 四輩) or "four orders" (*siyi* 四宜), terms adapted from Buddhism and referring to lay men, lay women, monks, and nuns. Among them, moreover, there were a large number of specific ranks and titles given to people who had taken a certain number of precepts (*jie* 戒) and received certain specific registers (*lu* 籙), talismans (*fu* 符), and scriptures (*jing* 經), and knew how to activate them with the help of ritual methods (*fa* 法). As the *Fengdao kejie* outlines in section 13, the lowest ranks were often given to children, beginning at age seven, and involved the transmission of registers with the names of certain protective generals. They included the following titles:

Disciple of the Great Dao (*dadao dizi* 大道弟子)
Disciple of the Heavenly Worthy (*tianzun dizi* 天尊弟子)

12. Edward Schafer speculates that the change in terminology occurred in the early Tang and was due to the use of *nüguan* 女官 for female palace attendants (1978, 11). If this is correct, it would imply that the Dunhuang manuscripts of the *Fengdao kejie*, which consistently use *nüguan*, are dated either before or very early in the Tang.

Disciple of the Three Caverns (*sandong dizi* 參洞弟子)
Register Pupil (*lusheng* 籙生)
Register Pupil of Orthodox Unity (*zhengyi lusheng* 正一籙生)

Following this, the lowest level of the hierarchy, which Benn describes as ranks of "initiation" rather than "ordination" (1991, 74), involves titles of the Celestial Masters:

Male/Female Officer Governing the Parish So-and-so (*mou zhiqi nanguan nüguan* 某治氣男官女官)
Disciple of the Three Ones, Perfected of Red Yang *Qi* (*sanyi dizi chiyang zhenren* 三一弟子赤陽真人)
Disciple of the Dignified Covenant of Orthodox Unity Governing the Parish So-and-so (*mou zhiqi zhengyi mengwei dizi* 某治氣正一盟威弟子)
Disciple . . . of Yangping Parish and Perfected of Original Destiny (*yangping zhi . . . dizi yuanming zhenren* 陽平治弟子元命真人)
Disciple . . . of Great Mystery Section and Perfected of Original Destiny (*taixuan bu . . . dizi yuanming zhenren* 太玄部弟子元命真人)

Next in the hierarchy, according to Zhang Wanfu, is the formal taking of the ten precepts, which marks the first level of ordination and allows people to carry the title Disciple of Pure Faith (*qingxin dizi* 清信弟子).[13]

Following this are a rank and title given to people who have received talismans, registers, and precepts associated with the *Shenzhou jing* 神咒經 (Scripture of Divine Incantations), a text classified as Abyss Cavern (*dongyuan* 洞淵): Perfected Great Ancestor of the Divine Incantations of Abyss Cavern (*dongyuan shenzhou dazong zhenren* 洞淵神咒大宗真人).

The next higher level involves receiving materials related to the *Daode jing* and the hagiography of Lord Lao. Four ranks belong in this category:

Disciple of Laozi's Green Thread and Golden Knob (*Laozi qingsi jinniu dizi* 老子青絲金鈕弟子)[14]
Disciple of Eminent Mystery (*gaoxuan dizi* 高玄弟子)
Preceptor of Highest Eminent Mystery (*taishang gaoxuan fashi* 太上高玄法師)
Disciple of the Highest Lord (*taishang dizi* 太上弟子)

After this comes the reception of texts and talismans of the Spirit Cavern, materials associated with the Three Sovereigns and their powers over heaven and earth. People here can receive the following titles:

Disciple of Spirit Cavern (*dongshen dizi* 洞神弟子)
Preceptor of All-Highest Spirit Cavern (*wushang dongshen fashi* 無上洞神法師)

---

13. See Benn 1991, 77. The *Fengdao kejie* places this rank among the lowest of categories, with the Disciples of the Great Dao and the Register Pupils.

14. This title refers to the green & gold-colored garb worn by ordinands.

Next are the materials associated with the *Shengxuan jing*, a sixth-century text that already involves doctrines and practices of the integrated system of the Three Caverns. People receiving these are entitled to the rank of Preceptor of Ascension to the Mystery (*shengxuan fashi* 昇玄法師).

From here onward, the highest ranks are entered, those involving materials associated with the Numinous Treasure and Highest Purity schools, that is, the Mystery and Perfection Caverns. In each case they divide into two levels, one where only charts and registers are transmitted, and a second that involves the reception of the entire canon. They are:

> Disciple of Highest Mystery Cavern of Numinous Treasure (*taishang lingbao dongxuan dizi* 太上洞玄弟子)
> Preceptor of All-Highest Mystery Cavern (*wushang dongxuan fashi* 無上洞玄法師)
> Preceptor of Perfection Cavern (*dongzhen fashi* 洞真法師)
> Preceptor of All-Highest Perfection Cavern (*wushang dongzhen fashi* 無上洞真法師)

The very highest rank at the very top, moreover, which involves having not only the collected scriptures but also a variety of ritual paraphernalia, such as the "interlocking belt of Mystery Metropolis," is that of a Preceptor of the All-Highest Three Caverns (*wushang sandong fashi* 無上三洞法師).

This hierarchy was active both in the monasteries and among the priesthood, priests of higher ranks being by definition also ordained monks or nuns. In contrast to the extensive information on this aspect of Daoist medieval organization, there are no titles or descriptions of institutional offices transmitted in the texts—with the sole exception of the title "abbot" (*guanzhu* 觀主), a sketchy list of monastic roles, and the standard description of ritual officers needed for the performance of great purgation rites (*Yaoxiu keyi* 8.7a–16a): the ritual master of lofty virtue (*gaode fashi* 高德法師), the cantor (*dujiang* 都講), the purgation overseer (*jianzhai* 監齋), the incense attendant (*shixiang* 侍香), and the lamp attendant (*shideng* 侍燈).[15]

The ritual master was the key protagonist of the rite; he visualized the gods and commanded the divine presence, and tended to remain in isolated purity to focus on his inner powers. The cantor orchestrated the movements of the ritual master, made sure the intention of the donor (to heal a disease, pray for good fortune, or offer repentance) was clearly expressed in the memorials, and scheduled all activities. The purgation overseer, next, made sure that the donor and his family were aware of the rules and stuck to the schedule. The incense and lamp attendants, finally, were in charge of the concrete setup, making sure that the burners were well stoked and the lamps lit in good time (see Kohn 2003).

All in all, medieval Daoists were organized very stringently and had a large number of specific ranks and titles, each associated not only with particular talismans, registers, scriptures, and precepts but also with vestments of a par-

---

15. The same officers are also described in the *Wushang biyao* and are still actively involved in Daoist ceremonies today (see Lagerwey 1987, 33).

ticular nature, color, and ornateness and other paraphernalia of ritual power. The organization was complex and the participants colorful, contributing significantly to the splendor and excellence of medieval life. The *Fengdao kejie* is an important source providing access to this otherwise hidden world, showing how Daoist life was envisioned in its ideal form and how religious attainment could be found under the concrete circumstances and through the organized daily practices of a religious institution.

PART II

Translation

Sandong Fengdao Kejie

*Rules and Precepts for Worshiping the Dao
According to the Three Caverns*

Translator's Note

The following translation is based on the edition of the text in DZ 1125, with supplementary sections from Dunhuang manuscripts and citations in Tang works.
The English rendition is based on the original Chinese, but makes occasional
use of Yoshioka's Japanese translation (1976, 161–219). Readings that were
reached particularly with his help and also those that differ significantly from it
are indicated in the footnotes. In addition, the earlier partial translation of the
text by Florian Reiter (1988; 1998) was examined but not used, since his reading
and interpretation differ significantly from mine.

The footnotes provide crossreferences to the manuscripts P. 2337 and S.
3863, which contain versions of *juan* 4–6 and parts of *juan* 1 (sec. 4), as well as
to other Daoist texts of the same period that contain comparable information, as
for example, the *Yinyuan jing*. They also explain technical terms and names and
titles mentioned, comment on the intention of the text, and explain the translation of specific ideosycretic phrases.

Preface

[1.1a] The [Master of the] Seven Perfected[1] said:

Investigating the great scriptures of the Three Caverns, I have generally drawn up [a survey of] the dignified observances[2] and rules and precepts [contained in them]. Regarding all Daoists, whether male or female, be it their deportment and actions, sitting and rising, sleeping and resting, clothing and vestments, food and drink, lodging and staying, or cells and residences, no activity is not written out in the instructions of the scriptures.

Be it the establishment of monasteries[3] or [procedures of] ordination,[4] the creation of sacred images or the copying of scriptures, the presentation of offerings or the performance of obeisances, the burning of incense or the lighting of lamps, the reading and recitation or the lecturing and explication [of the scriptures], the transmission [of precepts] or the invocation and request [of the gods], the precepts for rites of purgation[5] or the patterning of observances, personal cultivation or the practice of the divine law[6]—every single activity has its specific regulations!

All these are described in detailed entries whose origin goes back a long time. However, because their textual documentation is overwhelming and diffuse, it is not easy to get a clear grasp on them. People may have seen them once, yet forget them again later; they may have seen them but do not practice them; or

---

1. This appellation Qizhen 七真 refers to Jin Ming 金明, a Highest Purity master of the mid–sixth century, who received several revelations from high celestial deities and was divinized soon after his death. It is unlikely that he himself wrote the preface or any part of the *Fengdao kejie* we have today. See the introduction (also Kohn 1997a).

2. This translates *weiyi* 威儀, indicating the concrete behavioral rules in a ritual or monastic context.

3. This translates *guan* 觀. Another common term, also used by Reiter, is the term "belvedere," originally coined by Edward Schafer in reference to the first Daoist institution at Louguan, the lookout tower where Yin Xi spotted the emigrating Laozi. The term implies the function of Daoist sacred locations as observatories and places to communicate with the stars. Another common translation of *guan* is abbey (see Kohn and Kirkland 2000), indicating the presence of an abbot or abbess and the community role of the institution, its location for ritual and festival services for lay benefits and with extensive lay participation. In this translation, I prefer the term "monastery" for *guan* as being the most neutral.

4. This translates *duren* 度人, lit. "saving people." The expression occurs in the Lingbao scriptures with reference to "universal salvation" (e.g., *Duren jing*; see Bokenkamp 1997), and in Buddhist and monastic texts indicates "ordination," the ritual by which the practitioner is already considered part of the Dao and thereby "saved."

5. This renders *zhai* 齋, a complex term that has four distinct meanings in medieval Daoism: "purification," "vegetarian feast," "temporary renunciation," and "rite of purgation," "festival." See Malek 1985; Yamada 1999; Benn 2000.

6. This term translates *fa* 法, the word used in ancient China for "law" and in Buddhism for "dharma." In Daoism, the connotation is the holy system and organization of the religion, thus "divine law."

they practice them but not all the way. Then again, practitioners may follow their own inclinations, letting themselves be guided by their personal feelings.

In this way, each [group of Daoists] has [now developed] different sets of dignified observances on how to ascend the altar and enter the oratory.[7] [1b] Each individual has created his or her own patterned regulations on how to perform ritual repentances and scripture recitations. There is no mutual interaction or joint obedient worship any more. As a result, neither the older disciples nor the beginners have any idea of who or what is right. Already practitioners have gone off in many directions and lost the Dao. They proceed with only little understanding and follow the path of error, spending their days in laziness and willfully switching around the times of the dignified observances. Worse than that, they compete in ornate speeches and measure their skills against each other. At the hours of invocation, they perform according to ever new systems; on the days of confession, they completely abolish the old observances.

As years and months pass by, the rules and precepts are increasingly abandoned and destroyed, the accumulated new customs become regular, and [of the true rules] not one in ten survives. Anyone following the scriptural precepts and complying with the rules in his activities is being ridiculed and accused of not complying with the orthodox canon. Already, thus, there is much darkness and little enlightenment, and the further one advances the more error one gets into. The keeping of the divine law is negligent, falling ever deeper into destruction.

Carefully examining previous generations, I find them already quite decadent; looking down to consider practitioners today and beyond, I think they will be mired [in corruption] like a deep valley. For this reason, I herewith proceed to lay out the essentials of cultivation schedule and practice in 520 entries and eight sections of observances. Dividing them into three *juan*, I entitle the collection "Rules and Precepts for Worshiping the Dao According to the Three Caverns."[8] All [information contained therein] issues directly from the scriptures and records and is not based on empty talk, [2a] so that in a general way the ten thousand [ways of] antiquity are joined together in one organizational structure, and the [rules of the] ten directions are unified in one set of regulations. All being equal in myself, I present them to be spread widely, each rule in its proper section and each item under a systematic heading.

---

7. The "altar" (*tan* 壇) is an outdoor platform, usually of three or more layers, that symbolizes the division of the cosmos in heaven, earth, and humanity, and forms a central axis of communication with the divine (Lagerwey 1987, 25–48). The "oratory" (*jing* 靜, *jingshi* 靜室) is also called the "chamber of silence"; it consists of a single, isolated room with a low bench and an incense burner in which the practitioner communes with the gods (Schipper 1984, 205–7; Yoshikawa 1987).

8. Except for a listing in the *Chongwen zongmu* 崇文總目 catalog of the Song (Loon 1984, 85), no three-juan edition of the text has been detected anywhere. Even the Dunhuang version had at least five juan, the fifth of which survives in P. 2337. Neither could the 520 entries be located. Counting the various items under "The Rules say" together with those headed "The *Scripture* says," one comes to only about half that number. Counting every itemized list, on the other hand, there are far too many. The "eight sections of observances," however, are clear: they refer to the last eight sections of the text, also contained in P. 2337, which each have the word *yi* ("observance") in the title. See the introduction (also Kohn 1997a).

Section 1

Retribution of Sins[1]

[1.2a] (1) The *Scripture* says: Anyone who desecrates or destroys statues or sacred images of the Heavenly Worthies or the Great Dao after death will fall into the nine realms of darkness or the eighteen hells. After ten thousand kalpas [*Yinyuan jing* (hereafter abbreviated YYJ): of receiving pain, the pain will stop and] he will be born again [YYJ: among humanity], in a body suffering from leprosy [YYJ: which will make his whole body ooze pus and blood, be foul-smelling and stinking of rot, so that people will not be pleased to look at him.].

(2) The *Scripture* says: Anyone who curses or destroys the scriptures and manuals of the Three Caverns or the great divine law after death will pass through the nine realms of darkness and the eighteen hells [YYJ: and the palaces of the dead in Fengdu]. After one hundred [YYJ: million] kalpas he will [YYJ: meet a sage who will rescue him from there to] be born again in the body of a wild beast. [YYJ As such he will suffer pain without measure, then] when he returns to the human plane, the root of his tongue will rot and decay, [YYJ: he will always have a tight, constricted throat, and suffer from an ailment in his eyes].

(3) The *Scripture* says: Anyone who slanders the holy person of an ordained monk or nun,[2] in this life will have worms and suffer from leprosy. Having passed through this,[3] he will be born among the six domestic animals.[4]

---

1. This section is an abbreviated citation of section 3 of the *Yinyuan jing* (DZ 336, 2.4a–10a), entitled "Retribution of Bad Deeds" (*wubao* 惡報). For details on this text and a discussion of its karmic doctrines and their Buddhist precursors, see Kohn 1998. A comparative matching of this section in the two texts, including a numeration of entries, is found in Yoshioka 1976, 117–27. To make the work more easily accessible, I have similarly numbered the various items from 1 to 81.

Within the section, entries 1–27 are rather abbreviated in the *Fengdao kejie*, the *Yinyuan jing* giving more details, such as larger numbers of years and more drastic descriptions of punishments. Exceptions are numbers 13 and 21, which are not there at all, and items 17 and 22, which contain longer descriptions. The second part of the text, entries 28–81, is largely identical in both texts, with the following exceptions: numbers 31 and 36 are not contained in the *Yinyuan jing*, and items 33, 39, 47, and 49 have longer explanations.

For reasons of space, I do not point out every single variation between the two texts but limit myself to general annotation throughout and a supplementing of the *Yinyuan jing* version if it adds to the understanding of the text.

2. This renders *chujia fashen* 出家法身. *Chujia* means "leaving the family" and is the technical term for an ordained monk or nun; *fashen* is taken from the Buddhist term for *dharmakâya* and refers to the concrete and holy body or person of a Daoist.

3. This is the literal rendition of *guoqu* 過去, most commonly used to mean "the past." It means here something like "once this has become past." This usage of the term is highly unusual and limited to the *Yinyuan jing*. Yoshioka translates it as "in the future" (1976, 162).

4. These are the horse, cow, sheep, chicken, dog, and pig. They were originally the six types of animals used in sacrifices (*Zhouli* 周禮, "Tianguan 天官;" *Zuozhuan* 左傳, Xi 19).

[2b] (4) The *Scripture* says: Anyone who desecrates or destroys the [YYJ: sage images or] sacred altar in a numinous monastery in this life will have his eyebrows and beard fall out and body rot from within. [YYJ: His hips will drag and his thighs rub. After death, he will fall into the ice-cold hells. When he has suffered there sufficiently,] having passed through this, he will be born in the body of a poisonous snake.

(5) The *Scripture* says: Anyone who is disrespectful to the [YYJ: holy persons of the] Heavenly Worthies or the Great Dao in this life will be stupid and dimwitted, [YYJ: foolish and short, and afflicted by bouts of madness]. Having passed through this, he will be born among the six domestic animals.

(6) The *Scripture* says: Anyone who does not believe in the scriptures and the divine law or the rewards and retribution of fate they describe in this life will be blind and deaf. Having passed through this, he will be born among the wild birds and beasts [YYJ: and only be liberated after uncountable kalpas have passed.]

(7) The *Scripture* says: Anyone who does not believe in the karmic cause and retribution of suffering and good fortune in this life will become a slave. Having passed through this, he will be born among the six barbarian tribes [YYJ: where it is hard to encounter the right law].[5]

(8) The *Scripture* says: Anyone who treats the holy person of an ordained monk or nun with contempt in this life will be crippled. Having passed through this, he will be born among the pigs and dogs [YYJ: where urine and excrement are his constant food and drink. Whoever treats the Three Treasures[6] with contempt will receive a punishment like this].

[3a] (9) The *Scripture* says: Anyone who defiles the auspicious places of the Three Treasures [YYJ: fixed assets] in this life will have a foul-smelling body. Having passed through this, he will be born among manure and filth. [YYJ: After being there for a million kalpas, he will be born in a stagnant pool to live there as a slimy worm.]

(10) The *Scripture* says: Anyone who lasciviously violates the holy person of an ordained monk or nun in this life will be orphaned and widowed and hated and shunned by people. Having passed through this, he will be born among [YYJ: worms feeding on] excrement.

(11) The *Scripture* says: Anyone who commits debauchery and indulges in sex in this life will suffer from insanity. Having passed through this, he will be born among the sows and boars. [YYJ: After being there for several kalpas, he will be born among the wild bulls.]

(12) The *Scripture* says: Anyone who steals the materials or goods of the Three Treasures in this life will be poor and destitute. Having passed through this, he will be born among slaves or the six domestic animals [YYJ: or among the wild birds and beasts, where it is difficult to again obtain a human body.][7]

(13) The *Scripture* says: Anyone who steals anything from the fixed assets [of the monastery] in this life will suffer from wind-induced disorders.

5. These, as described in the *Hou Hanshu* 後漢書 (biography of Ran Youyi), are the Yi of the east, the Man of the south, the Yi of the southwest, the Jiang and Yu of the west, and the Xiongnu of the north.

6. The Three Treasures (*sanbao* 三寶), a term developed under Buddhist influence, are the Dao, the scriptures, and the living masters. See Lagerwey 1981, 31; Benn 1991, 66; Zürcher 1980, 115.

7. Strong rules against stealing from holy monasteries are also found in *Qianzhen ke* 11b.

Having passed through this, he will be born among the pigs, sheep, or other six domestic animals.

[3b] (14) The *Scripture* says: Anyone who steals the goods of any believer or benefactor among the four ranks[8] in this life will go mad [YYJ: so that he cannot hear the name of the Three Treasures]. Having passed through this, he will be born among lunatics.

(15) The *Scripture* says: Anyone who greedily devours the fruit and vegetables of the Three Treasures in this life will suffer from pathological hunger and thirst. Having passed through this, he will be born among the hungry tigers and poisonous snakes, [YYJ: beaten and hunted by people. After suffering from this punishment for a long time, he will be reborn among humanity but still suffer from pathological thirst.]

(16) The *Scripture* says: Anyone who steals ceremonial food or holy food laid out in offerings in this life will be hit by claps of thunder and be killed by malevolent demons. Having passed through this, he will be born in the body of a python snake and, after dying again, become one of the hungry ghosts.

(17) The *Scripture* says: Anyone who steals objects used for offerings or rites of purgation in this life will become a slave. He will be hungry and cold and never manage to get hold of sufficient food and clothing. Having passed through this, he will be born among mangy dogs and poisonous snakes.[9]

(18) The *Scripture* says: Anyone who steals any of the materials or goods surrounding the scriptures and sacred images in this life will suffer leprosy. After death, he will be fall into hell, where he will not obtain pardon for a myriad kalpas. [YYJ: He will then be reborn as a poisonous snake or evil worm.]

[4a] (19) The *Scripture* says: Anyone who curses or scolds the holy person of an ordained monk or nun in this life will suffer from epilepsy. Having passed through this, he will be born among mad dogs.

(20) The *Scripture* says: Anyone who humiliates or shames the holy person of an ordained monk or nun in this life will be put into the kangue and [YYJ: thrown into] prison. Having passed through this, he will be born among the flies and maggots.

(21) The *Scripture* says: Anyone who breaks the precepts in this life will encounter all three kinds of disasters.[10] Having passed through this, he will be born among the stinging hornets or [if human] be deaf and blind.

(22) The *Scripture* says: Anyone who breaks the [fasts during] purgations in this life will suffer from the choking sickness [YYJ: and from a tightly constricted throat]. Having passed through this, he will be born among hungry tigers [YYJ: panthers, or wolves.]

---

8. The four ranks (*sibei* 四輩) indicate the four types of religious followers: monks, nuns, and male and female lay devotees, based on the Buddhist classification of bhikhu, bhikhuni, upâsaka, and upâsikâ. See Mochizuki 1936, 1800a; Zürcher 1980, 116.

9. The *Yinyuan jing* here has: "Anyone who steals vessels, implements, or other objects used for offerings or festivals, in this life will become a lowly beggar who will never be satiated. Anyone who desecrates the statues and images of the Great Dao in this life will be like the mangy dogs and poisonous snakes, hungry and cold without respite and forever unable to find food. Having passed through this, he will be born among the monkeys" (2.5b–6a).

10. *Sanzai* 三災, lit. "three disasters," is also the rendition of Sanskrit *vipatti*; the term indicates major catastrophes that occur at the end of kalpa cycles. A lesser kalpa ends with war, famine, and epidemics; a greater kalpa with scournges by fire, water, and wind. See Mochizuki 1936, 1510a.

(23) The *Scripture* says: Anyone who kills or harms a living being in this life will have a short life span [YYJ: suffer from insanity,] and spend much time in prison and bodily peril. Having passed through this, he will be born among the six domestic animals [YYJ: or nasty beasts].

(24) The *Scripture* says: Anyone who eats meat [YYJ: of wild or other animals] in this life will suffer from the hundred diseases. Having passed through this, he will be born among the wild deer.

[4b] (25) The *Scripture* says: Anyone who craves alcohol [YYJ: or indulges in sex] in this life will become insane and encounter fierce conflagrations. Having passed through this, he will be born in mud and dirt.

(26) The *Scripture* says: Anyone who likes to eat strong-smelling vegetables[11] and defiling foods in this life will have a foul-smelling body. Having passed through this, he will be born among manure and filth.

(27) The *Scripture* says: Anyone who does not keep his mind under firm control and indulges in baiting the ordained monks and nuns in this life will be [as lowly as] a monkey. After death, he will be thrown into the boiling cauldron [of hell].

(28) The *Scripture* says: [YYJ: Obtaining the retribution of] having hands and feet that are bent and broken [YYJ: in all cases] comes from not having paid obeisance and respect to the Three Treasures.

(29) The *Scripture* says: Having hands and feet that are amputated and crippled [YYJ: down to a one-inch stump] comes from not having venerated or properly respected the Three Treasures.

(30) The *Scripture* says: Being blind in both eyes comes from not having believed in the divine law of the scriptures and having treated the Three Treasures lightly.

(31) The *Scripture* says: Catching a nasty disease comes from having been lazy in presenting offerings to the Three Treasures.

[5a] (32) The *Scripture* says: Having a rotting tongue comes from having cursed the scriptural teachings of the Three Caverns and the Great Vehicle.

(33) The *Scripture* says: Being dumb and unable to speak comes from having spoken badly about the holy persons of the ordained monks or nuns [YYJ: or the preceptors] of the Three Treasures.

(34) The *Scripture* says: Having a stuffy nose and being unable to smell either fragrance or stink comes from having indulged in wine, meat, and the five strong-smelling vegetables [YYJ: or from having insulted the Three Treasures].

(35) The *Scripture* says: Having a rotting body [YYJ: with joint after joint falling apart] comes from having desecrated or destroyed the Three Treasures.

---

11. The five strong-smelling vegetables are leeks, scallions, onions, garlic, and ginger. Originally part of the diet of Daoist hermits and immortals (see Yamada 1989), they were not encouraged by Daoist communal practitioners, such as the Celestial Masters, because of their socially disruptive tendencies (*Laojun yibai bashi jie* 老君一百 八十戒, DZ 786, no. 10). They also occur in Buddhism, where they are prohibited in the *Fanwang jing* 梵網經 (Brahmajâla sûtra, T. 1484, 24.997a–1010a), an apocryphon of the mid–fifth century (see Groner 1990; Kusuyama 1982; Yoshioka 1961). The *Lengyan jing* 楞嚴經 (*Surangama sûtra*, T. 945, 19.105–55), in addition to emphasizing their smelly nature, also attributes aphrodisiac and anger-inducing qualities to them (19.141c; Ch'en 1973, 98).

(36) The *Scripture* says: Having one's eyebrows and hair fall out comes from having slandered the Three Treasures.

(37) The *Scripture* says: Having rotting lips that expose the teeth [YYJ: and teeth falling out] and a collapsing nasal bone comes from having desecrated or destroyed the sacred space of the Dao.[12]

(38) The *Scripture* says: Having crooked hips, a bent chest, a twisted spine, and short legs comes from having boasted to or cheated on the Three Treasures.

[5b] (39) The *Scripture* says: Being mad, insane, and deluded comes from not having believed in the karmic cause and retribution of suffering and good fortune.

(40) The *Scripture* says: Having a body and face made ugly and repulsive by boils and contusions comes from having cursed and yelled at the Three Treasures.

(41) The *Scripture* says: Having red eyes, a slanted mouth, and a crooked nose comes from having slandered or ridiculed the holy person of an ordained monk or nun.

(42) The *Scripture* says: Suffering from long-term stupidity and dimwittedness, one's intention and knowledge entirely insufficient, comes from having deceived or doubted the Three Treasures, or again from having cheated on them or treated them with carelessness.

(43) The *Scripture* says: Encountering brigands and robbers and suffering personal harm and loss of goods comes from having stolen the materials and goods of the Three Treasures.

(44) The *Scripture* says: Being submerged in water, carried off and drowned comes from having drunk alcohol [YYJ: and eaten smelly foods] and having been foul or disrespectful [YYJ: to the Three Treasures].

[6a] (45) The *Scripture* says: Being burnt by fire, scorched and roasted, comes from having wasted the wealth of the Three Treasures.

(46) The *Scripture* says: Being bitten and devoured by a poisonous snake comes from having killed or harmed an ordained monk or nun.

(47) The *Scripture* says: Being infected by snake poison [YYJ: or a nasty insect] in one's nose or mouth comes from having spoken vicious and evil curses.

(48) The *Scripture* says: Being devoured by a tiger, wolf, or other wild animal comes from having secretly plotted viciousness and evil.

(49) The *Scripture* says: Being hungry and cold to the point of freezing and starvation, never having enough clothing and food, comes from having pilfered ceremonial food [YYJ: or fruit prepared for offerings or purgations but not yet properly set out in the sacred space of the Dao] or stolen the materials or goods of the fixed assets [monastic community] or the Three Treasures.

---

12. *Daochang* 道場, literally "place of the Dao," has two major meanings in medieval China: a specially created sacred area for the performance of rituals; and the place where a Daoist institution is located, a "Daoist ritual center." Today, in China the term indicates also a major sequence within Daoist ritual, the "Land of the Way" (Lagerwey 1987, 106–48); in Japan (*dôjô*), it is a training center of a religious-cum-sportive nature, where both martial arts, such as kendô or karate, and exorcistic rites, as those of the Mahikari new religion, are being practiced (see Davis 1980).

(50) The *Scripture* says: Being separated from parents, wife, and children, never able to live together with them, comes from having engaged in jealousy and adultery and thereby destroyed other people's harmony and separated them from their [YYJ: loving] kin.

(51) The *Scripture* says: Being poor and destitute, surrounded by hardship and suffering, comes from having broken the precepts and [fasts during] purgations.

(52) The *Scripture* says: Being a slave and of lowly status comes from having stolen and been stingy and greedy.

[6b] (53) The *Scripture* says: Being the object of jealousy and hatred in this life comes from having had an attitude of arrogant contempt and prideful boasting before.

(54) The *Scripture* says: Being addicted to lasciviousness and unable to avoid the revulsion of kin and strangers in this life comes from having been a dog, pig, or other of the six domestic animals before.

(55) The *Scripture* says: Craving alcohol and being mad in this life comes from having been a fish, turtle, shrimp, frog [YYJ: or other water creature] before.

(56) The *Scripture* says: Craving meat and loving to kill in this life comes from having been a poisonous insect or wild beast before.[13]

(57) The *Scripture* says: Being unclean and foul-smelling in this life comes from having been a tadpole or worm before.

(58) The *Scripture* says: Having a foul-smelling and unclean body given to lasciviousness comes from having indulged in the five strong-smelling vegetables or having been a pig or dog before.

(59) The *Scripture* says: Life as one of the six domestic animals comes from having to atone for killing living beings.

(60) The *Scripture* says: Life as a wild animal or deer comes from having eaten meat and stolen.

[7a] 61) The *Scripture* says: Life as a poisonous python snake comes from having been jealous and harmed others.

(62) The *Scripture* says: Life as a hungry tiger comes from having cheated, oppressed, or robbed others.

(63) The *Scripture* says: Life as a worm nourishing on excrement comes from having been lascivious, debauched, and unclean.

(64) The *Scripture* says: Life as a shrimp, frog, or tadpole comes from not having presented offerings to the Three Treasures.

(65) The *Scripture* says: Life as a fish or turtle comes from having despised or divulged the precious scriptures [YYJ: of the Great Dao].

(66) The *Scripture* says: Life as a small insect or ant comes from having violated the teaching of the scriptures.

(67) The *Scripture* says: Life as a fierce dog or wild pig comes from having turned one's back on the teachers and abandoned the root.

---

13. Yoshioka leaves this item out of his translation (1976, 156).

(68) The *Scripture* says: Life as a swallow or sparrow comes from having been a loudmouth and criticized the teaching of the scriptures.[14]

(69) The *Scripture* says: Life as a pigeon or dove [YYJ; or other similar bird] comes from having liked to think oneself right and done things differently from the divine law.

(70) The *Scripture* says: Life as an eagle or hawk [YYJ: or other similar bird] comes from having broken the precepts, disobeyed the scriptures, or treated the divine law with contempt.

[7b] (71) The *Scripture* says: Life orphaned and alone, destitute and cold [YYJ: in difficulties and pain], comes from having harmed the holy person of an ordained monk or nun or from having undertaken abortions.

(72) The *Scripture* says: Having an ugly and repulsive body or face comes from having slandered or ridiculed the Three Treasures or haughtily boasted to an ordained monk or nun.[15]

(73) The *Scripture* says: Suffering from insanity, epilepsy, or confusion comes from having accepted charity without giving anything back,[16] or from undertaking abortions.

(74) The *Scripture* says: Having a big belly and thin neck comes from having violated the sacred altar in a numinous monastery with lascivious desires.

(75) The *Scripture* says: Being imprisoned, locked in the kangue, or maimed comes from having spread rumors and poison and having engaged in [the forming of] cliques.

(76) The *Scripture* says: Being flogged with the whip or the heavy bamboo comes from having poisoned or harmed living beings without compassion.

(77) The *Scripture* says: Life as a cat [YYJ: otter, skunk, or other such animal] comes from having entered the sacred altar [area] in a numinous monastery after eating meat.

[8a] (78) The *Scripture* says: Life as a worm or louse comes from having approached the Three Treasures after eating strong-smelling vegetables.

(79) The *Scripture* says: Life as a jackal or wolf comes from having been stingy and not given donations.

(80) The *Scripture* says: Life as a raccoon or fox comes from having spread empty lies and deceived [others].

(81) The *Scripture* says: Life as a rat or weasel comes from having greedily devoured the leftovers from rites of purgation, drunk alcohol, and eaten meat.[17]

The *Rules* say: These eighty-one entries describing rules and precepts regarding the karmic cause and retribution of sins are taken from the "Highest Scripture on Karmic Rewards, Causes, and Retributions" (*Taishang yebao yinyuan jing*). In all cases, if one commits sins during life, one will pass through

---

14. Yoshioka here translates *duokou* 多口 ("loudmouth") as "for egoistic ends" (1976, 166).

15. Yoshioka here translates *aodan* 傲誕 ("haughtily boast") with "contemptingly insult" (1976, 166).

16. Yoshioka restructures the sentence to read "not giving charity" (1976, 166).

17. The *Yinyuan jing* goes on for six more entries, to no. 87, specifying the bad deeds that lead to rebirth as a centipede or millipede (82), a bee, dragonfly, viper, or grub (83), a gecko, chameleon, jellyfish, or cricket (84), a spider or earthworm (85), a mosquito, gadfly, flea, or louse (86), or a "border barbarian with bald head, stubble hair, sunk eyes, a long nose, and a foul-smelling body" (87; 2.9b).

hell after death; in accordance with the rules, one then receives retribution for one's sins and receives a particular form of life until one gets to have this very body. There is also retribution already in this life, so that all conditions of one's present life are based on the retribution for violations committed earlier. Thus, as all the scriptures and manuals agree, all Daoists, whether male or female,[18] should always, with their most essential heart, trust and worship [the rules], to brightly illuminate them for future followers. [8b] Thereby they cause practitioners both within and without the institution never to break the rules and precepts by which they eventually attain the perfection of the Dao.

Section 2

Retribution of Good Deeds[1]

[1.8b] (1) The *Scripture* says: Whoever generously produces scriptures and sacred images, erects monasteries and sponsors ordinations, gives donations and honors the precepts and purgation periods,[2] prays for the dead and helps save the living, who furthermore universally rescues all beings, greatly [YYJ: swears the vow, establishes great fields of blessedness, never cuts off his roots of goodness,] spreads happiness and goodness, and benefits and increases the multitude of living creatures, will be born in the body of an emperor and ruler of a country.[3]

(2) The *Scripture* says: Whoever upholds the scriptures and honors the precepts, recites and chants them and pays obeisance, widely [YYJ: merges his mind with and pours his imagination into the perfected countenances, burns incense

18. The *Yinyuan jing*, on which this paragraph is based, has the same words but is formulated as the direct command by the Lord of the Dao to Puji zhenren 普濟真人, the Perfected of Universal Salvation, ordering him specifically to become a model and cause others to behave religiously.

1. This section is an abbreviated citation of section 2 of the *Yinyuan jing* (DZ 336, 2.1a–4a), entitled "Rewards for Good Deeds" (*shandui* 善對). A comparative matching of this section in the two texts, including a numeration of entries, is found in Yoshioka 1976, 117–27. To make the work more easily accessible, I have also numbered the various items from 1 to 38. Simple additions to the text found in the *Yinyuan jing* are noted in brackets after the abbreviation "YYJ." Longer or more complex variants are noted in the footnotes. The *Yinyuan jing* also repeats much of the basic information in its section 18, "Rewards of Blessedness" (7.12a–13b).

2. This refers to the third meaning of *zhai* 齋, "temporary renunciation." Certain days were set aside for an enhanced practice of cultivation and devotion, complete with additional precepts, fasting after noon, and attendance of rituals or meditations. See Soymié 1977.

3. The text literally has "heavenly king" 天王, but in the reverse list hereafter, no. 18, *tian* 天 (heaven) is replaced by *di* 帝 (emperor), making it clear that rebirth in an elevated status on earth is indicated rather than a celestial position.

and pays obeisance to the Three Treasures and the great Dao,] establishing fields of blessedness, will be born in the body of an empress and mother of a country.

(3) The *Scripture* says: Whoever presents offerings to the Three Treasures, burns incense and lights lamps [for them], never tiring morning and evening, who also sponsors the production of scriptures and casting of sacred images, will be born in the family of an emperor.

(4) The *Scripture* says: Whoever trusts and rejoices in the scriptures and the divine law, worships and practices in accordance with the rules, observes the purgation periods and is mindful of the Dao,[4] gives donations and establishes merit, will be born in the body of a rich and noble, [YYJ: wise and majestic] person.

[9a] (5) The *Scripture* says: Whoever upholds the scriptures and honors precepts,[5] recites and chants them and holds on to them steadfastly, will be born in the body of a bright and perceptive, [YYJ: noble and superior] person.

(6) The *Scripture* says: Whoever, in the seventh generation,[6] rejoices in the Dao, honors the precepts and recites the scriptures, [YYJ: follows the divine law,] gives freely in donation and aids the poor, prays for the living and helps save the dead, always acts with compassion and sympathy, and presents offerings to the Three Treasures without being slack or lazy, will be born in the body of an ordained monk or nun.

(7) The *Scripture* says: Whoever, generation after generation, accumulates goodness, widely establishes fields of blessedness, upholds the purgation periods and honors the precepts, pays respectful obeisance to the Three Treasures, recites and chants the [texts of the] Great Vehicle, [YYJ: cultivates himself and performs services dutifully,] and never incurs a violation in his cultivation and [ritual] practice, will be born in the body of a preceptor of great virtue, venerated by the multitude of people.

(8) The *Scripture* says: Whoever [YYJ: life after life] worships and has faith in the great divine law of the Three Caverns, [YYJ: surrendering to the Three Treasures [*sangui*] and honoring the great law,] follows cultivation and ritual practice, and presents offerings [to the Dao], will be born among the celestials and in this world will be exceptionally pure and long-lived.[7]

[9b] (9) The *Scripture* says: Whoever presents offerings to the [YYJ: Three Treasures and the] holy person of an ordained monk or nun, will be born in the body of a long-lived and upright person.

(10) The *Scripture* says: Whoever sponsors the building of monastic residences and holy altars, will be born in the body of a wealthy and noble person.

---

4. This translates *niandao* 念道, in adaptation of *nianfo* 念佛, being mindful of the Buddha and reciting his name, a common practice in medieval China (see Kiyota 1978). The Daoist practice involves remembering the divine in all activities and is described in *Yaoxiu keyi* 12.3b.

5. The phrase is *chifeng jingjie* 持奉經戒, lit. "uphold and honor scriptures and precepts," which inverts the more common *chijing fengjie* 持經奉戒.

6. The YYJ here has "over seven lives," which is closer to the original Indian idea that karmic guilt and blessings accumulate over a series of personal lifetimes. In China, this was merged with indigenous ancestor worship and the notion of "inherited evil" (see Hendrischke 1991) to come out as "seven generations" of family lineage. See also Kamitsuka 1993; 1998.

7. The *Housheng daojun lieji* 後聖道君列紀 (Annals of the Latter-day Sage, Lord of the Dao, DZ 442; see Mollier 1990, 23; Strickmann 1981), also cited in *Sandong zhunang* 三洞珠囊 (8.16a–18a), has a detailed list of thirteen possible ranks of celestials with their matching earthly looks and personality. For a discussion of these, see Kohn 1996.

(11) The *Scripture* says: Whoever has faith in and venerates the Heavenly Worthies and the Great Dao, pouring [YYJ: merging] his whole heart into taking refuge in them, will be born in the body of an unimpaired and contented person.

(12) The *Scripture* says: Whoever has faith in the scriptures and honors the precepts [YYJ: never gives rise to dualistic thinking but maintains his fate and openness of inner nature, knowing] his karma and station in life, will be born in the body of a noble and respected, [YYJ: honored and well-beloved] person.

(13) The *Scripture* says: Whoever [YYJ: respects and honors the Three Treasures, loves to] gives donations and aids the poor, accumulating merit and virtue without even a trace of stinginess, will be born in the Middle Kingdom in the body of a long-lived, noble, and rich person.

(14) The *Scripture* says: Whoever abstains from killing living beings, stealing others' goods, [YYJ: getting addicted to] drinking alcohol, and eating meat, will be born in the body of a long-lived, unimpaired, and contented person.

(15) The *Scripture* says: Whoever delights in reciting the scriptures and precepts [YYJ: teachings], practices purgations for extended periods,[8] and worships the Dao, will be born in the body of an ordained monk or nun treated with great respect.

(16) The *Scripture* says: Whoever presents offerings to ordained monks or nuns [YYJ: as well as to preceptors and other virtuous persons], cherishes and is mindful of [YYJ: respects and honors all] the holy persons of the Three Treasures, will be born in the body of a pure and upright person.

[10a] (17) The *Scripture* says: Whoever is always mindful of and sympathetic toward all living beings, feeling compassion and sympathy for them [YYJ: all that wriggles and runs], will be born as a noble and high-ranking, aristocratic person.

(18) The *Scripture* says: Life [YYJ: in this generation] as an emperor and ruler of a country comes from having cultivated purgations and widely established fields of blessedness for a succession of kalpas.[9]

(19) The *Scripture* says: Life as an empress and mother of a country comes from having, for uncountable generations, widely set up fields of blessedness and presented offerings to the Heavenly Worthies and the Great Dao.[10]

(20) The *Scripture* says: Life as an emperor's son or grandson, as a princess or imperial concubine, comes from having, over several kalpas, cultivated goodness and accumulated [YYJ: planted many seeds of] karma.

(21) The *Scripture* says: Life as a person of high longevity and ripe old age comes from having upheld the purgation periods, honored the precepts, and compassionately aided all beings.

[10b] (22) The *Scripture* says: Life as a person with numerous descendants, of high longevity, great wealth, and nobility comes from having presented offerings to the Heavenly Worthies and the Great Dao.

8. This refers to the designation of entire months as purgation times, most commonly the first, third, fifth, seventh, ninth, and/or eleventh. See *Yaoxiu keyi* 8.4a.

9. This is considerably shorter than the *Yinyuan jing* version (2.2ab), which adds that one has to set up purgation rites and serve the Dao over many lives, rescuing both the living and the dead, and showing concern for all. It also supplies the information that after death, an emperor will go to reside in a wonderful heavenly paradise.

10. This entry rephrases the *Yinyuan jing*, which uses the formula applied earlier: do such-and-such and you will be born in such-and-such a body (2.2b). The phrasing here matches the overall pattern in this part of the section.

(23) The *Scripture* says: Life [in a family] where father and son, husband and wife, sons and daughters always live together comes from having been soft and yielding, harmonious and peaceful, never causing any disruption of familial love.

(24) The *Scripture* says: Life in a respected position with luscious provisions and beautiful clothes [YYJ: food] that keep the body covered and the mouth satisfied comes from having constantly established fields of blessedness.

(25) The *Scripture* says: Life as an aristocratic and high-ranking person, venerated and superior [YYJ: honored], whom others regard with awe and respect, comes from having devotedly believed in the Three Treasures.

(26) The *Scripture* says: Life as a wealthy and opulent person comes from having given donations, upheld the purgation periods, set up fields of blessedness, and aided the poor and destitute.

[11a] 27) The *Scripture* says: Life as a bright, perceptive, [YYJ: exceedingly] wise, and insightful person comes from having delighted in reciting the scriptures and the divine law and having been able to uphold them always.

(28) The *Scripture* says: Life with an erect and upright body and appearance comes from having presented offerings to the holy persons of the ordained monks and nuns of the Three Treasures.

(29) The *Scripture* says: Life as a [YYJ: pure man or woman or in the] holy person of an ordained monk or nun, whom people respect and honor, comes from having explained the divine law to teach and educate [people], [YYJ: from having upheld the purifications and honored the precepts,] and from having established fields of blessedness by upholding the purgation periods and honored the precepts.

(30) The *Scripture* says: Life as a wealthy and noble person who is held in great awe and does not weaken even over kalpas comes from having established fields of blessedness by giving donations toward the permanent establishment [of monasteries].

(31) The *Scripture* says: Life as a person who is venerated, respected, loved, and looked up to by people everywhere comes from having given donations, upheld the scriptures, and honored the precepts.

[11b] 32) The *Scripture* says: Life as a person who is pure in body and mind and radiant in wisdom and insight [YYJ: and perspicacity] comes from having protected and upheld the Great Vehicle of the Three Caverns.

(33) The *Scripture* says: Life as a person who is happy everywhere and always free from disasters and dangers comes from having freed and aided living beings, never harming any life.

(34) The *Scripture* says: Life as a person who is fragrant and clean in body, whom [YYJ: all] people look at with love and good thoughts, comes from having always maintained purity by not drinking alcohol, eating meat, or consuming strong-smelling vegetables.

(35) The *Scripture* says: Life as a person with abundant descendants and a plenitude of wealth and nobility comes from having given widely in donation, [YYJ: repaired tumbling bridges and passages,] established [YYJ: many fields of] blessedness, [YYJ: and created all kinds of merit and virtue].

(36) The *Scripture* says: Life as a woman who gives birth to healthy [YYJ: and noble] sons and is respected and loved by her family comes from having had a devoted mind found through the teaching at the Daoist ritual center.

[12a] 37) The *Scripture* says: Life on this earth with a clear and elegant voice comes from having chanted verses of praise at the Daoist ritual center [YYJ: and from having had respect and faith in the Three Treasures].

(38) The *Scripture* says: Life on this earth as a person of a cheerful disposition and with natural good fortune comes from having been single-minded and [YYJ: utterly] sincere at the Daoist ritual center, hearing about the divine law, listening to the scriptures, and giving widely in donation.[11]

The *Rules* say: These thirty-eight entries describing the karmic interrelation between good fortune and good deeds are taken from the "Highest Scripture on Karmic Rewards, Causes, and Retributions." They all detail the karmic retribution attained in one's present body as caused by the actions and seeds planted either in one's own earlier lives or in those of one's ancestors, or again the rewards one receives in the present life from the good deeds accumulated in this body. All Daoists, whether male or female, should always obey the rules and become models to ordinary men and women, causing them to venerate the rules and observe the precepts, thus enabling them to attain good fortune without measure.[12]

Section 3

Comprehensive Structures

[1.12a] The Rules say: According to the "Statutes of Mystery Metropolis"[1] and the "Code of Orthodox Unity,"[2] all Daoists, whether male or female, and even

---

11. The *Yinyuan jing* (2.3b–4a) continues this list with two further entries (nos. 39 and 40): people of an erect appearance, a laughing and harmonious, peaceable and sage disposition beloved by all used to present offerings to ordained monks and nuns; those who are assured of a continuously ample supply of clothing and beautiful ornaments in a former life had given ritual vestments to the Daoist community.

12. Except for the first sentence, this too rephrases the *Yinyuan jing* (2.4a), with two variants: instead of "all Daoists," the text addresses Puji zhenren; and for "uphold the rules and precepts" it has "recognize the good rewards inherent in karma and fate."

1. *Xuandu lüwen* 玄都律文 (DZ 188), a text of the southern Celestial Masters, commonly dated to the sixth century. It contains various lists of precepts and gives exact numbers for faults just as the *Fengdao kejie*. For a discussion, see Nickerson 2000.

2. *Zhengyi fawen* 正一法文, originally in 60 juan, now lost, with only about half surviving, often in fragments and citations. While there are similarities in basic outlook, especially with the *Zhengyi fawen jing* (DZ 1204), the text makes no mention of specific numbers associated with faults.

ordinary followers, receive a subtraction in reckoning if they disobey the scriptures and precepts. According to one system, a subtraction in reckoning means that one reckoning [unit] is subtracted from a person's life expectancy so that longevity cannot be extended. [12b] According to another, one reckoning [unit] means sixty days. The two theories are different, thus I present them both.[3]

Moreover, according to some, after the subtraction in reckoning takes effect, the person dies. Others have it that even in life, as one commits more sins, subtractions from the life span are made in accordance with standardized rules. An increase in life expectancy similarly means an addition in reckoning and an appropriate extension of life. All Daoists, whether male or female, should thus know the rules and precepts and honor and practice them in accordance with the divine law.

The *Rules* say: According to yet another source, whether one is in disobedience, breaks a rule, or commits a sin, one will inevitably receive [bad karma in] retribution in accordance with a specific set of standardized rules.[4]

Section 4

Setting Up Monasteries

[1.12b] The *Rules* say:[1] The realms on-high of the Three Purities and the ten continents, the five sacred mountains and the various renowned mountains, even the grotto heavens and the openness of the Great Void[2]—they all are places governed[3] by sage beings.

---

3. Yoshioka leaves this sentence out in his translation (1976, 170).

4. For earlier sources on this kind of lifetime calculation, see Yoshioka 1970, 167–96. Among the earliest is the *Chisongzi zhongjie jing* 赤松子中戒經 (Essential Precepts of Master Redpine, DZ 185) of the fourth century. For a discussion, see Kohn 1998a.

1. The introductory paragraph of this section, to the first three lines on page 13b, is also cited in *Miaomen youqi* 妙門由起 (DZ 1123) 12ab (Yoshioka 1976, 95). The variants between the two texts are minimal and will be noted specifically. The *Zhengyi weiyi jing* (DZ 791) in its item on monasteries describes them as a place to live in harmony and be free from sin, practicing repentance for past evils and services to maintain communication with the divine (18a).

2. This is a concise summary of Daoist sacred geography. The Three Purities 三清 (Highest, Jade, and Great Purity) are the highest heavens of the universe, where the sacred scriptures are stored; the ten continents 十洲 are the paradises of the immortals, including Penglai 蓬萊 and Kunlun 崑崙 (see Smith 1990). The five sacred mountains 五嶽 are the pillars of the earth in the four cardinal directions and the center, supported by a number of lesser but still renowned mountains where holy beings make their home. The grotto heavens 洞天 number thirty-six and are underground passageways that connect sacred mountains and also open up a link to the heavens (see Miura 1983). The Great Void 太虛, moreover, encompasses the larger space of the open universe. For a general summary, see Hahn 2000.

3. The *Miaomen youqi* here has *li* 理, "controlled," for *zhi* 治, "governed."

[13a] In some cases, coagulating *qi* forms towers and pavilions, halls and sanctuaries; in others, accumulating clouds create terraces and kiosks, palaces and chambers. Sometimes [wondrous beings] live among[4] the sun and the moon, the planets and stars; or they reside in interiors formed by misty clouds and rosy vapors. In some cases, the residences emerge from spontaneous transformation; in others, they are produced through divine power. Some [sacred residences] are embellished and expanded over a succession of kalpas; others are set up in a single moment. There are the round[5] peaks of Penglai and Fangzhang, the spread of orchards on Yingzhou, and the hanging gardens of Lanfeng and Mount Kunlun.[6] There are twelve-storied jade towers and three thousand golden turrets, and other wondrous constructions with ten thousand appellations and a thousand different names—impossible to count them all!

They are all traces of the transformations of the Heavenly Worthies and the Highest Lords, places governed[7] by celestials of the ranks of sage, perfected, or immortal. Recorded in the various scriptures, they can yet never be described in enough detail. Inevitably people and celestials return to them, while the foolish and the wise gaze at them in wonder.[8] Thus, people imitate structures found in the heavens and set up numinous monasteries over here, creating auspicious places[9] and residences fit for immortals.

As regards the building ground for such monasteries, each case has to comply with its specific organizational patterns, but in general there are six areas to consider:

1. Mountain areas[10]
2. Walled cities and suburbs
3. Palace apartments
4. Villages and neighborhoods
5. Isolated environments
6. Among the people

[13b] Also in all cases, the institution must be sponsored and protected by an emperor or king, built and maintained with the help of the ministers and officials [of the government]. Thereby they can help ordain male and female Daoists and allow them to inhabit [the institution] in perpetuity and present offerings.[11] This is foremost among all good [karmic] deeds, with effects unimaginable.

[Once a location has been decided,] build the following:[12]
Sanctuary to the Heavenly Worthies [1]

---

4. Following the *Miaomen youqi* and reading *jian* 間, "among," instead of *men* 門, "gate."

5. Here the *Miaomen youqi* reads "cinnabar" (*dan* 丹).

6. Yoshioka reads "round peaks," "spread of orchards," and "hanging gardens" as additional names (1976, 170). The locations are paradises and form part of the ten continents (see Smith 1990).

7. The *Miaomen youqi* again has *li* 理, "controlled," for *zhi* 治, "governed."

8. This sentence is obscure. The reading follows Yoshioka (1976, 171).

9. This translates *fudi* 福地, a term often associated with the number 72 and indicating a lesser type of grotto heaven. *Fudi* are locations where particularly beneficial *qi* forms and where divine beings like to reside. A more recent Western equivalent would be "power spot." For more details, see Hahn 2000.

10. Following the *Miaomen youqi* and again reading *jian* 間, "in" or "area," instead of *men* 門, "gate."

11. Here ends the passage cited in the *Miaomen youqi*.

12. The numbers were added by the translator to make the list more accessible.

Hall to the Heavenly Worthies [2]
Scriptural lecture hall [3][13]
Building for the explanation of the divine law [4]
Scripture tower [5]
Bell pavilion [6]
Masters' chambers [15]
Corridors [20]
Balustrades
Gate towers and lodges [13]
Holy altar [19]
Refectory [7]
Kitchen [8]
Scriptorium [9]
    Copy hall
    Correction hall
    Airing hall
    Fumigation hall
Bath house [10]
Incense building [18]
Ascension building [17]
Transmission building [16]
Meditation building [11]
Servants' quarters [21]
Stables and carriage houses [22]
Lay guest quarters [24]
Ordained visitors' residences [23]
Water mills [28]
Terraces, pavilions, and towers [12]:
    Terrace to Search Perfection
    Terrace to Refine *Qi*
    Terrace for Prayers to the Perfected
    Terrace to Inhale Luminant Essences
    Terrace to Scatter Florescence
    Terrace to Wait for the Immortals
    Terrace to Gather Dew
    Terrace of the Nine Purities
    Pavilion of Wandering Immortals
    Pavilion of Concentrated Numen
    Pavilion of Striding on the Clouds
    Pavilion of Flying Phoenixes
    Pavilion of Extending Numen
    Pavilion of Meeting the Wind
    Tower of the Nine Immortals

13. Yoshioka joins items two and three to read "Heavenly Worthies Scriptural Lecture Hall" (1976, 171), although a division is borne out by the discussion hereafter.

Tower for Extending Perfection
Tower of Dancing Phoenixes
Tower for Free and Easy Wandering
Tower of Tranquil Mindfulness
Tower for Meeting the Wind
Tower of the Nine Perfections
Tower for Burning Incense
Tower[14] for Preparing Medicines
and so on.

[14a] All these have to be planned and built in accordance with the relevant present circumstances,[15] which determine whether to build large or small, spacious or narrow, in ornate format or with basic simplicity. In each case, [construction] should be managed in accordance with the available resources.[16]

In addition, there should be an herb garden [25], an orchard [26], and vegetable plots [27],[17] sporting well-known trees and rare shrubs, clear ponds and fragrant flowers of all different kinds. They should all grow vigorously together to be used in the presentation of offerings. All together, this will create a truly auspicious place, which can be justly called a "pure residence." For eternal kalpas, it can be inhabited in perpetuity, never allowing it to deteriorate or fall into disrepair. [Building such an enclave] gives good fortune without measure; it is first among all the deeds that generate merit and virtue.

(1) Sanctuary to the Heavenly Worthies. The *Rules* say: The sanctuary to the Heavenly Worthies should be built either three, five, seven, nine, eleven, or thirteen bays in size.[18] How large or small it is depends on the relevant present circumstances, how decorative or imposing it is will vary according to the available resources, but in all cases it should be surrounded by gardens on all sides.[19]

"Sanctuary" is what we call a residence of the divine sages, while "hall" refers to a place occupied and used by humanity.

In constructing any type of residence or structure, six general rules are to be observed:

1. Use high-quality wood as numinous material
2. Proceed in accordance with the relevant present circumstances
3. Use gold and jade in ornamental carvings
4. Lay solid foundations in tamped earth or stone
5. Paint the walls with murals using cinnabar and green
6. Use clay tiles or thatch for the roof

[14b] One may also [for ornamentation] carve phoenixes and sculpt dragons, paint clouds and depict the moon, show hanging plants or growing lichens,

---

14. Reading *lou* 樓 for *tang* 堂 ("hall") to match the preceding list.

15. The word translated with this rather clumsy phrase is simply *shi* 時, "time," but the phrase occurs often and the meaning is highly technical, thus warranting this English rendition.

16. This again is a short phrase in Chinese, rendered rather technically: *renli* 任力, "depending on strength."

17. The latter is not mentioned in this initial listing but appears later on and has thus been supplied from the later context.

18. A "bay" (*jian* 簡) is the space between two pillars in a traditional building. It measures roughly five meters.

19. This reading follows Yoshioka (1976, 171).

lotus ponds or flowery seas. There may be bright pendants and glistening jade disks, engraved railings and ornate balustrades, cinnabar porches and turquoise tiles, turquoise side chains and green patterns.

There may also be golden niches and silver corners, ridges of rosy mist and beams of cloudy designs. There may be sun openings and moon windows, yin gates and yang sliding doors. Above [the ceiling] may reach out to the vaporous expanse, below [the floor] may be covered with [patterns of] mysterious mist.

[While all this is possible,] the actual dimensions of the structure and its opulence have to be decided on in accordance with the relevant present circumstances. There is no fixed model to follow.

(2) Hall of the Heavenly Worthies. The *Rules* say: The hall of the Heavenly Worthies should be build either one, two, three, or five bays in size. Whether large or small, spacious or narrow depends on the relevant present circumstances.

(3) Scriptural Lecture Hall. The *Rules* say: The hall of the divine law[20] is where is the law is explained and the teaching clarified. It should be located behind the sanctuary to the Heavenly Worthies to permit easy access to the [monastic] crowd. However, it is also possible to have it in another location, depending on what is suitable in the given situation.

[15a] *(4) Building for the Explanation of the Divine Law.* The *Rules* say: The building[21] for the explanation of the divine law should be built to the right or left of the sanctuary to the Heavenly Worthies. It should be built especially wide and spacious with the main purpose to admit large crowds of listeners.[22] How exactly to arrange the rooms within the building is then decided in accordance with relevant present circumstances.

(5) Scripture Tower. The *Rules* say: The scripture tower can be built high or low, large or small, ornate or simple; it depends on the available human and material resources. Still, in all cases it should allow the precious scriptures of the Three Caverns and the mysterious writings of the Four Supplements to be easily accessible and clearly present. Wind and sunlight should flow freely through it, while rain and dew should be kept out completely. This is the first and cardinal rule for erecting [a scripture tower]. The remainder is left to [local] convenience and suitability. There is no unchangeable system.[23]

(6) Bell Pavilion. The *Rules* say: The organizational system for erecting a bell pavilion is the same as that of the scripture tower. Just make sure that the frame is solid, while the four walls are open and thin. This will allow the sound of the bell to pass out without hindrance, whenever it is rung to indicate the six periods.[24] The bell pavilion had best be placed in front of the sanctuary to the

---

20. This translates *fatang* 法堂, a Buddhist expression, most commonly rendered "dharma hall."

21. The word translated "building" here is *yuan* 院, commonly used in Buddhist contexts, where it is rendered "cloister" and indicative of a separate facility or residence within a larger monastery complex.

22. This follows Yoshioka (1976, 172). The word *bie* 別 could also mean "not," indicating that the building should not be too wide and spacious, so that people can listen with more ease.

23. Yoshioka leaves out this last sentence (1976, 172).

24. These are the six major times of worship used in Buddhist and Daoist institutions: cockcrow, sunrise noon, sunset, midevening, and midnight. For a historical discussion, see Pas 1987.

Heavenly Worthies and opposite the scripture tower: the bell on the left, the scriptures on the right, one may put the meditation building separate yet nearby.

(7) Refectory. The *Rules* say: The refectory is usually built as a separate building on the eastern border [of the compound]. Whether big or small, spacious or narrow, depends on what is suitable in the relevant present circumstances. [15b] Wide doors and open windows should allow easy access, but the main entrance should be covered with a curtain and open to a throne of the Heavenly Worthies. To their right and left, benches and seats, rugs and thick mats should be laid out in accordance with the divine law. Immediately in front of the Heavenly Worthies, place incense burners, flowery pendants, and clean cloths; then arrange the refectory benches, tables, and mats in proper accordance with the divine law.

(8) Kitchen. The *Rules* say: The kitchen is best built very close to the refectory. Cauldrons and stoves, storerooms and warehouses, and all other things necessary for the communal provision should be not be too far to get to.

(9) Scriptorium. The *Rules* say: In all monasteries, one must build a scriptorium in a separate building that is off limits to ordinary people. Whether the structure is just a small hut or a spacious lodge, it must in all cases contain a hall for editing the scriptures, a wash house, and a stove.

Moreover, the place where the paper is being prepared has to have cloth-beating stones with appropriate clubs, sharp cutting knives, fresh benches, tree stumps, and whetting stones that are kept clean with cloth and fabric rinsed in the wash house. To fumigate and spread the scriptures, a rack has to be prepared and a hut set up. All mortars, clubs, and other necessary utensils should also be stored in the scriptorium. [16a] Under all circumstances they have to be maintained in pristine purity and must never be allowed to come in contact with ordinary people, be defiled by worldly confusion, or be deficient even for a limited period: this is most important to be avoided.

(10) Bath House. The *Rules* say: In any monastery, a bath house must be built, located in a separate building and private facility.[25] Setting it up is an urgent priority, because [baths are required every time Daoists] perform rites to the Dao, recite the scriptures, ascend to the altar, or enter meditation; [they need baths] also before formal announcements or prayer incantations, rites of repentance and confession, and whenever someone has violated the rules of the outside [world] or gone against the precepts of the perfected within [the monastery]. Also, baths are essential to wash of dirt and sweat [after labor] and to get rid of dust and defiling substances.[26] If even a small spot is left impure or unclean, one will violate the numinous offices, offend the immortal officials, and make good *qi* go awry.

In all these situations, Daoists must thoroughly bathe to cleanse and purify their bodies and minds. They have to make sure they are engulfed in a good, clean fragrance, and only then can they perform the services. Therefore on all days when rites to the Dao are scheduled, all participants must take baths in fragrant hot water. All the necessary implements—cauldrons and boiling pans,

---

25. Details on bathing and its facilities are also found in *Daoxue keyi* 1.13a–15a; *Qianzhen ke* 14b.
26. Details on defilements and their eradication are described in *Daoxue keyi* 1.15a–16a.

wells and stoves, benches and mats, fragrances and powders—must be readied properly.

(11) Meditation Building. The *Rules* say: The meditation building should be well away from all noise and disturbance. It should be pure and clean and free from defilements. [16b] Thus it must be set up as a separate building, in utter isolation and tranquility. Then, whether it is east or west, north or south, far or near, spacious or narrow can be decided according to the relevant present circumstances, suitability, and convenience.[27]

A proper sanctuary to the Heavenly Worthies, a chamber to enter meditation, a place to refine *qi*, a bath house, and a medicine hall are thus essentials for the use of the masters. These [facilities] must all be set up adequately—make sure they lack in nothing!

(12) Terraces, Pavilions, and Towers. The *Rules* say: All the various terraces, pavilions, towers, and so on—such as the Terraces to Search Perfection, to Refine *Qi*, for Prayers to the Perfected, to Inhale Luminant Essences, to Scatter Florescence, to Wait for the Immortals, to Gather Dew, and of the Nine Purities; the Pavilions of Wandering Immortals, of Concentrated Numen, of Striding on the Clouds, of Flying Phoenixes, of Extending Numen, and of Meeting the Wind; the Towers of the Nine Immortals, for Extending Perfection, of Dancing Phoenixes, for Free and Easy Wandering, of the Nine Perfections, for Burning Incense, of Tranquil Mindfulness, and so on—are dedicated to the ecstatic excursions of male and female Daoists.

There they soar up in imagination to the highways of the clouds, ascend in true sincerity to the roadways of the stars. They wander in their minds outside of all known bounds and send their eyes to the center of the universe. They rise to the provinces of the Eight Luminants and approach the swinging assemblies of the ten kinds of immortals. As [these terraces, pavilions, and towers] represent extraordinary endeavors,[28] they must be far away and thoroughly cut off. They should, however, be accessible from the meditation building and the two main halls.

In all cases, they must be built so that wind and dew cannot invade them, while clouds and haze meet no obstacle.[29] Also, one must be able to gaze up into the Milky Way from them, to watch the distant course of the stars. [17a] On the outside, the buildings should have doors to the Four Luminants; on the sides, windows should be open to the Eight Winds. This will allow the carriages of the immortals to freely enter and leave, the steeds of the perfected to easily come and go.

The buildings should be admirable and rare, lofty and spacious,[30] so that practitioners join the immortals hand in hand, cherishing their closeness in their day-to-day lives and seeing them both morning and evening.[31]

---

27. The same requirement is also stated in *Qianzhen ke* 9b.

28. From here to the end of item 20, the text is also available in a Dunhuang manuscript (S. 3863; Ôfuchi 1979b, 219).

29. S. 3863 here has *he* 閡 for *ai* 礙, "obstruction."

30. S. 3863 writes the emphatic particle *mi* 彌 with an abbreviated character.

31. This last sentence is highly obscure. Unfortunately, or maybe because of this, Yoshioka does not translate it (1976, 173).

(13) Gate Towers and Lodges. The *Rules* say: The gate to all wonders,[32] is the passageway[33] for coming and going; the door of the perfected crowd is the route of entering and leaving. It can be compared to the mouth in the human body, to the eyes in the human face:[34] they must never be missing. Thus, all monastery gates must be built with a special lodge or with a tower, standing above and in front of the institution like the forehead [in a human face], signaling its outstanding and exceptional nature.

The number of stories and size [of the gate] depend on the relevant present circumstances. Similarly, the question of whether there should be two major gates[35] is decided according to the financial opulence or constraints at the time of building. In any case, all major gates have to be separate buildings and must be built in an imposing and majestic style with appropriate carvings[36] and ornamentation. In each case, the monastery has to do what is most suitable. There is no single fixed[37] standard but only a general model to be followed.[38]

(14) Carriage Gates. The *Rules* say: To the right or left of the monastery gate there should be separate doorways[39] to allow carriages and draft animals— horses, mules, and oxen—to enter and leave. They must not pass through the main gate proper when they come and go.

[17b] *(15) Masters' Chambers.* The *Rules* say: The chambers of the masters should be located near the sanctuary and hall to the Heavenly Worthies in any of the four directions.[40] Their size and number depend on the relevant present circumstances of each institution.

(16) Transmission Building. The *Rules* say: When a Daoist, whether male or female,[41] enters the Dao, he or she must receive the scriptures and precepts,[42] talismans and registers. For this reason, a separate transmission building with its own altar should be erected. It is best located opposite the refectory and the meditation building, so that all necessities for ordination can easily be prepared.

(17) Ascension Building. The *Rules* say: For the time when a male or female Daoist leaves this body, a separate ascension building[43] must be erected. It should be a building standing all by itself. When constructing the hall and its chambers,[44] also prepare all the implements necessary for its proper functioning.

32. This is a citation from the first chapter of the *Daode jing.*
33. S. 3863 writes *jing* with radical no. 60 instead of no. 162.
34. Following S. 3863, which supplies the words "compared to the mouth" 如口之在身 and thus makes the parallelism clear with the eyes in the face. Yoshioka, not using the manuscript, leaves out the comparison to the mouth (1976, 173).
35. The word for "major gate" is *sanmen* 三門, literally "triple gate," a Buddhist term.
36. S. 3863 uses a simplified version for this character.
37. S. 3863 has *heng* 恆, "constant," for *ding* 定, "fixed."
38. Yoshioka leaves out this last sentence (1976, 174).
39. S. 3863 supplies the word *men* 門 here, which is left out in the *Daozang* edition.
40. S. 3863 has *mian* 面, "sides," for *fang* 方, "directions."
41. S. 3863, here and elsewhere, has the expression "female officer" (*nüguan* 女官) instead of "female hat" (*nüguan* 女冠) commonly used in the *Daozang* version.
42. S. 3863 writes *jie* 戒 with the "speech" radical 誡.
43. S. 3863 calls this the "Building for Transformation into an Immortal" (*xianhua yuan* 仙化院). Under this name, it is described in more details in *Qianzhen ke* 20ab and *Yaoxiu keyi* 15.11a.
44. S. 3863 has *rong* 容, "structure," instead of *shi* 室, "chambers."

(18) Incense Building. The *Rules* say:[45] When a male or female Daoist has died, the host of the divine law should feel with them and support them to attain final salvation. For this purpose, near the ascension building there should be an incense building, equipped with tables and mats, beds and seats, having every-thing necessary[46] [for proper worship] immediately available.

[18a] *(19) Holy Altar.* The *Rules* say: In all monasteries, in front of the sanc-tuary to the Heavenly Worthies, one should set up a mound of earth, layered bricks,[47] or piled stones, on which a wooden scaffold is erected. This serves as the altar platform. It normally consists of three or five layers, but can also have as many as twenty.[48] Instructions are detailed in the original scriptures. Inscrip-tions on the railings and plaques on the gate, moreover, should be affixed in accordance with the divine law.

(20) Corridors. The *Rules* say: Between the different structures—sanctuary, halls, towers, pavilions, terraces, kiosks, and the various separate[49] buildings—one should build covered corridors for passage and perambulation. They should be like houses themselves, enclosed on all four sides.[50]

(21) Servants' Quarters. The *Rules* say: The servants'[51] quarters should be in yet another separate building, with its own gate, windows, well, and stoves, all built as described above. But this building must not in any way be connected to the masters' chambers; and servants coming in only on a temporary basis should again be housed separately.

(22) Stables and Carriage Houses. The *Rules* say: Houses for carriages and stables for oxen, mules, and horses should be built close to the servants' quarters in a separate building. Under no circumstances must they be in direct contact with the master's chambers or the refectory kitchen. Nor should anyone enter-ing or leaving the stables pass near a well or stove.

[18b] *(23) Ordained Visitors' Residences.* The *Rules* say: For Daoists of the ten directions, practitioners of the divine law, or other karmically privileged visitors to the monastery and their servants and animals, a separate residential quarter should be erected. Unless such visitors have attained the rank of master, they must stay in the visitors' residences. If there is as yet no separate building for them, they should be lodged in the servants' quarters. Their mounts and draft animals should be placed in the monastery stables. Visitors should pay in compensation for whatever costs they incur to the fixed assets of the in-stitution.[52] In no case must they inconvenience the masters or the host of the divine law.

(24) Lay Guest Quarters. The *Rules* say: Lay guests, new disciples, or officials of the local administration should be housed in special guest quarters. The

---

45. The building is also described in *Yaoxiu keyi* 15.11a.
46. Literally, "one thing and more" (*yishi yishang* 一事已上). S. 3863 has *yishang* 一事以上.
47. S. 3863 writes *zhuan* 磚 with the "earth" 土 radical.
48. S. 3863 adds the word *nai* 乃 in this sentence.
49. S. 3863 here has correctly *bie* 別, not *yin* 引.
50. Here ends the passage also found in S. 3863.
51. The term used for "servants" is *jingren* 淨人, lit. "pure people," a technical term borrowed from Buddhism.
52. This reading follows Yoshioka (1976, 175).

servants and animals they bring must in no way harm or reduce the fixed assets of the institution. They may stay only if they pay proper compensation.[53]

(25) Herb Gardens. The *Rules* say: For the production of medicines necessary to cure ailments, there should be a separate herb garden. Everything that can grow [in the specific location] should be cultivated there with care.

(26) Orchards. The *Rules* say: Flowers and fruits to be used in the presentation of offerings should abound in the monastery.[54] Between the various separate buildings, inside and out of the covered corridors and lodges, [19a] everywhere should be flowers and fruit trees, rare plants and herbs. They should be picked according to season and presented in offerings to the Three Treasures.

(27) Vegetable Plots. The *Rules* say: The vegetables necessary for the vegetarian meals, except the five strong-smelling vegetables, should be planted according to season [in suitable vegetable plots]. Things like leafy greens, cucumbers, and squash, should all be planted and grown.

(28) Water Mills. The *Rules* say: Agricultural estates and water mills are central to the fixed assets of the institution.[55] They are to be set up, as each location allows, in due accordance with the regulations of the divine law, separated into pure and defiled, and clearly evaluated. Their management should in all cases be in accordance with the relevant present circumstances and comply with the orders of the monastic official in charge.

(29) Residences. The *Rules* say: All ordained Daoists must maintain strict purity and simplicity and do away with all pride and luxury. They must keep their residences frugal and sparingly furnished. Under no circumstances must they embellish them with flowery ornaments, high beds and thick mats, or fancy objects for personal amusement. They should keep their residences stark and plain, and never make them like the places of ordinary people. Inside and outside should communicate freely, within and beyond should be without obstruction. Never should they use curtains and awnings to hide themselves away.

[19b] The rope-bed and bench can be placed according to individual taste, with the incense burner and ritual implements on their right or left. Any objects not of ritual character, however, or anything used only for personal amusement must not be kept. This is a very strict precept for all practicing Daoists.

(30) Workshops. The *Rules* say: Every monastery should also have a separate workshop building, with rooms in accordance with the divine law. Here [statues of] the Heavenly Worthies and other objects are made and repaired. To allow the proper merit and virtue, a wash house with cauldrons, stoves, and the like should be in readiness there.

(31) Greenery. The *Rules* say: Within and without the sanctuary and hall to the Heavenly Worthies as well as in and around all the various separate buildings and private quarters, greenery should be planted: fruit trees interspersed with blossoming shrubs, green bamboo next to shimmering ponds. Precious herbs

---

53. The *Qianzhen ke* also allows for lay visitors to stay in the servants' quarters (9b).

54. A similar statement is also made in *Zhengyi weiyi jing* (DZ 791) 18b.

55. This point is also made in *Zhengyi weiyi jing* 18b. For a discussion of the role of water mills in Buddhist monasteries of the Tang, see Ch'en 1973; Gernet 1995. For more on their economic situation, see also Twitchett 1956; 1957.

and fragrant flowers should divide the areas and separate the buildings. They will shed radiance on the sanctuary and halls, and shade the living quarters in serenity. Their fragrance will rise in a numinous wind, their petals will shine with the light of wisdom. Time and again, lovely birds will come and sing in them, attracting the perfected from on high.

Thus, imitating the jasper terraces above and looking like golden towers below, [the monastery is] a place to elevate the heart, a record of [celestial] sojourn [on earth].

Section 5

Making Sacred Images[1]

[2.1a] The *Rules* say: Great images do not have form, the fully perfected is free from physical aspects.[2] Utterly clear, they are empty and serene. Sight and hearing cannot match them, and yet they change and transform to be apparent in physical shape. Visible for a little while, they again return into hiding. For this reason, to visualize the perfected, one must first develop an imagination of their sage countenances. To aid this process, one uses cinnabar and green, gold and turquoise to create depictions and shape representations; one makes sacred images of the perfected countenances adorned with powder of white lead.

Before, then, engaging the mind [in meditative visualization], one must first make sacred images.[3] There are six kinds of representations, to be made and venerated in this order:

First, make [representations of] the All-Highest King of the Divine Law, the Heavenly Worthy of Primordial Beginning; the Highest Sovereign of Emptiness, the Great Dao of Jade Dawn; and the Eminent Lord Laozi, the Heavenly Worthy of Great Unity.[4]

Second, make representations of the immeasurable sages, perfected, and immortals of the Three Purities, below the heaven of Grand Network and above Great Purity.[5]

---

1. An earlier English translation of this entire section is found in Reiter 1988, 60–6 (and again in Reiter 1998, 84–91). I have not made use of it, as my reading, both in terminology and syntax, differs significantly from it.

2. This translates *se*, the Chinese rendition of Skt. *rupa*, "physical form."

3. Yoshioka leaves out this sentence (1976, 176).

4. This group of deities is the Daoist trinity, joined from the highest gods of the major Daoist schools (see Kohn 1998b, 121–9). First statues of the trinity are found in the early sixth century (see Kamitsuka 1993; 1998).

5. These refer to the highest four of the thirty-six Daoist heavens, Grand Network (Daluo 大羅), Highest Purity (Shangqing 上清), Jade Purity (Yuqing 玉清), and Great Purity (Taiqing 太清). See Kohn 1993, 69.

Third, make representations of the limitless sages of past, present, and future.

Fourth, make paintings of the perfected and immortals of the stars and Dippers in the various heavens.

[1b] Fifth, make representations of the innumerable sages with the rank of sage, perfected, or immortal.[6]

Sixth, make representations of the infinite sages, perfected, and immortals[7] who follow the karmic chain of impulse and response.

Develop your mind in accordance with the hierarchy of these deities.

Now, there are eighteen ways to fashion the perfected countenances:

1. Carved in precious jade, jasper, carneole, and other precious stones like the Seven Treasures[8]
2. Cast in yellow gold
3. Cast in white silver
4. Cast in red bronze
5. Cast in green iron
6. Cast in tin and pewter
7. Carved in fragrant wood, like aloeswood[9]
8. Woven into fabric
9. Stitched in embroidery
10. Modeled in clay
11. Pressed in hemp
12. Painted on silk
13. Painted on walls
14. Chiseled in caves
15. Etched in stone
16. Erected on steles
17. Printed on fragrant wood pulp
18. Printed on paper, modeled in mud, scratched on bricks, made from assembled earth, engraved on tiles, chiseled in bone, carved in ivory, cut in wood, shaped in piled-up snow, or painted in ashes

[2a] If one can make any of these images with concentrated thought and a full heart, one will gain good fortune without measure.

Now, the size of a given image can be anywhere from one inch to two, three, four, or five inches, even up to a foot.[10] There is no fixed standard regarding size, nor is there a limit to quantity. The image can therefore also be any number of feet in size: one, two, three, four, five, ten, twenty, thirty, forty, fifty, sixty, a

---

6. These are the three major types of celestial officials as described in Tao Hongjing's 陶弘景 *Zhenling weiye tu* 真靈位業圖 (Chart of the Ranks and Duties of the Numinous Perfected, DZ 167). See Ishii 1983.

7. Reading *xian* 仙, "immortal," for *xing* 形, "body."

8. These are precious materials used in Buddhism: gold, silver, lapis lazuli, crystal, agnate, pearls, and cornelian. See Nakamura 1975, 587.

9. This wood is famous for making a particularly fragrant incense. See Schafer 1963, 163; Read 1982, 70.

10. A Chinese inch is about three centimeter; a foot about thirty centimeter. For a complete list of medieval Chinese weights and measurements, which changed over time and place, see Hansen 1995, ix.

hundred, a thousand, even ten thousand. Images can moreover be placed in one, ten, a hundred, a thousand, even ten thousand districts;[11] in one, ten, a hundred, a thousand, even ten thousand shrines; in one, ten, a hundred, a thousand, even ten thousand niches; on one, ten, a hundred, a thousand, even ten thousand *juan*; on one, ten, a hundred, a thousand, even ten thousand high seats; in one, ten, a hundred, a thousand, even ten thousand chambers; or in one, ten, a hundred, a thousand, even ten thousand halls. They may even number in the billions.

There can be one Heavenly Worthy, two Heavenly Worthies; then again, as many as ten, a hundred, a thousand, or a million can be grouped together. There can be perfected, immortals, and sages; jade lads and jade maidens; [2b] imperial kings of the various heavens; diamond gods and divine kings, incense officials and messengers; dragon and tiger incense attendants; as well as lions and evil-dispellers. There may be sanctuaries and halls with curtained high seats, flowery banners and bannered canopies, flying celestial musicians and all sorts of attendants and guards.

In each case, follow your inclination and resources, and use the images to present offerings, pay obeisance, and burn incense. Be mindful of them day and night as if you were facing their actual perfected body. Then, having done so, your good fortune in the future will be without measure, and you will certainly attain the Dao of perfection.

The *Rules* say: Whenever one makes a sacred image, one must follow the scriptures in fashioning its proper characteristics. The Heavenly Worthy has fifty million such characteristics; the Lord of the Dao, seventy-two; the Lord Lao, thirty-two; and other perfected, twenty-four.[12]

Their vestments and headdresses, as well as their flowery high seats, also must conform to the divine law. The Heavenly Worthies, therefore, should wear capes of nine-colored loose gauze or five-colored cloudy mist over long robes of yellow variegated brocade with mountain-and-river patterns. Their gold or jade headdresses should have tassels and pendants to the right and left; then again, these gold and jade headdresses can be inlaid in multiple colors.

[3a] Their upper capes must never be executed [one-colored] in pure purple, cinnabar, blue, or turquoise, nor must the perfected be depicted with loose hair, long ears, or a single horn. On the other hand, they may wear headdresses showing [patterns of] hibiscus flowers, flying clouds, primordial beginning, or the like, but they must never wear flat headdresses that show the two forces or caps of the young deer type.[13]

The two perfected [acolytes] on their left and right should be shown presenting offerings, holding scriptures, grasping audience tablets, or with

---

11. This passage is an expansion of a highly similar list in the *Zhengyi fawen jing* (DZ 1204), according to which statutes of the Heavenly Worthies of the ten directions can be produced in "one statue, in ten, a hundred, a thousand, even ten thousand statues, as many as one's resources permit" (5b).

12. These numbers do not occur elsewhere in this manner. Typically the Buddha has thirty-two primary characteristics, while Laozi, the Highest Lord Lao, has seventy-two. For an analysis of these, see Kohn 1996.

13. Living Daoists, on the other hand, often wore deerskin caps and kerchiefs tied to represent the two forces. In addition, those of higher ranks also sported headdresses of more intricate designs, including hibiscus flowers and primordial beginning. See Schafer 1978. Other sources on Daoist medieval headgear include the *Fafu kejie wen* 法服科戒文 (DZ 788), 5b; and the *Wushang biyao* 無上秘要 (DZ 1138), 43.1a (see Lagerwey 1981, 140).

fragrant flowers in their hands. They should be referential and dignified, their hands and feet not too far extended or their garments hanging oddly to one side. The Heavenly Worthies themselves sit upright, their fingers entwined in the hand sign of Great Nonbeing,[14] never holding even a *ruyi* scepter or a deer-tail whisk. Their hands are simply empty, that is all.

The *Rules* say: On the left and right of the Heavenly Worthy, Lord of the Dao, and Lord Lao, there are various perfected, jade lads and jade maidens, incense and scripture attendants, incense officials and messengers. Also to their left and right, there are dragon and tiger lords, official messengers of the left and right. In addition, there are heavenly Ding deities[15] and demigods [*vîras*], diamond gods [*vajras*] and divine kings [*râjâs*], lions and demon-eaters, dragons and unicorns, fierce beasts and flying pythons, divine tigers, phoenixes and peacocks, gold-winged birds and scarlet sparrows, the four heraldic animals and the eight dignified creatures, [3b] the protectors of the divine law and the gods of good deeds—all standing to support and protect the Heavenly Worthies on the left and right, each and every one installed according to the available resources.

The *Rules* say: The names and titles of the perfected are exceedingly many and cannot be enumerated. They all, based on karmic causes planted in former kalpas, have completed the Dao and reached the highest fruit, thus they now stand on guard and present invocations to the left and right of the Heavenly Worthy, Lord of the Dao, and Lord Lao. Part of the universal transformations, they are spontaneously wherever the Worthies reside, following them always to assist and guard.

The *Rules* say: Jade lads and jade maidens are all born from transformations of Dao-*qi* and do not grow in wombs. They all have official functions: attending on the scriptures, attending on incense, scattering flowers, presenting addresses, assisting the immortals, or serving those who have attained the Dao. Ranked hierarchically, they can also be demoted for committing errors.

The *Rules* say: Scripture and incense attendants are all born from the coagulation of *qi*. They are always in the same place as the Heavenly Worthies and the perfected scriptures. They transmit memorials in smooth flow and keep records of good and bad deeds.

[4a] The *Rules* say: Diamond kings [*vajras*][16] are the four boundary gods of heaven, positioned at its four corners. They serve at the gates of heaven and at the doors of earth.[17] They are twelve thousand feet tall, carry swords and hold staffs. Their bodies enveloped in heavenly garb, they wear precious headdresses of

14. Daoist hand signs developed independently in a medical, *qi*-guiding context, then merged actively with the Buddhist culture of mudras in the Tang dynasty. For details, see Mitamura 2002.

15. These deities may either be "heavenly soldiers," reading *bing* for *ding*, or refer to the Six Ding 六丁. The latter are six gods of the cyclical signs, typically coupled with the six Jia 六甲 deities. First abstract symbols that merely represented the stems of the hours and days, they became jade maidens in Highest Purity and then advanced to more powerful protector deities. For a study, see Inoue 1992.

16. Adding the particle *zhe* 者 after *jingang* 金鋼 to match the pattern of the other entries.

17. These are specific corners of heaven and earth that allow communication between the realms and have accordingly to be guarded closely. For a study, see Matsumura 1992.

flying cloud. Their feet step on huge mountains, divine beasts, large boulders, or various demons. Standing strong, they have the power to kill demons, controlling all those demons and spirits under heaven and above the earth who go against the divine law. Faced with their angry eyes and biting voices, all noxious sprites are awed and subdued.

Their images should be installed to the left and right of the gates and windows in all sanctuaries and halls governed by the Heavenly Worthies. There they serve as guardians and protectors. They transform and change without end, never remaining in one firm body—again because they are born from the fierce *qi* of the Dao and did not grow in wombs. In monasteries today, set up their images at all gates and windows of sanctuaries, halls, and scripture repositories.

The *Rules* say: Divine kings [*râjâs*] are the rulers of the host of the gods. They are of three types: first, coagulated from *qi*; second, born due to divine reward; and third, caused by a succession of [good] karma.

Those condensed from *qi* were not born from wombs but came forth as part of the *qi* of spontaneity. Those born due to divine reward received life in their present bodies because they served [to control] the various demons and spirits and thus earned merit in the Dao. [4b] Those caused by a succession of [good] karma accumulated karmic actions over many kalpas and thus became masters of their bodies. Originally ordinary people who completed perfection and attained the Dao, they have become supervisors of salvation.

The names of the divine kings are without number. They all wear armor and helmets, and [bear] lances, hold knives, and carry swords. Either standing or sitting, they are not steady in their bodily appearance. They govern and control the multitude of demons, drive out and expel all unlucky and noxious [powers]. More on them is found in the various scriptures and declarations, so I will not go into further detail here.

The *Rules* say: Demon kings similarly belong to the line of the divine kings.[18] They come in three types:

1. Demon kings of the three heavens
2. Demon kings of the five emperors
3. Demon kings of the flying celestials [*apsaras*]

They caution and refine, protect and support all students of the Dao and practitioners. Thus these great meritorious demon kings protect and support even yourself.

The *Rules* say: The heavenly Ding deities and demigods, dragons and tigers to the left and right, incense officials and messengers were equally born from transformations of *qi*. In accordance with karmic causes, they emerge to subdue evil and command demons, transmit messages and serve as couriers. They are numinous officials who protect the divine law.

---

18. A type of divine warrior first inspired by Buddhist demon kings, these are positive and protective deities of the Dao. For a study, see Kamitsuka 1996.

[5a] The *Rules* say: The eight dignified creatures are the poisonous dragon, fierce tiger, flying python, beast of lightning, long tooth [beast], rampaging bull, ape of heaven, and piercing thunder. They were all evil creatures who had accumulated bad karma. The Heavenly Worthy subdued them with his might and made them stand ready at gates and guard passages. In caves and caverns, at walls and boundaries, they ward off baleful influences.

The *Rules* say: The four heraldic animals are the turtle, dragon, unicorn, and phoenix. They correspond to constellations in the sky and in their different energies combine the blossoms of the five phases.[19] Sometimes their mouths recite numinous texts while their bodies bring forth charts and registers. They know the patterns of retreat and advance, and at the right time descend into the world. Residing in the gardens of the Heavenly Worthy, they are truly auspicious birds and wondrous animals.

The *Rules* say: The Heavenly Worthies must have a high seat, which can come in any of the following eight forms:

1. A thousand-petaled lotus flower
2. A five-colored lion
3. A seven-jeweled golden couch
4. A nine-layered jade throne
5. Nine crouching dragons
6. Eight coiled-up snakes
7. A seat of cloudy empyrean
8. A seat of smoky mist

[5b] On any of these [the Heavenly Worthies] manifest physically in accordance with the transformations, come to reside as the situation warrants. High seats today that are screened off with a curtain and adorned with the seven treasures, eight gems, pearls and jade, gold and turquoise, on the other hand, contain mere imitation images and are not at all the real thing.[20]

The *Rules* say: The various representations of the Heavenly Worthy, Lord of the Dao, and Lord Lao, as well as those of the sages, perfected, and immortals, as years grow long and time deepens may sustain damage through blowing wind and driving rain. If that happens, repair and restore them in good time, not allowing the perfected countenances to break or collapse. Doing so, you will attain good fortune without measure.

The *Rules* say: The sacred images of the Heavenly Worthies [in their concrete form] of gold, bronze, jewels, and jade, should once every month, on the fifteenth day, be properly purified by being washed with hot fragrant water. If the image is pressed on hemp or carved in wood, it should be wiped and polished so it sparkles with cleanliness. Doing so, you will gain tremendous merit and virtue.

---

19. Usually they are identified as the green dragon, white tiger, red bird, and turtle-cum-snake. See Major 1986. They go back to starry constellations and represent the five phases. For a map, see Staal 1984.

20. The translation of this rather obscure passage follows Yoshioka (1976, 179).

Section 6

Copying Scriptures

[2.5b] The *Rules* say: The scriptures are the teaching as handed down by the sages, they guarantee its smooth and orderly transmission.[1] They encourage and transform [beings in] the various universes[2] and bring forth the host of the sages.

[6a] Following the scriptures, one awakens to the Dao; pursuing this awakening, one realizes perfection. The scriptures open salvation for all five hundred million celestials and people, and help teach and convert all three thousand countries; they create a path toward the ascent to perfection and provide the karmic conditions necessary for going beyond the world. The scriptures contain the continuous practice [transmitted from] ten thousand [years of] antiquity and maintain the eternal models [set by] the Three Purities.

Combined from flying mysterious *qi*, scattered in verses of great purple [characters], the scriptures appear in phoenix seals or dragon scripts, in jasper texts or precious registers. Their characters are ten square feet in size, their eight corners suspended in empty vastness. Their sacred texts consist of ten sections and contain the secret instructions of the Three Vehicles.[3] Enveloped in book wrappers of clouds and hidden behind banks of morning mist, they are arranged according to the Three Caverns to divide the major schools and the Four Supplements to set off the different traditions. They are truly the efficacious medicine for celestials and people,[4] and serve as the bridge of the divine law that leads out of-life-and-death.[5] They cause the host of living beings to pass through the ford of the Five Turbidities and together climb on the Six Ferries to the other shore [of salvation].[6]

There are twelve forms in which the perfect scriptures can be produced:

1. Texts engraved on gold tablets
2. Characters sealed on silver plaques
3. Writings chiseled on flat stone

---

1. Supplementary information regarding the concrete preparations and procedures of copying the scriptures is found in *Zhengyi xiuzhen lueyi* 正一修真略儀 (DZ 1239) 19a–20b.

2. The word *tian* 天, "heaven," here indicates not only the supernatural but also the various natural worlds.

3. This refers to the canonical classification of the Three Caverns, as based on the Buddhist system of the Three Vehicles or *triyāna*. For details, see Ōfuchi 1979a.

4. This recalls the section of good deeds as medicines for the Dao described in the *Xuandu lüwen* (DZ 188).

5. This translates *shengsi* 生死, the technical term for *samsāra* in Buddhism. See Nakamura 1975, 707.

6. These are both terms taken over from Buddhism. The Five Turbidities 五濁 refer to periods of increasing decline, beginning with an overall decay, and passing through the development of egoistic views, afflictions, misery of all beings, and a short life expectancy (Nakamura 1975, 353). The Six Ferries 六度 are the six *pāramitās* or perfections leading to enlightenment: donations, morality, tolerance, effort, *samādhi* (concentration), and wisdom (Nakamura 1975, 1457). In Daoism, the meaning is slightly changed, the Five Turbidities referring to miserable states now rather than to periods in history.

4. Characters carved in wood
5. Writings on silk
6. Writings on lacquer
7. Characters in gold [6b]
8. Characters in silver
9. Bamboo tablets
10. Writings on walls
11. Writings on paper
12. Writings on leaves

Whether old script or new script, seal script or office script, whether using the jade characters of the heavenly writing or imitating the golden stanzas of cloudy *qi*—any of the eight forms of characters and six styles of calligraphy will do.[7] Just follow your heart's desire.

More particularly, there are generally two methods of copying: the integrated and the separate.[8] According to the integrated method, one treats the entire precious repository of the Three Caverns and goes through all the mysterious writings of the Four Supplements, copying them all in smooth flow in one or the other of the twelve forms named above. According to the separate method, one concentrates on each character, each sentence, each scroll, and each wrapper, following one's inclination and widely copying texts as a way to present offerings.

In all cases, the writing and copying should be essential and wondrous, paper and ink should be fresh and clear, the entries and scrolls should be full-bodied and extensive, and the wrappers and cases should be carefully stored and venerated. Burn incense and pay obeisance, for kalpas eternal presenting offerings. You will attain good fortune without measure and beyond belief.

The *Rules* say: The heavenly scriptures must be collected in a repository.[9] This again can be of two kinds, either integrated or separate. An integrated repository assembles all the writings of the Three Caverns and Four Supplements into one collection. Whether top or bottom, right or left, front or back, all texts are arranged in levels and marked with the formal title "Repository of Precious Scriptures of the Three Caverns."

[7a] A separate repository divides the writings of the Three Caverns and Four Supplements into various separate collections. Of these it contains seven:

1. Collection of the perfect scriptures of Great Pervasion
2. Collection of the precious scriptures of Mystery Cavern
3. Collection of the immortal scriptures of Spirit Cavern
4. Collection of the scriptures of Great Mystery
5. Collection of the scriptures of Great Peace

---

7. The six styles of calligraphy are the classical forms of Chinese writing: greater seal script, lesser seal script, office script, standard script, cursive script, and artistic script. See Barnhardt 1990.

8. The integrated method is also described in *Zhengyi fawen* 5b.

9. This also is taken over from Buddhism. Originally a set of shelves or racks, not unlike the construction described here, the Buddhist repository in the Middle Ages became a big revolving case, established in a building of its own and allowing the monks to turn the entire canon at one time. For a discussion of the latter, see Goodrich 1942.

6. Collection of the scriptures of Great Purity
7. Collection of the scriptures of Orthodox Unity[10]

In all cases, supply clear titles, so the separate parts can be clearly distinguished.

Whether one arranges the scriptures comprehensively or each in its own collection, in all cases one should follow the proper storing method, placing them in a special scripture terrace or in the sanctuary to the Heavenly Worthies. There they should be spread out[11] to the left and right, with the Three Caverns to the left and the Four Supplements to the right. Each collection should have its own platform and be set up properly so it does not fall to the ground or get its wrappers and scrolls broken and confused. Also, in accordance with the divine law, set up benches and lecterns with incense burners and dragon seals, so you can burn incense and light lamps to visualize and be mindful of them.

[7b] The size of the collection and repository depends on the relevant present circumstances. There are no further general rules.[12]

Section 7

Conditions for Ordination

[2.7b] The *Rules* say: The Dao is spread through people; the teaching is attained by following the masters. Unless efforts are made to ordain people, the bridge of the divine law is broken. For this reason, the spreading of the teaching lies first with ordaining people.

There are twelve different kinds of people that can be ordained:

1. Sons and grandsons of emperors
2. Great officials and prime ministers
3. Empresses and consorts
4. The intelligent and wise
5. The knowledgeable and perspicacious
6. The rich and noble, whether male or female
7. The physically erect and awe-inspiring
8. The widely benevolent and those of encompassing faith

---

10. This corresponds to the classic division of the Daoist Canon. For a study of its origins, see Ôfuchi 1979a.
11. Reading yang 揚, "spread out," for yang 陽, "yang."
12. Another rule regarding the proper storage and treatment of scriptures is found in a citation in the section on "Protecting and Guarding" in the *Shishi weiyi* (see the introduction).

9. Those keenly painstaking in work and practice[1]
10. Those keenly enthusiastic in lecturing and chanting
11. Those keenly presenting courage and bravery
12. Anyone with a strong mind [toward the Dao]

Among these twelve, those who indeed become ordained monks or nuns begin with one single person and go on to millions of people, all handing down the teaching of the divine law and widely unfolding the transmission of the scriptures.

Then again there are twenty-five kinds of people who can be caused to become ordained monks or nuns:[2]

1. Those whose families over generations have worshiped the Dao and who believe and delight in the divine law of the scriptures[3]

[8a] 2. Those who themselves over several lives[4] have worshiped the Dao and who believe and delight in the divine law of the scriptures

3. Those who in this body actively worship the Dao and who believe and delight in the divine law of the scriptures

4. Those whose families over generations have been pure and good and have believed and worshiped right perfection[5]

5. Those who themselves over several lives have been pure and good and have believed and worshiped right perfection

6. Those who in this body are pure and good and who believe and worship right perfection

7. Those who excel in their devotion to the scriptures

8. Those who are keenly painstaking in [spiritual] work and practice

9. Those who refine *qi* and abstain from grains

10. Those who are singleminded and sincere towards the Dao

11. Those who vow to spread the great Dao

12. Those who are determined to distribute the teaching of the scriptures[6]

13. Those who have practiced the Dao for a long time

14. Those who cleanse and purify their body and mind

15. Those without a mind of strong lusts

---

1. The word translated as "keen" in this section is *jing* 精, lit. "essential."

2. A short description of the ideal student of the Dao is also found in *Qianzhen ke* 2ab.

3. This translates *jingfa* 經法, a term adopted from Buddhism where it indicates "the doctrines of the sûtras" and is commonly used as another term for "dharma." See Nakamura 1975, 237.

4. This translates *jianshi* 見世, an expression used in earlier sections to denote "in this life." The translation here is in contrast to the next item, which specifies actions taken in "this life," using the expression "in one's own body" (*jishen* 已身).

5. This translates *zhengzhen* 正真. The word *zheng* 正 signifies "orthodoxy," "rightness," and the "right path," and as such appears among the Celestial Masters who call their school Zhengyi 正一 (Orthodox Unity). In Buddhism, *zheng* is used to translate *samyak* or *sât*, "right," "correct," "just." It refers to actions and attitudes that are "right" in that they will lead to liberation and enlightenment, and as such occurs in the steps of the Eightfold Path, e.g. "right livelihood," "right views," "right speech." See Nakamura 1975, 697.

6. This translates *jingjiao* 經教, a term similarly used in Buddhism to render "the teaching of the sûtras" and often another word for "dharma." See Nakamura 1975, 235.

16. Those without a mind of worldly love and attachments
17. Those without a mind of worldly victory and defeat
18. Those without a mind of worldly hatred and contempt
19. Those without a mind of worldly pride and recklessness
20. Those without a mind of worldly praise and condemnation
21. Those who develop their minds and raise their intentions, so their only wish is to become ordained monks or nuns
[8b] 22. Those who vow to become ordained monks or nuns and hand down the right divine law[7]
23. Those who vow to become ordained monks or nuns and give up all their bodies, lives, and wealth to live only for the Dao
24. Those who vow to become ordained monks or nuns and establish great good fortune and benefit for emperors and rulers and all lords, ministers, and officials governing under heaven and above the earth
25. Those who vow to become ordained monks or nuns and, on behalf of all living beings, establish fields of bliss within life-and-death by giving explanatory lectures about the Great Vehicle and widely opening all ignorance and darkness to lead all [beings] to awaken in the Dao.

On the other hand, there are ten kinds of people who must not be allowed to become ordained monks or nuns:

1. Fired ministers or rejected sons
2. Descendants of executed criminals
3. Murderers of [Daoist] masters or rebels against the Dao
4. Disbelievers in the great divine law
5. Butchers, wine-sellers, and prostitutes
6. Thieves and adulterers
7. Wine-drinkers and meat-eaters
8. Rejecters of fate and karmic retribution
9. Cripples and handicapped people
10. Murderers and lunatics

Anyone in these ten categories must not be allowed to take ordination, lest he or she diminishes the dignity of the Dao and desecrate the teaching of the divine law. [9a]

In addition, there are twenty-five kinds of people not suitable for entering the Dao:

1. Those whose families for generations have engaged in defamation and slander, never believing in the divine law of the scriptures
2. Those who themselves over several lives have engaged in defamation and slander, never believing in the divine law of the scriptures

---

7. This translates *zhengfa* 正法, an adaptation of the Buddhist term *sad-dharma* for the correct principles or truth of the teaching. It also appears as another term for "dharma." See Nakamura 1975, 704.

3. Those who in this body have engaged in defamation and slander, never believing in the divine law of the scriptures
4. Those whose families for generations have engaged in frivolity and hypocrisy, never worshiping right perfection
5. Those who themselves over several lives have engaged in frivolity and hypocrisy, never worshiping right perfection
6. Those who in this life have engaged in frivolity and hypocrisy, never worshiping right perfection
7. Those who are addicted to alcohol and have strong cravings to eat meat
8. Those who do not worship the Dao in their hearts
9. Those who have desecrated or destroyed the great Dao
10. Those who are not mindful of the divine law of the scriptures
11. Those who laze about and indulge in sensual desires
12. Those who singlemindedly pursue worldly affairs
13. Those who are defiled and evil in body and mind
14. Those who harbor strong lusts in their minds
15. Those who pass [judgment of] right and wrong in their minds
16. Those who love and are attached to sounds and sights
17. Those who care about worldly victory and defeat
18. Those who feel worldly hatred and contempt
19. Those who harbor worldly pride and recklessness
20. Those who always think about indulgence and licentiousness [9b]
21. Those who lack a mind for worshiping the divine law
22. Those who only crave for worldly benefits
23. Those who have a dissolute and unfocused mind
24. Those who are lazy and lack diligence
25. Those who only think of how to benefit themselves and not how to benefit all beings

At the time of ordination, rely on these rules to select [proper candidates]. They must meet the conditions of the divine law; only then can they become ordained monks or nuns.

Among all the fields of blessedness—be they [rites] for emperors and kings, heaven and earth, or the sun and the moon, at ancestral temples or the shrines for soil and grain, for your parents or yourself, your wife, children, or other relatives, for the dead or the living, for those coming of age or those newly born, for those without peace beyond the eight directions or the four kinds of sentient beings, be they because wind and rain are not coming in order or because the stars and lunar mansions are off course, because people have been stricken by epidemics and poison or the crops of grain have been destroyed by floods and droughts—among all the many, many fields of blessedness, ordaining people is the highest! It brings merit and virtue truly beyond belief!

The *Rules* say: There are thirty kinds of people ready to undergo initial ordination:

1. Those who always practice keen progress and are free from worldly defilements [10a]

2. Those who always practice courage and bravery and do not slacken [in their efforts] for the Dao
3. Those who always practice compassion and sympathy and never kill any living beings
4. Those who always practice care and mindfulness and aid the salvation of all creatures
5. Those who always practice forbearance and humility and never harbor rage or anger
6. Those who always practice joy and cheerfulness, leading and guiding all [to the Dao]
7. Those who always give rise to a mind of goodwill and [are eager to] hand down the Three Treasures
8. Those who always give rise to a mind of generosity and help to repair and manage the numinous monasteries
9. Those who always give rise to a mind of generosity and widely spread the teaching of the scriptures
10. Those who always pray[8] that they may develop a mind to encourage and guide all beings, causing them to take refuge in the orthodox Dao
11. Those who always pray that they may develop a mind to explain and lecture on the Great Vehicle, thereby to arouse awakening among ignorance and darkness
12. Those who always pray that they may develop a mind to establish great good fortune and benefits for emperors and rulers
13. Those who always pray that they may develop a mind to establish fields of blessedness for all great officials and prime ministers
14. Those who always pray that they may develop a mind to work for living beings so they can all be freed from suffering
15. Those who always pray that the ruler may live ten thousand years and the country be prosperous and at peace [10b]
16. Those who always pray that all under heaven may have great peace and the five grains grow in abundance
17. Those who always pray that the teaching of the scriptures is spread widely and that all attain awakening and liberation
18. Those who always pray that all beings under heaven turn toward the great Dao
19. Those who always observe the precepts and purgation periods, never slackening with each consecutive mind
20. Those who always honor the divine law of the scriptures, practicing its cultivation with each consecutive thought
21. Those who always burn incense for the Heavenly Worthies and perform rites to the Dao
22. Those who widely copy the teaching of the scriptures and distribute it freely among the people

8. This translates *yuan* 願, lit. "wish," "resolve." The term is also used for the bodhisattva vow, and in monastic manuals refers either to communal prayers or to good intentions/wishes the practitioner is to develop on behalf of all beings.

23. Those who widely support numinous monasteries, causing all beings to turn to them
24. Those who always pray that their holy persons stand firm and stable and be without slackening
25. Those who greatly establish fields of blessedness that reach everywhere and to everyone
26. Those who widely encourage donations[9] to create much merit and virtue
27. Those who widely radiate a compassionate mind and help save all creatures
28. Those who widely practice compassion and sympathy, extending wisdom to all
29. Those who always maintain the formalities of the divine law, never compromising in its dignified observances [11a]
30. Those who apply the highest and wondrous divine law on behalf of beings currently in the three bad rebirths or the hells, causing them all to ascend to salvation and be forever free from darkness and suffering

The above thirty items present a profile in the divine law of those qualified to become ordained monks or nuns. They should always pray [for people] in all the three periods—past, present, and future—with each consecutive thought and never slackening. They should also always be conscious of themselves as holy persons, never resting or being lazy. Handing down the great Dao, they establish good fortune and benefit for all living beings without measure, causing all creatures of the world, whether they have consciousness or not—indeed *all* living creatures to realize the highest Dao.

The *Rules* say: All Daoists, whether male or female, after they have been first ordained, must first of all establish themselves [in the Dao] by following guidelines for the orderly pursuit of the teaching of the divine law. There are specifically five guidelines:

1. They should make sure that their Daoist practice is pure and strong. Their minds should always be devoted to the divine law and not egotistically focus on themselves. They should pray for successful realization.
2. They should make sure that their pure honesty is proper and upright. They should never inflict harm upon any being but have their wills fully set on establishing fields of blessedness.
3. They should make sure that their practice of virtue is lofty and far-reaching. They should illuminate and defend the teaching of the divine law, using skillful means to guide both Daoists and ordinary people to take refuge [in the Dao]. [11b]
4. They should make sure that their wondrous consciousness serves in accordance with the relevant present circumstances. They should

9. The text here has *qiqu* 乞趣, lit. "beg and receive." Since begging in medieval China was not encouraged, not even among Buddhists, I have rendered the phrase as "encouraging donations."

match their minds to the current situation of the world and never go against the teaching of the scriptures.

5. They should make sure that their painstaking efforts are full of goodness and ability. They should always work toward initiating benefits and increasing advantages for all followers of the divine law.

Making sure of these five sets up a system of proper guidelines for the orderly pursuit of the teaching of the divine law. If even one of them is neglected by the followers of the divine law, they cannot establish [themselves in the Dao]. There may, for instance, be some vain and reckless people who are proud of their [Daoist] status and practice in name, but in their emotions still pursue only their personal advancement. Such people are impossible to establish [in the Dao]. Then again, there may be some who have genuine purity and diligence but in their minds do not pray for happiness. People like these have to be examined closely as to whether they can be established [in the Dao] or not.

Furthermore, there are ten conditions that make someone's full establishment utterly impossible:

1. Not believing in fate and the karmic retribution of suffering and good fortune
2. Not knowing humility and shame, and only desiring personal benefits
3. Presuming on nobility and aristocratic power, and not developing sensitivities for supporting the [monastic] crowd
4. Following one's mind and paying heed only to one's own will, seriously diminishing the permanent [monastic] residents
5. Whenever a donation is received, always giving rise to a calculating mind
6. Not understanding the scriptural precepts nor respecting them [12a]
7. Not accepting one's times of duty but shedding wolf's tears to get one's own way
8. Being clean on the outside but filthy within, ignorant outside but knowing within, true outside but false within, modest outside but greedy within, saying "yea" on the outside but thinking "nay" within
9. Never benefiting living beings, while yet not actually harming them, thus emptily occupying a position in the divine law
10. Developing egoistic desires and personal convenience because one occupies a position in the divine law, using the guidelines only to pursue personal benefits

Anyone showing any of these ten tendencies cannot be allowed to stay [in the monastery]. Also, any responsible leader who does not rely on these rules but bends them to promote his protégés will receive a subtraction of 3,600 [days of life].

The *Rules* say: Also, there are twenty-five directions that disciplined followers of the divine law should always honor and uphold:

1. Do not develop a cheating and ungrateful mind toward the materials and goods belonging to the Three Treasures.

2. Do not develop a cheating and ungrateful mind toward the various possessions of the permanent residents.
3. Do not develop a cheating and ungrateful mind toward goods donated by [members of] the four ranks.
4. Do not develop an overbearing and careless mind toward the various worthies [masters] of great virtue. [12b]
5. Do not develop an overbearing and careless mind toward middle-aged members of the [four] ranks.
6. Do not develop an overbearing and careless mind toward those of lesser standing or later birth.
7. Do not develop an overbearing and careless mind toward those of lesser or humbler station.
8. In your body honor the rules and precepts, following them without any violations.
9. Become good at [spreading] harmony and joy, soothing and cherishing both high and low.
10. Become skilled at applying skillful means in guiding the followers of the divine law.
11. Be deeply conscious of the suitability and rightness of all benefits and advantages.
12. Always maintain an upright mind toward all that belongs to the Three Treasures.
13. Never inflict any damage or desecration on the living quarters of the permanent residents.
14. Do not develop evaluations about what you receive, giving rise to love and hatred toward it.
15. Do not develop a one-sided or partisan mind toward the host of the divine law.
16. Do not entertain personal inclinations toward the various affairs and opportunities.
17. Maintain a proper and upright mind, never allowing yourself to be misguided by material things.
18. Develop a positive mind toward all tasks and always pray for their successful completion.
19. Never harm even the tiniest bit of the various materials and goods. [13a]
20. Develop the wish to benefit and increase the opulence and dignity of the Three Treasures and the permanent residents.
21. Become good at developing opportunities [for the Dao] and spread harmony and joy in worldly affairs, never allowing anyone to desecrate or destroy the Three Treasures.
22. Develop your ability to protect the host of the divine law, causing them never to be harmed from the outside.
23. Always instruct the host of the divine law, causing them to act in accordance with the rules and precepts.
24. Develop your ability to treat all people equally, whether noble or humble, insider or outsider. Whether thinking ahead or of the past, your mind should be firm and stable, as if one.

25. Widely radiate your sincere mind and successfully guide the followers of the divine law. See that nothing is ever desecrated or destroyed, thus establishing fields of blessedness for kalpas eternal, helping living beings of the future to plant good deeds and become recluses.

These twenty-five items create a comprehensive guideline for Daoist followers and help them gain merit and virtue. It thereby causes them to receive good fortune without measure in past, present, and future.

The *Rules* say: On the reverse, there are thirty items that cannot be used as guidelines for followers of the divine law. Use them to examine the permanent residents:

1. Developing a cheating and ungrateful mind toward the materials and goods belonging to the Three Treasures. [13b]
2. Developing a cheating and ungrateful mind toward the various possessions of the permanent residents.
3. Developing a cheating and ungrateful mind toward the goods donated by [members of] the four ranks.
4. Developing an overbearing and careless mind toward the various worthies of great virtue.
5. Developing an overbearing and careless mind toward middle-aged members of the [four] ranks.
6. Developing an overbearing and careless mind toward those of lesser standing or later birth.
7. In your body going against the rules and precepts, following them but violating them frequently.
8. Being unable to spread harmony and joy toward those both higher and lower.
9. Being unable to give guidance to the followers of the divine law.
10. Being unable to apply skillful means to the benefit and increase of all.
11. Not maintaining an upright mind toward all that belongs to the Three Treasures.
12. Always desiring to inflict damage or desecration on the living quarters of the permanent residents.
13. Never accepting anything without criticism and giving rise to a mind of love and hatred.
14. Not being of equal and common mind toward the host of the divine law.
15. Always finding personal use for the various affairs and opportunities.
16. Engaging in quarrels and cheating and acting with pride and recklessness.
17. Developing an attitude about each task and never bringing any to successful completion. [14a]
18. Feeling compelled to taking even the tiniest bit of the various materials and goods.
19. Never benefiting or increasing the Three Treasures and permanent residents, but always enriching oneself.

20. Never recognizing suitable opportunities [for the Dao] but going against and spoiling worldly affairs, allowing the outside crowds to invade and harm, diminish and destroy the Three Treasures.
21. Being unable to protect the host of the divine law, thus increasing and abetting the nonritual.
22. Failing to instruct the followers of the divine law, thus multiplying their infractions of the rules and precepts.
23. Preventing insiders or outsiders, the noble and humble, from receiving equal refuge in one's mind.
24. Whether thinking ahead or of the past, never having stability and method.
25. Radiating a one-sided and crooked mind, never successfully completing anything, thus causing the followers of the divine law to desecrate and destroy [the institution] and ruin or lose their fields of blessedness.
26. Relying on one's power and rank in the scriptural order to sell and barter [the effects of] the Three Treasures.
27. Relying on the trust of followers of the divine law to garner personal benefits and thus defile the teaching of the scriptures.
28. Selling the might of the Three Treasures [for money], giving free rein to one's passions and [raising judgments of] right and wrong.
29. Listening to people's opinions and criticism and frequently committing nonritual acts. [14b]
30. Taking and diminishing [the goods of] the Three Treasures and the permanent residents to give satisfaction to one's own body and mind.

One must not commit even one of these thirty. Any violation will lead to future rebirth among wild or domestic animals, where it depends on people whether one is killed or allowed to live and where one forever loses the human realm. While still in this life, one will become blind and deaf, mute and dumb, crippled in hands and lame in feet, maimed in body and appearance. Thus all Daoists, whether male or female, should clearly understand these rules and precepts and act in accordance with them without incurring any violations.

The Rules say: All Daoists, whether male or female, following the guidelines must worship and perform [rites to] the Dao in accordance with the divine law, diligently proclaiming all the rules and precepts and being a model of instruction for the host of followers. Anyone who violates the rules must be punished in accordance with the divine law, by offering incense and oil, sounding the bell and paying obeisance. Anyone who repeats the violation without showing penitence must be controlled more severely by being made to work hard repairing the monastery [buildings] on the inside or strengthening bridges [in the outside world]. Anyone, finally, who still does not comply is judged by the rules of the divine law, expelled from the order, and returned to his or her original [lay] state.

Mere ignorant fools, on the other hand, must be guided [patiently] to turn toward the Dao and refrain from violating the rules and precepts. They will thus learn to stick to the right [path] and not be led astray into disturbing the rules and codes. [15a] Failure to comply carries a subtraction of 2,400 [days of life].

Section 8

Ritual Implements

[3.1a] The *Rules* say: Ritual implements are first in the presentation of offerings and form the foundation of the dignified observances of all Daoists, male or female.[1] They cannot be left aside. All that is necessary for handling the scriptures, especially in the monastery [halls] but also in personal cells, at any occasion when offerings are being presented, the [utensils necessary] are comprehensively called ritual implements.

The *Rules* say:[2] Bells are what calls the four ranks to assemble for the major services at the six daily times [of worship]. If this utensil were being left aside, gatherings of the divine law would deviate from the proper order. The *Scripture* says, "When [the participants of] the long purgation assemble in Mystery Metropolis, they strike jade [pieces] and ring jasper bells."[3] And: "Drums of the divine law call the host of immortals to assemble. Joining in numinous song, none sounds quite the same as the other." This is just it.

[1b] Bells produced are of five kinds: (1) gold; (2) silver; (3) cast from five-metal alloy; (4) copper; (5) iron. They can have nine corners or eight, four corners or two, or even be without corners altogether. Big ones may be as large as ten thousand piculs, while small ones may measure no more than a single peck—depending on the relevant present circumstances. Once produced, all bells must be engraved with an inscription to record the current reign title and year, as well as the names of the local prefecture, district, and monastery. Their purpose in all cases is to let the ten thousand generations come together at the six daily times without fail.

The *Rules* say: Chimes[4] are used to give rhythm to the dignified observances, allowing them to stay with the essentials. They are of six kinds: (1) jade; (2) gold; (3) silver; (4) copper; (5) iron; (6) stone.

They can have two corners or four, nine corners or none, appear shaped like hooks or in any other recognizable shape. Whenever offerings are being presented, there must be bells and chimes. For them all one should create racks to suspend them.

The *Rules* say: For the sanctuary and hall of the Heavenly Worthies and any other place where scriptures or sacred images are housed, one must make screened high seats and bannered canopies, flags and streamers, staffs and

---

1. A discussion of various types and classes of ritual implements, including scriptures and sacred images, is also found in *Qianzhen ke* 10b–11a.

2. Details on bells and their use are also found in *Daoxue keyi* 1.16a–17b; *Zhengyi weiyi jing* 13a–14a. For modern uses, see Lagerwey 1987, 55. For bells in Buddhism, see Saunders 1960, 146–7.

3. The same citation is also found in *Daoxue keyi* 1.16b as from the *Zhongyuan jing* 中元經.

4. Musical stones 磬, also called lithophones, but not necessarily made from stone.

sedan chairs, incense burners and flowery jade pendants. There should also be benches and lecterns, veiling adornments and streamers on poles, platforms and racks for lamps, candle holders and lamp frames, altar frames, door plaques, and incense holders.

[2a] Ritual implements come in all types and kinds: made from gauze or woven silk, brocade or plain silk, ornamented with gold or chiseled jade, with halcyon feathers or kingfisher plumage, red pearls or green jade disks, with opaque glass or tortoise shells, strung beads or piled-up pebbles, with the seven treasures and nine radiances, the three luminescences or six extraordinary signs. Whether flowery and ornate or simple and pure—any and all kinds are in accordance with the divine law.

Presenting offerings to the Heavenly Worthies creates fields of bliss for generations eternal—even one ritual implement must not be left aside! Thus producing them with great care is of utmost merit and virtue.

The *Rules* say: Banners are of twenty-one kinds: (1) interwoven gold; (2) beaded jade; (3) stringed pearls; (4) threaded silver; (5) stitched embroidery; (6) woven [silk]; (7) variegated brocade; (8) various gauze; (9) mixed colored silk; (10) carved engravings; (11) knotted silk; (12) connected silk threads; (13) cloudy mist; (14) changeable writings; (15) made from threads; (16) monochrome; (17) of mixed colors; (18) with no paintings; (19) with painted characters; (20) of five colors; (21) of nine colors.

[2b] Whether long or short, wide or narrow, three feet or five, seven feet or nine, ten feet or twenty, forty-nine feet or a hundred, or even a thousand; whether one piece or two, ten pieces or a hundred, a thousand or ten thousand— it all depends on the relevant present circumstances.

There are also [special banners] for the dead, which show how their spirits move about, their souls migrate, and themselves go beyond the world, [reaching] the nine heavens, the three lower rebirths, and the like. Then there are banners for the sick and those that help overcome danger, dissolve disasters, liberate from danger, extend the years, lengthen life, give protection, and more—all serving to keep daily life smooth and easy.

In addition, there are banners to invite good fortune, extend auspiciousness, improve life expectancy, protect long life, relieve old age, increase the life span, and so on. They all should be produced as permitted by the local resources, then suspended from long poles in the courtyard, to the left and right of the scriptures or sacred images, and on the sides of chambers, hallways, buildings, and residences, as well as wherever offerings are being made.

The *Rules* say: Incense burners are of fifteen kinds: (1) carved jade; (2) cast gold; (3) pure silver; (4) gilded stone; (5) cast copper; (6) pure iron; [3a] (7) the seven treasures; (8) carved wood; (9) with multicolored paintings; (10) pure lacquer; (11) porcelain; (12) brick; (13) stone; (14) bamboo; (15) other currently available materials.

Their size depends on the relevant present circumstances. [They may be ornamented with] dancing phoenixes or curling dragons, flying clouds or rolling mists, lotus blossoms, thousand [petaled] leaves, or fragrant hills. They may be carved or engraved, ornamented either with insets or in relief, kept plain and simple, or merely have a straight line around them. They may have three feet or six, nine feet, or just a single central stand—in all cases following what is locally suitable.

The *Rules* say: Kerchiefs are of eight kinds: (1) variegated brocade; (2) variegated gauze; (3) variegated plain silk; (4) woven; (5) embroidered; (6) intricately colored; (7) monochrome; (8) with colored paintings.

Their size depends on the relevant present circumstances. They may be short and highly functional or [adorned with] engraved gold, suspended [pieces of] jade, strings of pearls, or bands of flowers. There can be many different kinds of ornaments, but in all cases the kerchiefs should be carefully folded and stored safely in boxes and caskets.

[3b] The *Rules* say: Scriptures must be carefully wrapped by section or at least in packs of five or ten scrolls. Of wrappers there are five kinds: (1) brocade; (2) woven; (3) embroidered; (4) pure variegated silk; (5) painted cloth. Place [the scriptures] inside [these wrappers] and tie them up in accordance with the divine law. In all cases mark them with the title of the text, saying: "So-and-so Scripture."

The *Rules* say: Scripture cases come in twelve different kinds: (1) carved jade; (2) pure gold; (3) pure silver; (4) gold engraved; (5) silver engraved; (6) pure lacquer; (7) painted wood; (8) painted in color; (9) ornamented in gold; (10) studded with jewels; (11) stone; (12) iron. Their size varies according to convenience.

The *Rules* say: Scripture chests come in six kinds: (1) studded with jewels; (2) fragrant and ornamented; [4a] (3) with gold and silver engravings or relief; (4) pure lacquer; (5) aloeswood; (6) other excellent woods. Their size depends on the relevant present circumstances.

The *Rules* say: Scripture repositories should be lacquered on the outside and lined with sandalwood or aloeswood within. They can also, both within and without, be made from pure lacquer, studded with jewels, adorned with colorful paintings, or be made from an excellent wood and kept simple and pure. Each case follows the relevant present circumstances; their size and quantity depend on the available resources.

Repositories can be built [vertically] in seven layers, one above the next; they can also [be horizontal and] have three sections next to each other. These can be three spaces apart or seven spaces, but they should always be placed in accordance with the division of the Three Caverns and Four Supplements. Their doors should have locks and keys; to their right and left likenesses of the diamond gods and divine kings should be painted [as guardians]. In all cases, make sure that the repository is erected on a platform and never placed directly on the ground.

The *Rules* say: The high seat for lecturing on the scriptures should be nine feet [2.7 meters] high and ten feet [3 meters] square. Its four pillars should be straight and coated with vermilion lacquer or made from plain wood. In all cases, it should have paintings of the diamond gods and divine kings [as guardians]. Whether there are ten high seats or a hundred—[4b] they should always be set up in matching pavilions with proper balustrades and railings around them. All has to be done in accordance with the divine law.

The *Rules* say: The high seat for reciting the scriptures should be five feet [1.5 m] high and the same square. Its organization patterns are the same as those described for the high seat for lecturing above. Its ornaments, too, are the same as outlined above.

The *Rules* say: Scripture racks are of ten kinds: (1) jade; (2) gold; (3) silver; (4) aloeswood; (5) purple sandalwood; (6) white sandalwood; (7) yellow sandalwood; (8) other excellent woods; (9) pure lacquer; (10) with reliefs and insets of gold and silver or with designs in gold, jade, pearls, and colorful silk. In all cases make the racks elevated and never place them directly on the ground.

The *Rules* say: Scripture stands to be placed before the Heavenly Worthies and lecterns used for scripture reading are of six kinds: (1) jade; (2) gold; (3) silver; (4) stone; (5) fragrant wood; (6) other woods.

[5a] Their size is determined by convenience. A lectern, for example, could be one foot two inches [35 centimeters] wide, one foot eight inches [50 centimeters] long, and one foot five inches [42.5 centimeters] high, but there are many different kinds of execution and design depending on the relevant present circumstances. Still, whenever you ascend the lectern, make sure your kerchief is tied properly.

The *Rules* say:[5] As to the divine law regarding lamps, first make a lamp frame, then surround it with a lamp shade, so that the wind cannot blow out the light or insects enter. Hang them up everywhere: near the scriptures and sacred images, in all the buildings, at the doors to the residences, and along the walkways. They will give brilliant light both inside and out—do not disregard them or leave them aside.

The *Rules* say: All other scripture utensils, such as satchels, cases, boxes, tablets, covers, collections, and so on, should be made in accordance with the relevant present circumstances. Also, whether you use pearls and jade, variegated brocade, or fine silk gauze, depends entirely on the available resources.

The *Rules* say: The canopies suspended above the sacred images of the Heavenly Worthies and the perfected are of ten kinds: (1) flying clouds; (2) soaring phoenixes; (3) dancing phoenixes; (4) lotus blossoms; (5) immortal fungi; [5b] (6) the seven treasures; (7) embroidered silk; (8) combinations of different patterns; (9) monochrome; (10) with colored paintings.

Ornaments, such as pearls and jade, jade pendants, flowing perilla, suspended bells, and strings of jade should be added in accordance with the relevant present circumstances. However, any canopies held by Daoists, whether male or female, must be either kingfisher or turquoise. Canopies can have eight corners or four, they can be square or round, as is warranted by the relevant situation. But the holes and hooks necessary for the various hangings and attachments should be properly covered—for this reason the [painted] figures hold morning flowers in their hands.

The *Rules* say: Comfortable sedan chairs and cloth-covered carriages are what the immortals and sages come riding in during the presentation of offerings and the dignified observances. Build them as you would those for a contemporary king.

---

5. Details on the use and making of lamps are also found in *Daoxue keyi* 2.1a–2a.

The *Rules* say: Flag poles and standards are what the gods and immortals hold [during their descent]. Described in the scriptures and manuals, they are important requisites for the dignified observances. Pattern them on those used in contemporary affairs of state.

The *Rules* say: Blossomy branches and flowery lanterns are necessary for inducing and guiding [the immortals below]. Every monastery must have them. Make a rack and place it before the Heavenly Worthies, then create paper lanterns without saving material or effort. Failure to comply carries a subtraction of 180 [days of life].

[6a] The *Rules* say: All fire braziers to burn incense and their related implements, such as seven-pronged tongs to regulated the fire, bowls to transfer the fire, sieves and holders for the ashes, containers and baskets for the charcoal, nine-layered carriers for the charcoal, covers against [flying] ashes, cloths to wipe the braziers, racks for the seven-pronged fire tongs, as well as the nine-layered vessels to regulate the fire, should all be produced harmoniously and following the local convenience. Place them in the sanctuary to the Heavenly Worthies or into niches on its right and left. Failure to comply carries a subtraction of 680 [days of life].

The *Rules* say:[6] All roped beds, knee supports, *ruyi* scepters, slanted benches, brooms, and water pitchers are not urgently needed on the immediate right and left of the Heavenly Worthies, yet they are essential for all Daoists, whether male or female, when they present offerings. They should be made in accordance with the relevant present circumstances—do not leave them aside or disregard them.

Section 9

Ritual Vestments[1]

[3.6b] The *Rules* say: All Daoists, whether male or female, each have ritual vestments of the Three Caverns, which come with specific observances and regula-

---

6. The following are utensils used in the residences of Daoists. They are listed again, with more discussion, in section 10.

1. Vestments are also discussed in *Wushang biyao* 43.1a–2b; *Daoxue keyi* 1.5a–9a; *Zhengyi weiyi jing* 5b–6a; *Qianzhe ke* 6a, 7A; and *Yaoxiu keyi* 9.1a–3b. The most detailed presentation is in the *Fafu kejie wen* (DZ 788), which contains an outline of the ritual ranks, both celestial and on earth, with their various robes, plus forty-six practical rules on vestments. For a partial translation of the latter, see Kohn 1993, 336–43.

tions, all described in the fundamental scriptures. Practitioners must wear them according to the regulations of the divine law, as is expounded below.

[In general,] the various capes in their adornments with mountain patterns, swirling mists, luminous paintings, and so on, must not imitate the appearance of the nine-colored variegated gauze worn by the figures of the Heavenly Worthies.

Now, preceptors of great virtue who lecture to explain the Great Vehicle of the Three Caverns, widely expose the wondrous Dao, and otherwise ascend the high seat, have formal vestments that they wear whenever they approach the divine law, climb the altar platform, enter the oratory, announce a purgation rite, perform rites to the Dao, or serve as the head in reading a formal presentation. Similarly, the cultivation of the divine law of the scriptures and the transmission of scriptural precepts are dignified observances that necessitate [the wearing of ritual vestments].

However, these affairs are limited and of short duration; once they are over, the vestments should be returned immediately. Except on these occasions, they are not to be put on. Failure to comply carries a subtraction of 1,200 [days of life].

The *Rules* say: Female Daoists wear skirts with green borders around the hem. For dyeing [the main garment], use gardenia to achieve a deep yellow color. The sleeves of the garment should be wide, just as those of the male Daoists. In no case must it be of a light, dull, or mixed color. Failure to comply carries a subtraction of 240 [days of life].

[7a] The *Rules* say: When Daoists, whether male or female, prepare [to put on] their vestments, they must first divest themselves of everything that does not comply with the rules. Their upper, middle, and lower garments must all be of a light yellow color and might even, if the dye contains some powdery earth, turn into a rather dull [tone of] yellow. The length and size in each case depend on the individual's body.

Among the monastic residents, masters of the presentation of offerings, senior monks of high virtue, artisans who work on the ornamentation of scriptures and sacred images, and officers in the monastery administration must all wear such garb. They are collectively called office-holders.

All Daoists, whether male or female, must wear breeches and leggings, tunics and shirts of dusty yellow. They must not use any other color, including white. Failure to comply carries a subtraction of 360 [days of life].

The *Rules* say: All Daoists, whether male or female, have headdresses and kerchiefs that have many kinds of names and come in different shapes and patterns. They are specified in the scriptures and outlined below.

They can be made from grain husks or the shell of bamboo shoots, from birds' down or pure lacquer, depending on their basic shape. They must, however, in no case be of deerskin or adorned with pearls, jade, or damask.

[7b] For hairpins,[2] the use of ivory, jade, bone, and horn is within the limits of the divine law. They should be kept in cases and boxes and not left openly

---

2. For more on hairpins, see also *Yunji qiqian* 47.2a.

exposed, lest ordinary people harm or defile them. Failure to comply carries a subtraction of 260 [days of life].

The *Rules* say:[3] All Daoists, whether male or female, have shoes with a round tip or representing the two forces. They should be made from leather, cloth, or raw silk and adorned with the colors yellow and black. They must not be made from gauze, damask, brocade, or embroidery, nor should they be painted or embroidered, studded with fake pearls or contain hidden pouches. Daoists' shoes must in no way be like the shoes of ordinary people, who use green and purple brocade and often embroider them.

The stockings of Daoists must be pure and plain and made from ordinary cloth or raw silk. Boots should have round tips and broad, flat soles. Overshoes should be made from nothing but plain hemp. Aside from these, Daoists should not afford any luxuries. Failure to comply carries a subtraction of 240 [days of life].

The *Rules* say: All Daoists, whether male or female, should use bedding made from coarse linen and dyed a dull yellow or a light acacia brown. Anything blue, green, turquoise, scarlet or purple, made from brocade, damask, or gobelin, anything that shines brilliantly and is of variegated colors, must not be used.

[8a] The same rule applies to all cushions and mats, bedspreads and coverlets, with the exception that coverlets may on occasion be purple, turquoise, or brown in color. Pillows[4] should be made from wood or pure lacquer and always rectangular in shape. They should not be slanted, curved, or have any kind of fanciful shape. Nor should they have a special groove for the top knot or be engraved or adorned with gold and silver. Always spread a clean cloth beneath them. Failure to comply carries a subtraction of 360 [days of life].

The *Rules* say: All Daoists, whether male or female, should carry [bits of] scripture, precepts, talismans, and registers suspended from their belts. With the celestial writing on their bodies, the perfected stay near them, the *qi* of the Dao supports and protects them, and the numen of the immortals gives them something to rely on. The formal garments and headdresses they wear are called ritual vestments. They all contain spirits and numinous powers, so treat them with respect and care, even when sitting and lying down. Always keep them particularly pure and clean.

When pursuing karmic connections and going into the world to teach and educate ordinary people, never allow your holy person to be defiled by ordinary affairs. Common people's beds[5] and mats are full of defiled *qi*, and they make distinctions of noble and humble in their clothing. You must, therefore, make sure to be properly separate from them. Also, whenever you sit down, first spread a seat-cloth, which should be four feet square in size and inscribed on both sides with seal script. Senior Daoists of high virtue, preceptors, and advanced practitioners of the divine law can use purple for their seat-cloth; all others should use acacia brown.

---

3. Shoes are also described in *Zhengyi weiyi jing* 16a.

4. Extensive details on pillows, with a list of herbs to be placed inside them, are found in *Daoxue keyi* 2.6b–7b; *Yaoxiu keyi* 14.11b–12b.

5. Reading *chuang* 床, "bed," for *zhuang* 狀, "appearance."

[8b] In no case must anyone take objects of brocade, damask, pearls, or fine silk with them when coming and going among ordinary people. The reason is that going among ordinary folk, they will have no need [for such finery]. Failure to comply carries a subtraction of 360 [days of life].

Section 10

Residences

[3.8b] The *Rules* say: All Daoists, whether male or female, have residences and sleeping places that should be surrounded by four walls and built for single occupancy. There should not be several bunks [in the same room] either in front or behind each other. Whether sitting or sleeping, Daoists should always be alone and one per bed. Failure to comply carries a subtraction of 120 [days of life].[1]

The *Rules* say: All Daoists, whether male or female, have sleeping and sitting places that should not be surrounded by curtains, screens, or wind shields. If the hut has holes or leaks so that wind and dust come in easily, they may patch it up with simple cloth or plain silk or set up an enveloping silk curtain, but nothing else. Failure to comply carries a subtraction of 120 [days of life].

[9a] The *Rules* say: All Daoists, whether male or female, should always keep their residences empty and clean, simple and stark. There may be a slanted bench, a knee-support, a *ruyi*, a broom, an incense burner, an incense holder, a scripture stand, a kerchief, a chest of wood or bamboo, a seat coverlet, a rope bed, a scripture repository, a lamp stand, various plates and bowls for food, and a water pitcher.[2] All other objects, especially if nonritual and for play only, must not be kept or used. Failure to comply carries a subtraction of 360 [days of life].

The *Rules* say:[3] All Daoists, whether male or female, should have eating utensils of the following five kinds: (1) pure lacquer; (2) copper; (3) stone; (4) iron; (5) earthenware. They come in three sizes:

1. Large, holding five pints [3.5 liters]
2. Medium, holding three pints [2.1 liters]
3. Small, holding one pint [0.7 liters]

---

1. A similar rule is also found in *Zhengyi weiyi jing* 15b–16a.
2. A similar list of Daoist utensils is also found in *Zhengyi weiyi jing* 15b.
3. Rules on eating utensils are also found in *Shishi weiyi* 8b–9a.

These five [three?] cover all necessary eating utensils. There should also be an earthenware alms bowl that holds one-half pint [0.35 liters]. Spoons and chopsticks can be made from copper or lacquer, nothing more fancy. After each use, wipe them with a clean cloth.

A second set of utensils is reserved for use in the refectory. This is to be kept separate from the other ware and must never be used for other purposes but should be maintained clean and pure at all times. It is called the "refectory set." After each use, wash and wipe it, then store it on a special dish rack. Never mix it with other dishes. Failure to comply carries a subtraction of 280 [days of life].

[9b] The *Rules* say: All Daoists, whether male or female, should have a bath house built near their residences. Here they clean themselves inside and out, washing off all violations and defilements, sweat and dirt. Failure to comply carries a subtraction of 120 [days of life].

The *Rules* say: All Daoists, whether male or female, should build their residences near a fresh spring or well. It has to be kept clean and pure, never allowing defilements or mixed [substances] to despoil it, nor even the excrements of domestic animals. In any case, before using the water, it should be filtered. Failure to comply carries a subtraction of 120 [days of life].

The *Rules* say:[4] All Daoists, whether male or female, in their residences should be provided with a water pitcher, pouring basin, or any other vessel suitable to collect clear water and carry [it to the house]. This is for rinsing the mouth and washing the hands. The vessel can be made from gold, silver, copper, or earthenware, as the relevant present circumstances permit. The container with the water should be kept covered, so that the water is not made dirty by dust or insects. Use a clean cloth to put on top. Failure to comply carries a subtraction of 80 [days of life].

The *Rules* say:[5] All Daoists, whether male or female, should set up an outhouse near their residences. For this, hollow out a more or less shallow pit from the earth and erect a small hut over it. [10a] The place should be kept scrupulously clean both inside and out; no defilement or dirt must be openly apparent. Failure to comply carries a subtraction of 120 [days of life].

---

4. A detailed description of the water pitcher and its use is also found in *Shishi weiyi* 7ab.
5. Another description of the outhouse and its use is also found in *Daoxue keyi* 2.12ab.

Section 11

Reciting the Scriptures[1]

[4.1a] When you first enter the hall, perform incantations[2] and ablutions as pre-scribed by the divine law. Offer incense three times, then circumabulate the scripture once all the way round, and again offer incense three times. Depending on your rank either fold your hands [on your chest] or hold your ritual tablet, then, with erect posture, each bow in respect [and say]:

> With all my heart, I knock my head to the Highest Non-Ultimate Great Dao!
> With all my heart, I knock my head to the worthy scriptures in thirty-six sections!
> With all my heart, I knock my head to the great preceptors of the mysterious center!

While intoning this formula, kneel on your seat as prescribed by the divine law, then sprinkle purified water. This done, one [specially selected] person takes incense and swings it for fumigation and purification. Thereafter he brings out the scripture and again swings the incense to fumigate.

Next, he chants the encomium as prescribed by the divine law. Then all offer an incantation, which runs:

> For our fate and destiny, we now have faith,
> Weak vessels, we hope to speak of nonbeing.
> Mostly desiring to see only what is before our eyes, [1b]
> We yet try to go beyond the eyes and come to address anxiety.

> As with greater wisdom we begin to understand the teaching of the Dao,
> In sorrowful distress, we mourn the obstinate.
> Weeping bitterly, we think of their deep suffering;
> As we care deeply, they make us feel so sad.

---

1. This section, as do all sections to the end of the *Daozang* edition (11–18), has the word *yi* 儀, "observances," in the title. This title thus reads literally "observances for reciting the scriptures." For stylistic reasons in English, I have left the word untranslated, although its meaning is clearly implied. All sections, from here to the end of the DZ text, are also contained in the manuscript P. 2337, reprinted and discussed in Yoshioka 1955. Similar instructions on scripture recitation are also found in *Daoxue keyi* 1.19a–20a; *Zhengyi weiyi jing* 6b–7a; and *Zhengyi fawen jing* (DZ 1204), 6ab.

2. This refers to short verses said at different occasions in order to raise the person's awareness. For example, there are verses used while getting up, putting on robes, combing the hair, washing the face, cleaning the teeth, and so on. They are first documented in the section on "Purifying Practice" of the *Avatamsaka sûtra* (*Huayan jing* 華嚴經), which was translated as part of Kumârajîva's project in 417. See Cleary 1984.

Following this, practice silent mindfulness as prescribed by the divine law. Then place your hand tablet on the bench nearby, kneel with straight back, make your hands into fists, and clap your teeth thirty-six times. Close your eyes and visualize a five-colored cloudy *qi*-vapor that completely fills the room. Then see the green dragon, white tiger, great lion, dark turtle, red bird, and wondrous phoenix stand guard at your front and back. Immortal lads and jade maidens, the five emperors and numinous officials, spirit immortals and soldiers and horses—a crowd of ninety million—guard you to the left and right.

Now rock your body three times and offer the following incantation:[3]

> Lonely and solitary, in the line of utmost nonbeing,
> Empty and steep, for kalpas never ending,
> Abysmal and deep—the mysterious writings of the Caverns,
> Who could measure their depth and reach?
> Once having entered the path of the Great Vehicle,
> Who can count the years and numerous kalpas?
>
> No more life and no more death,
> I wish to be born following the lotus blossom,
> To go beyond the realms of all Three Worlds,
> And with compassionate heart look at the worldly net.
> As a perfected of all-highest virtue,
> Generation after generation a member of immortals.

The latter is intoned by all together as a common recitation.

[2a] Next, each is mindful of the names of the Highest Worthies seven times. This done, [the selected person] intones the request for turning the wheel of the divine law. At this time, he first opens the scripture. Unless another person is chosen to ascend to the high seat and perform the scripture recitation, now he intones the request for the preceptor to come up. The preceptor duly rises and, holding his ritual tablet, bows three times to the scripture and the sacred images, facing first south, then west and north. After this he ascends to the high seat and turns left about to face east. He claps his teeth and meditates as prescribed by the divine law. To step down again from the high seat, he reverses the procedures, beginning with the south, and bowing three times.

This is the ritual prescribed for [scriptures of] Mystery Cavern. The others, Perfection Cavern and Spirit Cavern, each have their own fundamental rituals. To cultivate and practice their scriptural rites, rely on their specific rules. I will not present them in detail here.[4]

After concluding the reading of the scripture, it is rolled up again. Then a [specially selected] person brings water to sprinkle on it for purification and fumigates it again by swinging incense. Once the proper purifications are concluded, all chant the encomium as prescribed by the divine law. Then all intoning members bow in respect [to the scripture] and offer incense three times.

---

3. The text of this incantation is also found in the Shangqing work *Yujing baojue* 玉經寶訣 (Precious Formulas of the Jade Scriptures, DZ 425). See Yoshioka 1976, 145. It is repeated again in section 12.

4. A description of the complete rites of all the various ritual ranks is found in *Yaoxiu keyi* 2.2a–5a.

Holding their ritual tablets and standing up straight, they surrender their lives with all their hearts to the three Highest Worthies, the [gods of the] ten directions, the host of the sages, and [the masters of] superior virtue. Finally, another [specially selected] person, with deep awe for the scripture, offers a formal invocation and prayer. It runs:

> Now, the precious scriptures of the Three Caverns, the superior models of the myriad heavens, are combined from flying mysterious *qi* and created from cloud-seal verses. [2b] The crown of [deep] meaning, they are without birth; writings suspended [in emptiness], they endure for kalpas eternal. Therefore, heaven and earth hold on to them and are divided; the sun and the moon follow them and establish their course; demons and spirits honor them and transform pervasively; human beings worship them and attain salvation.
>
> For this reason, whoever chants them will traverse the scarlet empyrean in his body; whoever listens to them will be born in turquoise openness in his spirit.[5] All humans and celestials rely on them; all life and death depends on them. They serve as the ford and bridge of the multitude of creatures, are truly the door and window of the host of the perfected. Too unfathomable to be described, they are the pure accumulation of the Great Vehicle.
>
> I, so-and-so, today on behalf of such-and-such an affair, turn the scripture so-and-so, *juan* so-and-so, for so-and-so many times.[6] As I open its case and unfold its depth, the scripture's rustling penetrates the three thousand [worlds]. As I hold its scroll and hum its mysterious [words], the scripture's sound carries through the five billion layers [of the universe].
>
> I therefore pray that a golden incense maid gathers the smoky characters in the heavens, while a jade scripture lad presents the scripture's text on his tablet, thus causing all our faults of bygone kalpas to dissolve and good fortune to descend to our present time. Whether alive or dead, all rejoice in the grace of creation and prosperity; whether animal or plant, all delight in the virtue of life and growth.
>
> [3a] As thus the excellent goodness [of the scripture] spreads its majesty everywhere, all beings in the three bad rebirths cease their distressed and hurtful toils, those in the nine [dark] nights end their bitter and painful suffering. Then all anxious and concerned people, all wriggling and crawling creatures, climb on the boat of the Six Ferries [Perfections] to ascend the shore of the Three Purities.

5. "Turquoise openness" translates *biluo* 碧落, a technical term for one of the higher heavens. See Bokenkamp 1991.

6. The term "turn" (*zhuan* 轉) in the context of scriptural recitation means to "recite repeatedly." See Bokenkamp 1997, 390.

Thus I pray:
After my turning of this scripture—
May the myriad goodnesses be widely held on to
And the thousand disasters be destroyed completely!
With all my heart I knock my head
To the Three Treasures of Right Perfection!

Thus I pray:
After my turning of this scripture—
May good fortune envelope the dark and bright,
While merit soaks the far and near!
With all my heart I knock my head
To the Three Treasures of Right Perfection!

Thus I pray:
Through my turning of this scripture—
May merit and virtue protect and envelope all
And the host of living beings be freed from suffering and find
    liberation!
With all my heart I knock my head
To the host of all the sages!

In regular rites of scripture cultivation, practitioners should [conclude the session by] reciting one of several possible encomia to honor the scripture: the Encomium of the Scripture of the Great Ultimate, in seven stanzas; the Praise of the Four Heavenly Kings of the Numinous Book, in four stanzas; or the Encomium of the Perfected Writings of the Eight Luminants. These will not be further specified here.

[3b] The Rules say: Whenever you read or recite a scripture, proceed in accordance with these observances. Failure to comply carries a subtraction of 2,400 [days of life].

Section 12

Lecturing on the Scriptures[1]

[4.3b] The preceptor washes and rinses, then dons his headdress and belt as prescribed by the divine law. A disciple holding incense and flowers bows to him and requests to be guided [in the teaching], using the formula prescribed in the *Rules*. Then the preceptor climbs to the mat before the scriptures and sacred images and collects his mind, standing upright with an incense burner in his hands.

This done, he intones [the refuges], while all members of the congregation bow in respect. They take refuge in the great Dao, praying that all living beings may be liberated and awakened to right perfection and develop a mind that encompasses the all-highest; they take refuge in the divine law of the scriptures, praying that all living beings may find penetrating wisdom and insight as deep and wide as the ocean; they take refuge in the preceptors of the mystery, praying that all living beings may discern the darkness and overcome all obstacles, widely spreading the orthodox Dao.

Next, the preceptor ascends to the [lecturing] high seat, while the participants,[2] after having stood for intoning [the refuges], kneel with straight backs and wait for him to offer incense three times. This done, he chants again, then practices silent mindfulness as prescribed by the divine law. After a further visualizing mindfulness, he intones the chant of the [scriptural] encomium as prescribed by the divine law. It goes:[3]

> Lonely and solitary, in the line of utmost nonbeing,
> Empty and steep, for kalpas never ending,
> Abysmal and deep—the mysterious writings of the Caverns,
> Who could measure their depth and reach?
> Once having entered the path of the Great Vehicle,
> Who can count the years and numerous kalpas? [4a]
> No more life and no more death,
> I wish to be born following the lotus blossom,
> To go beyond the realms of all Three Worlds,
> And with compassionate heart look at the worldly net.
> As a perfected of all-highest virtue,
> Generation after generation a member of immortals.

---

1. Details on scriptural lectures are also found in *Shishi weiyi* 12a–13b; *Daoxue keyi* 1.2a–3b; *Zhengyi weiyi jing* 8ab. For details on washing the hands and rinsing the mouth, see *Shishi weiyi* 7b–8b.

2. Reading *dao* 道 as *daoshi* 道士.

3. The same chant as practiced during scripture recitation; this also appears in section 11 (4.1b). A different set of chants for the same occasion, based on the *Benxiang jing*, is found in *Yaoxiu keyi* 2.8b–9a.

Then all intone the request for turning the wheel of the divine law. Intoning in a common recitation, all chant the names of the Highest Worthies seven times.

Next, the cantor arranges the scripture and begins to recite it, while the preceptor remains beneath the high seat. After each section, the latter bows to the scripture once, then gives a detailed explanation of the text. Whenever he completes his lecturing, he falls silent, allowing harmony and delight [to spread] without anything to be heard. When the entire lecturing session is over, the preceptor takes the incense burner and adds a pinch of incense to it, praying that this lecture on the scriptures may produce strong and vigorous merit and virtue. [He says]:

> May
> Our sovereign emperor and imperial princes,
> All our kings, lords and nobles, governors and overseers,
> All magistrates and elders of prefectures and districts,
> All the people in the wide empire,
> All the faithful believers in the scriptural lectures,
> All present followers of the divine law,
> All living beings,
> All those suffering in the three bad rebirths,
> May they all with the help of this root of goodness
> Attain bodily liberation in the Great Vehicle
> And take refuge with their hearts in the orthodox Dao!
> May they all come out of the river of passions
> And freely wander in the ocean of the divine law!

Next, the congregation intones communally, with each member bowing in respect: "With all my heart I surrender my life to the three Highest Worthies, the [gods of the] ten directions, and the host of the sages." [4b]

Then they pray:

> May our sovereign emperor
> Have a hundred kinds of good fortune, strong and vigorous,
> And ten thousand good deeds that assemble like the clouds!
> With all my heart I knock my head
> To the Three Treasures of Right Perfection!

> Through this lecturing on the scriptures
> May merit and virtue protect and envelope all,
> And the host of living beings be freed from suffering and find
>   liberation!
> With all my heart I knock my head
> To the host of sages and those who have attained the Dao!

In accordance with the divine law, a disciple now takes the incense and the flowers and escorts the preceptor back to his residential quarters. All bow as prescribed by the divine law.

The *Rules* say: Whenever you lecture on a scripture, proceed in accordance with the divine law as described here. Failure to comply carries a subtraction of 1,200 [days of life].

Section 13

The Ritual Order[1]

[4.4b] The *Rules* say: All Daoists, whether male or female, have ritual ranks, formal order, and religious titles, each of their specific class. You must know which is superior and inferior, higher and lower, so there is neither favoritism nor abuse of power. For this reason I have set them out in detail below. Familiarize yourself thoroughly with them. Failure to comply in each case carries a subtraction of 1,200 [days of life].

[5a] The *Rules* say: The wise ones among the people of the Dao are called believers. Those among the good men and good women who actively practice [the Dao] are known as male and female Daoists. These are appellations for those ahead of ordinary people; they are not merely restrictive names to be used in court when disputing charges. In addition, there are preceptors, masters of great virtue, venerated masters, and elders. These appellations are for men outside of ordinary society who have become ordained monks. Their titles are not mere convenient appellations for presenting petitions or submitting memorials, either.

Then again there are the "poor Daoists," which is another, rather deprecating way to call ordained monks or nuns. "Disciples," on the other hand, is a humble term for all those still living in the common world. It should not be used before the Three Treasures. It is different in this respect from the term "Disciples of the Three Caverns," which is a name for the preceptors. Familiarize yourself thoroughly with the system. The following is a detailed outline.

MEN, WOMEN. *Note*: This is the appellation for commoners who have not yet taken the scriptural precepts.

HOUSEHOLD ELDERS. *Note*: People who make sincere contributions to Daoist lineage are called Household Ledger [holders].

DISCIPLES[2] OF THE GREAT DAO, DISCIPLES OF THE HEAVENLY WORTHIES, DISCIPLES OF THE THREE TREASURES. *Note*: Men and women who have surrendered their hearts to the great Dao and diligently follow the scriptural teaching have earned any of these titles.

DISCIPLES OF PURE FAITH.[3] *Note*: Anyone who has received the Heavenly Worthy's ten precepts and fourteen rules of self-control, the twelve resolutions for [control of] the six senses, or equivalent precepts, has earned this title. [5b]

---

1. The full list of ritual ranks and related scriptures, divided into eleven levels, as based on the work of Zhang Wanfu in combination with this text, is presented and discussed in Benn 1991, 78–97. For a complete and systematic description of the entire system, see Benn 2000.

2. Benn calls these "students" (1991, 77), but I prefer to maintain one translation for *dizi*, namely "disciples."

3. This is placed after the basic Orthodox Unity ranks and appears as level 4 in Benn (1991, 77). The ten precepts and fourteen rules of self-control go back to the Lingbao school and are contained most prominently in the *Shijie*

MALE PUPILS, FEMALE PUPILS. *Note*: Children of seven or eight years who have received the register of one general have earned this title.

REGISTER PUPILS. *Note*: Children of ten or over who have received the talismans and register of three or ten general and have taken the three refuges and five precepts have earned this title.

The *Rules* say: These ten titles have to be used whenever a man or woman delivers a memorial or makes a formal announcement. Before the Heavenly Worthies or the Great Dao, in all cases the humble appellation "so-and-so" should be applied and not a direct name. Failure to comply carries a subtraction of 360 [days of life].

As for the ritual ranks of Orthodox Unity,[4] lads have received the register of one, three, or ten generals. Register pupils have also received the *Sanjie wen* (Text of the Three Precepts) and the *Zhengyi jiewen* (Text of the Precepts of Orthodox Unity). *Note*: They are either children of seven or eight or again those of ten years and over. They are called REGISTER DISCIPLES OF ORTHODOX UNITY.

Qishiwu jiangjun lu	Register of 75 Generals
Bai wushi jiangjun lu	Register of 150 Generals[5]
Zhengyi zhenjuan	Perfected *Juan* of Orthodox Unity
Ershisi zhi zhengyi chaoyi	Observances for Audience Rites of the 24 Parishes[6]
Zhengyi bajie wen	Text of the Eight Precepts of Orthodox Unity

Note: Those who receive these have the title MALE OFFICER or FEMALE OFFICER GOVERNING THE PARISH SO-AND-SO.[7] [6a]

Huangchi quanqi	Tally Contract of Yellow and Red
Huangshu quanling	Contract Ordinances of the Yellow Book
Wuse qiling	Tally Ordinances of the Five Colors
Basheng jiugong qiling	Tally Ordinances of the Eight Life Energies and the Nine Palaces
Zhentian liujia quanling	Contract Ordinances of the Six Jia Gods of Perfect Heaven
Zhentian sanyi qiling	Tally Ordinances of the Three Ones of Perfect Heaven
Wudao baquan	Eight Contracts of the Five Realms

Note: Those who receive these have the title DISCIPLES OF THE THREE ONES, PERFECTED OF RED YANG.

---

jing 十戒經 (Scripture of the Ten Precepts), a popular and much-used text in medieval Daoism. It is contained in DZ 459 as well as in the Dunhuang manuscripts, S. 6454, P. 2347, P. 2350, P. 3770, and P. 3417 (Ōfuchi 1979b, 191–201). See also Fukui 1952, 197; Kusuyama 1982; Ren and Zhong 1991, 341. The precepts are listed fully in section 18. The twelve resolutions are found in the *Chishu yujue* 赤書玉訣 (Jade Formulas of the Book Written in Red, DZ 352), an early Lingbao work; see Bokenkamp 1989.

4. Reading *zheng* 正 "right," "true," instead of *zhi* 止, "stop," probably a copying error.
5. Also mentioned in *Zhengyi xiuzhen lueyi* 正一修真略儀 (DZ 1239), 4b–5a.
6. Also mentioned in *Zhengyi xiuzhen lueyi* 11a.
7. Benn calls these levels 1–3 and describes them as part of initiation, prior to ordination proper. He does not list the materials for this last rank (1991, 74–7).

Jiutian poyi [zhang]	[Verses of the] Nine Heavens That Destroy Sick ness
Jiugong hanwei duzhang	Complete Verses of the Nine Palaces against Danger[8]
Biyin sibu jinqi	Prohibition *Qi* to Neutralize Seals in All Four Areas
Liugong shenfu	Divine Talisman of the Six Palaces
Jiutian doutong zhanye dafu	Talisman of the Nine Heavens to Control All and Behead Evil
Jiuzhou sheling	Earth God Ordinances of the Nine Provinces
Tianling chiguan sanwu qi	Tally of the Celestial and Numinous Red Offi cials of Three and Five
Sanyuan jiangjun lu	Register of the Generals of the Three Primes[9]

Note: Those who receive these have the title DISCIPLES OF THE DIGNIFIED COVENANT OF ORTHODOX UNITY GOVERNING THE PARISH SO-AND-SO.

Yangping zhi dugong ban	Tablet of all Merit of Yangping Parish
Jiutian zhenfu	Perfect Talisman of the Nine Heavens
Jiutian bingfu	Military Talisman of the Nine Heavens[10]
Shangling zhao	Summons of Highest Numen
Xianling zhao	Summons of Immortal Numen
Shixing lu	Register of the Ten Stars
Ershiba su lu	Register of the 28 Lunar Mansions
Yuanming lu	Register of Primordial Destiny[11]

Note: Those who receive these have the title PERFECTED OF PRIMORDIAL DES- TINY, DISCIPLES OF THE DIGNIFIED COVENANT OF ORTHODOX UNITY IN YANGPING PARISH, WHO GOVERN THE TWENTY-FOUR ENERGIES OF LIFE AND THE HIGHEST *QI* OF THE CENTER.[12]

Sui tiandi guishen lu	Register to Pursue Demons and Spirits of Heaven and Earth
Zitai bilu	Secret Register of the Purple Terrace
Jingang badie xianlu	Immortal Register of the Eight-Faceted Diamond [6b]
Feibu tiangang lu	Register of Flying and Pacing the Heavenly Net
Tongtian lu	Register of Governing Heaven
Wanzhang guilu	Register of the Mile-High Demons
Qingjia chijia lu	Register of the Green and Red Jia Gods
Chibing lu	Register of the Red Bing Gods

---

8. Also mentioned in *Zhengyi xiuzhen lueyi* 7b.

9. The last four are also mentioned in *Zhengyi xiuzhen lueyi* 9a, 8b, 8a, 5b.

10. Also mentioned in *Zhengyi xiuzhen lueyi* 9a.

11. Also mentioned in *Zhengyi xiuzhen lueyi* 5b–6a.

12. Also mentioned in *Zhengyi xiuzhen lueyi* 5b–6a. These ranks appear as level 5 in Benn 1991, subdivided into four sections (79–81).

Taiyi wuzhong lu	Register of Never-Ending Great Unity
Dadi lu	Register of Great Earth
Sanyuan zhailu	Residential Register of the Three Primes
Liuren shilu	Controlling Register of the Six Ren Gods
Shi zhenshen lu	Register of Controlling Perfected and Spirits
Taixuan jinqi	Prohibition *Qi* of Great Mystery[13]
Qian erbai dazhang	1,200 Grand Petitions
Sanbai liushi zhang	360 Petitions
Zhengyi jing	Scripture of Orthodox Unity (27 *juan*)[14]
Laojun yibai bashi jie	180 Precepts of Lord Lao
Zhengyi zhaiyi	Purgation Observances of Orthodox Unity[15]
Laozi sanbu shenfu	Divine Talismans of Laozi in Three Sections

Note: Those who receive these have the title PERFECTED OF PRIMORDIAL LIFE, DISCIPLES OF THE DIGNIFIED COVENANT OF ORTHODOX UNITY, WHO GOVERN THE TWENTY-FOUR ENERGIES AND THE HIGHEST *QI* OF THE CENTER, CELESTIAL MASTERS OF THE ORTHODOX UNITY LINEAGE OF THE GREAT MYSTERY SECTION.[16]

Dongyuan shenzhou jing	Scripture of Divine Incantations of Abyss Cavern (10 *juan*)
Shenzhou quan	Contract of Divine Incantations
Shenzhou lu	Register of Divine Incantations
Sishen tu	Chart for Visualizing the Gods
Shenxian jinzhou jing	Scripture of Prohibiting Incantations of the Divine Immortals (2 *juan*)
Hengxing yunü zhouyin fa	Method of Imprinting the Jade Maiden's Incantation in Horizontal Lines
Huangshen chizhang	Red Petition of the Yellow God

Note: Those who receive these have the title PERFECTED OF THE LESSER OMEN, PRECEPTORS OF ABSORPTION,[17] GREAT ANCESTORS OF THE DIVINE INCANTATIONS OF THE ABYSS CAVERN.[18]

Laozi jinniu qingsi	Laozi's Green Thread and Gold Knob
Shijie shisi chishen jie	Ten Precepts and Fourteen Precepts of Self-Control

Note: Those who receive these have the title DISCIPLES OF LAOZI'S GREEN THREAD AND GOLD KNOB. [7a]

Laozi daode jing	Laozi's Scripture of the Dao and Its Virtue (2 *juan*)

---

13. Also mentioned in *Zhengyi xiuzhen lueyi* 6b–7a.
14. Also mentioned in *Zhengyi xiuzhen lueyi* 11a.
15. Also mentioned in *Zhengyi xiuzhen lueyi* 11a.
16. This is described as level 5, or second ordination level in Benn 1991 (81–2).
17. This translates *sanmei* 三昧, the transliteration of the Buddhist term *samâdhi* or "absorption."
18. Benn classifies this as level 6 or second ordination level (1991, 81–2).

Heshang zhenren zhu	Commentary by the Perfected on the River (2 *juan*)
Wuqianwen chaoyi zashuo	Miscellaneous Explanations on the Audience Observances of the Five Thousand Words (1 *juan*)
Guanling neizhuan	Esoteric Biography of the Guardian of the Pass (1 *juan*)
Jiewen	Precepts Text (1 *juan*)

Note: Those who receive these have the title DISCIPLES OF EMINENT MYSTERY.

Laozi miaozhen jing	Laozi's Scripture of Wondrous Perfection (2 *juan*)
Xisheng jing	Scripture of Western Ascension (2 *juan*)
Yuli jing	Scripture of the Jade Calendar (1 *juan*)
Lizang jing	Scripture of Successive Repositories (1 *juan*)
Laozi zhongjing	Central Scripture of Laozi (1 *juan*)
Laozi neijie	Esoteric Explanation of the *Laozi* (2 *juan*)
Laozi jiejie	Sectioned Explanation of the *Laozi* (2 *juan*)
Gaoshang Laozi neizhuan	Esoteric Biography of Laozi the Most High (1 *juan*)
Huangren sanyi biaowen	Text for Memorials to the Sovereign Three Ones

Note: Those who receive these have the title PRECEPTORS OF ALL-HIGHEST EMINENT MYSTERY.

Taiyi badie	Eight Leaves of Great Unity
Dunjia xianlu	Immortal Register for Jia Divining
Zigong yidu dalu	Great Register for Going Beyond to the Purple Palace
Laojun liujia bilu	Lord Lao's Secret Register of the Six Jia Gods[19]
Huangshen yuezhang	All-Surpassing Petition of the Yellow God

Note: Those who receive these have the title DISCIPLES OF THE HIGHEST LORD.[20] [7b]

Jingang tongzi lu	Register of the Diamond Lads
Zhushi fu	Talisman of the Bamboo Messenger
Puxia ban	Tablet of Puxia
Sanhuang neijing fu	Talisman of the Esoteric Essence of the Three Sovereigns
Sanhuang neizhen hui	Taboo Names of the Esoteric Perfected of the Three Sovereigns
Jiutian fabing fu	Talisman for Sending out Soldiers of the Nine Heavens
Tianshui feideng fu	Talisman for Flying to the River of Heaven

---

19. Also mentioned in *Zhengyi xiuzhen lueyi* 11b.
20. This appears as level 7, with four subdivisions, in Benn 1991, 82–7.

Badi lingshu neiwen	Esoteric Text and Numinous Book of the Eight Emperors
Huangdi danshu neiwen	Esoteric Text and Cinnabar Book of the Yellow Emperor
Bacheng wusheng shisan fu	Thirteen Talismans of the Eight Completions and Five Victories
Bashi lu	Register of the Eight Record-Keepers
Dongxi erjin	Two Prohibitions of East and West
Sanhuang sanjie wujie bajie wen	Three, Five, and Eight Precepts of the Three Sovereigns

Note: Those who receive these have the title DISCIPLES OF SPIRIT CAVERN.

Tianhuang neixue wen	Text of the Esoteric Study of the Heavenly Sovereign
Dihuang jishu wen	Text of the Recorded Writings of the Earthly Sovereign
Renhuang neiwen	Esoteric Text of the Human Sovereign
Sanhuang tianwen dazi	Celestial Texts and Great Characters of the Three Sovereigns
Huangnü shenfu	Divine Talisman of the Yellow Maiden
San jiangjun tu	Chart of the Three Generals
Jiuhuang tu	Chart of the Nine Sovereigns
Shengtian quan	Contract for Ascending to Heaven
Sanhuang chuanban	Transmission Tablet of the Three Sovereigns
Sanhuang zhenxing neihui ban	Tablet of the True Forms and Esoteric Names of the Three Sovereigns
Sanhuang sanyi zhenxing neihui ban	Tablet of the True Forms and Esoteric Names of the Three Ones and Three Sovereigns
Sanhuang jiutian zhenfu qiling	Tally Ordinance and Perfect Talisman of the Nine Heavens and Three Sovereigns
Sanhuang yin	Seal of the Three Sovereigns
Sanhuang yuquan	Jade Contract of the Three Sovereigns
Sanhuang biao	Memorial to the Three Sovereigns one wide belt collected scriptures of Spirit Cavern, in 14 *juan*.

Note: Those who receive these have the title PRECEPTORS OF ALL-HIGHEST SPIRIT CAVERN.[21] [8a]

Shengxuan neijiao jing[22]	Scripture of the Esoteric Teaching of Ascension to the Mystery (1 section, 10 *juan*)

21. These two ranks are classified as Level 8, fourth ordination rank with two subdivisions, in Benn 1991 (87–92).

22. This text begins with the classification *Taishang dongxuan lingbao* (Contained in the Mystery Cavern of Highest Numinous Treasure).

Shengxuan qishier zi dalu	Great Register of Ascension to the Mystery in 72 Characters

Note: Those who receive these have the title PRECEPTORS OF ASCENSION TO THE MYSTERY.[23]

Chishu zhenwen lu	Register of the Perfect Text Written in Red[24]
Ershisi shengtu[25]	Chart of the Twenty-Four of Life [Energies]
Sanbu bajing ziran zhizhen yulu	Jade Register of the Three Sections and Eight Luminants, Spontaneity and Utter Perfection
*Zhutian neiyin lu**	Register of the Esoteric Sounds of the Various Heavens
Lingbao ziran jingquan	Scriptural Contact of the Spontaneity of Numinous Treasure
Yuanshi lingce	Numinous Slips of Primordial Beginning

Note: Those who receive these have the title DISCIPLES OF THE HIGHEST MYSTERY CAVERN OF NUMINOUS TREASURE.

LINGBAO COVENANT SCRIPTURES

*Wupian zhenwen chishu**	Perfect Scripture in Five Tablets, Written in Red (2 *juan*) [LB 1, DZ 22][26]
*Yujue**	Jade Instructions (2 *juan*) [LB 2, DZ 352]
*Kongdong lingzhang jing**	Scripture of the Numinous Stanzas of the Cavern Heavens (1 *juan*) [LB 6, P. 2399]
Shengxuan buxu zhang	Stanzas on Ascending to the Mystery and Pacing the Void (1 *juan*) [LB 7, DZ 1439]; [8b]
*Jiutian shengshen zhangjing**	Scripture of Stanzas of the Vital Spirit of the Nine Heavens (1 *juan*) [LB 8, DZ 318]

23. This is Benn's level 9 (1991, 92–3).

24. This title begins with *Yuanshi dongxuan lingbao* (Contained in the Mystery Cavern of Primordial Beginning).

25. Titles marked with an asterisk all have the classification *Taishang dongxuan lingbao* (Contained in the Mystery Cavern of Numinous Treasure).

26. The Lingbao numbers in this section follow the classification in Yamada 2000. An alternative numbering, which uses this version of the Lingbao catalog rather than the earlier manuscript, is found in in Bokenkamp 1983. The first text of the list is also mentioned in *Zhengyi xiuzhen lueyi* 11b.

Lingbao ziran wucheng wen	Text of the Five Correspondences of Spontaneity of Numinous Treasure (1 *juan*) [LB 9, DZ 671]
Zhutian neiyin yuzi*	Esoteric Sounds and Jade Characters of the Various Heavens (2 *juan*) [LB 10, DZ 97][27]
Zhihui shangpin dajie jing*	Scripture of the Highest Great Pre cepts of Wisdom (1 *juan*) [LB 11, DZ 177]
Zuigen shangpin dajie jing*	Scripture of Highest Precepts Warding off the Roots of Sin (1 *juan*) [LB 12, DZ 457]
Changye fu jiuyou yugui mingzhen kejing*	Scripture of the Rules of the Luminous Perfected, Contained in a Jade Bookcase, That Ward off the Realm of Long Night and Ninefold Darkness (1 *juan*) [LB 15, DZ 1411]
Zhihui dingzhi tongwei miaojing*	Wondrous Scripture on Firming up Determination and Wisdom That Penetrates the Subtle (1 *juan*) [LB 16, DZ 352]
Taishang lingbao benxing shangpin	Highest Chapters of the Basic Endeavor of Highest Numinous Treasure (1 *juan*) [LB 17, P. 3022]
Xuanyi sanzhen quanjie zuifu falun miaojing*	Wondrous Scripture of the Exhortations and Precepts of the Mysterious One and the Three Perfected Regarding the Turning of the Wheel of Suffering and Good Fortune (1 *juan*) [LB 18, DZ 346]
Wuliang duren shangpin miaojing*	Wondrous Scripture and Highest Chapters on Limitless Universal Salvation (1 *juan*) [LB 19, DZ 1]
Zhutian lingshu duming miaojing*	Wondrous Scripture on the Salvation of Life in the Numinous Writing of the Various Heavens (1 *juan*) [LB 20, DZ 23] [9a]
Miedu wulian shengshi miaojing*	Wondrous Scripture of Salvation from Extinction through Fivefold Purification for Reviving the Dead (1 *juan*) [LB 21, DZ 369]
Sanyuan pinjie jing*	Scripture of the Precepts of the Three Primes (1 *juan*) [LB 22, DZ 456]

27. The text is also listed in *Zhengyi xiuzhen lueyi* 11b.

*Ershisi shengtu sanbu bajing ziran zhizhen shangjing**	Highest Scripture of Utmost Perfection with the Chart of 24 Life-*Qi*, 3 Sections, and 8 Luminants (1 *juan*) [LB 26, DZ 1407]
*Wufu xu jing**	Introduction to the Five Talismans (1 *juan*) [LBX 1, DZ 388][28]
*Zhenwen yaojie jing**	Scripture of Essential Explanations of the Perfect Texts (1 *juan*) [LBX 3, DZ 330]
Ziran jing	Scripture of Spontaneity (1 *juan*) [LBX 4, P. 2356]
*Fuzhai weiyi jing**	Scripture of Dignified Observances for Organizing Purgations (1 *juan*) [LBX 5, DZ 532]
*Anzhi benyuan dajie shangpin xiaomo jing**	Scripture to Dissolve Evil with Firm Determination, Original Vow, and Highest Prejects (1 *juan*) [LBX 6, DZ 344]
Xiangong qingwen	Questions of the Immortal Lord (2 *juan*) [LBX 7, S. 1351, DZ 1114]
Zhongsheng nanjing	Scripture of the Hardships of the Sagely Host (1 *juan*) [LBX 8, DZ 1115, P. 2454]
Taiji yinjue	Secret Instructions of the Great Ultimate (1 *juan*) [LBX 2, DZ 425]
Lingbao shangyuan jinlu jianwen	Bamboo Text on the Gold Register [Purgation] of the Upper Prime of Numinous Treasure (1 *juan*) [LBX 4, lost]
Lingbao xiayuan huanglu jianwen	Bamboo Text on the Yellow Register [Purgation] of the Lower Prime of Numinous Treasure (1 *juan*) [lost]
Lingbao chaoyi	Audience Observances of Numinous Treasure (1 *juan*)
Buxu zhu	Commentary on [the Stanzas on] Pacing the Void (1 *juan*) [9b]
Lingbao xiushen zhaiyi	Numinous Treasure Observances for Self-Cultivation Purgations (2 *juan*)
Lingbao baixing zhaiyi	Numinous Treasure Observances for Hundred Families Purgations (1 *juan*)
Lingbao sanyuan zhaiyi	Numinous Treasure Observances for Three Primes Purgations (1 *juan*)

---

28. The last two texts are also listed in *Zhengyi xiuzhen lueyi* 11b–12a.

Lingbao mingzhen zhaiyi	Numinous Treasure Observances for Luminous Perfected Purgations (1 *juan*)
Lingbao huanglu zhaiyi	Numinous Treasure Observances for Yellow Register Purgations (1 *juan*)
Lingbao jinlu zhaiyi	Numinous Treasure Observances for Golden Register Purgations (1 *juan*)
Lingbao du ziran quanyi	Numinous Treasure Observances for Contracts of Attaining Spontaneity (1 *juan*)
Lingbao dengtan gaomeng yi	Numinous Treasure Observances for Announcement on Ascending the Altar (1 *juan*)
Lingbao fu wuya licheng	Numinous Treasure Establishment of Perfection by Ingesting the Five Sprouts (1 *juan*)
Taishang zhihui shangpin jiewen	Text of the Highest Precepts of Wisdom (1 *juan*)
Lingbao zhong jianwen	Collected Bamboo Texts of Numinous Treasure (1 *juan*)
Zhongjing xu	Introduction to the Collected Scriptures (1 *juan*)

Note: Those who have received these texts are called PRECEPTORS OF THE ALL-HIGHEST MYSTERY CAVERN[29]

Wuyue zhenxing tu	Chart of the True Form of the Five Sacred Mountains[30]
Wuyue gongyang tu	Chart of the Presentation of Offerings to the Five Sacred Mountains
Wuyue zhenxing tu xu	Introduction to the True Form Chart of the Five Mountains
Lingbao wufu	The Five Talismans of Numinous Treasure
Wufu xu	Introduction to the Five Talismans
Wufu chuanban	Transmission Tablet of the Five Talismans
Shangqing beidi shenzhou wen	Highest Purity Divine Incantations to the Northern Emperor
Taixuan hetu	River Chart of Great Mystery[31]

---

29. This entire section appears as level 10 with two subdivisions in Benn 1991, 93–5. He does not include a full list of the Lingbao scriptures. Reiter has the complete list and also provides a chart comparing them with materials in the *Sandong zhunang* and *Shangqing daolei shixiang*. He uses Ôfuchi's catalog for his basic reference (1998, 137–41).

30. Also listed in *Zhengyi xiuzhen lueyi* 12a.

31. Also listed in *Zhengyi xiuzhen lueyi* 18a.

Jiuhuang baolu	Precious Registers of the Nine Sovereigns[32]
Dongzhen bawei zhaolong lu	Perfection Cavern Register of the Eight Majestic Beasts and to Summon Dragons
Dongzhen feixing sanjie lu	Perfection Cavern Register to Fly in the Three Worlds
Shangqing dadong zhongjing quan	Highest Purity Contract for the Collected Scriptures of Great Pervasion[33]
Shangqing dadong zhenjing quan	Highest Purity Contract for the Perfect Scripture of Great Pervasion [10a]
Shangqing basu quan	Highest Purity Contract for the Perfect Scripture of the Eight Simplicities
Shangqing bu wuxing quan	Highest Purity Contract for Pacing the Five Planets
Shangqing bu tiangang quan	Highest Purity Contract for Pacing the Heavenly Net
Shangqing sigui mingjing quan	Highest Purity Contract for [Using] the Bright Mirror with Four Dials
Shangqing feixing yuzhang quan	Highest Purity Contract for Flying with Wings[34]
Shangqing jinma qi	Highest Purity Tally of the Golden Horse
Shangqing yuma qi	Highest Purity Tally of the Jade Horse
Shangqing muma qi	Highest Purity Tally of the Wooden Horse
Shangqing huangting qi	Highest Purity Tally of the Yellow Court
Shangqing taishang yujing jiutian jinxiao weishen yuzhou	Highest Purity Dignified and Spiritual Jade Incantations of the Highest Jade Capital and Golden Empyrean of the Nine Heavens
Taishang shenhu yulu	Highest Jade Register of the Divine Tiger
Shangqing taishang taiwei tiandi jun jinhu yujing zhen fulu	Essential and Perfect Jade Talisman and Register of Highest Purity [in the Form] of the Golden Tiger,

32. The texts in this section so far are also listed in Zhang Wanfu's version of the ranks. The following are not and thus do not appear in Benn (1991, 95–6).

33. The last two are also listed in *Zhengyi xiuzhen lueyi* 18a and 17b.

34. Also listed in *Zhengyi xiuzhen lueyi* 17b.

	[Issued by the] Lord Emperor of the Heaven of Great Tenuity[35]
Shangqing taishang yujing jiutian jinxiao weishen yuzhou jing	Scripture of the Dignified and Spiritual Jade Incantations of Highest Purity in the Highest Jade Capital and Golden Empyrean of the Nine Heavens
Taishang da shenhu fulu	Highest Talisman and Register of the Divine Tiger
Shangqing taiwei huangshu balu zhenwen = Xuandu jiaodai lu	Perfect Text of Eight Registers of Highest Purity, for the Yellow Book of Great Tenuity Register of the Interlocking Belt of Mystery Metropolis
Shangqing taishang shanghuang ershisi gaozhen yulu	Twenty-four Eminent and Perfect Jade Registers of the Highest Sovereign of Highest Purity[36]
Shangqing gaoshang taishang daojun dongzhen jinxuan bajing yulu	Perfection Cavern Golden and Mysterious Jade Registers of the Eight Luminants of the Highest Lord of the Dao of Highest Purity
Shangqing taishang santian zhengfa chu liutian wen lu	Highest Purity Register of the Orthodox Law of the Highest Three Heavens to Abolish the Writ of the Six Heavens [10b]
Shangqing taiji zuo zhenren qusu juesi = Jiutian fengqi xuanqiu taizhen shulu	Highest Purity Instructive Verses on Winding Simplicity of the Left Perfected of Great Ultimate Book and Register of Great Perfection of the Wind and Hills of the Nine Heavens
Shangqing taiwei dijun huoluo qiyuan shang fulu	Superior Talisman and Register for Widely Opening the Seven Primes of the Lord Emperor of the Heaven of Great Tenuity of Highest Purity[37]
Shangqing taishang shijing jinguang zangjing lu	Highest Purity Register for Storing the Luminosity of Mineral Essences and Golden Radiance
Xingshe shanjing falu	Ritual Method and Register for Controlling Embodied Mountain Sprites

---

35. Also listed in *Zhengyi xiuzhen lueyi* 18a.
36. The last three texts are also listed in *Zhengyi xiuzhen lueyi* 18a and 17b.
37. These three texts are also listed in *Zhengyi xiuzhen lueyi* 17b–18a.

Shangqing taishang yuanshi bianhua baozhen shangjing	Highest Purity Precious and Perfect Highest Scripture on the Transformations of Primordial Beginning
Jiuling taimiao guishan yuanlu	Primordial Register of the Ninefold Numinous and Greatly Wondrous Turtle Mountain
Shangqing taishang shangyuan jiantian dalu	Highest Purity Great Register of Highest Upper Prime to Regulate the Heavens
Shangqing taishang zhongyuan jianxian zhenlu	Highest Purity Perfect Register of Middle Prime to Regulate the Immortals
Shangqing taishang xiayuan jiandi yulu	Highest Purity Jade Register of Lower Prime to Regulate Earth
Shangqing yujian jianren xianlu	Highest Purity Immortal Register of Jade Inspection to Regulate Humanity
Shangqing taishang suzou dan fulu	Highest Purity Highest Cinnabar Talisman and Register for Plain Announcements
Shangqing taishang qionggong lingfei liujia lu	Highest Purity Register of the Six Flying Jia Gods of the Highest Jasper Palace
Shangqing gaoshang yuanshi yuhuang jiutian pulu	Highest Purity Genealogical Register of the Eminent [Deities] Primordial Beginning, Jade Emperor, and the Nine Heavens
Shangqing zhongyang huanglao jun taidan yinshu liujin huoling lu	Highest Purity Register for [the Talismans] Flowing Gold and Fire Bell, from the "Great Cinnabar Secret Writings" by the Yellow Lord Lao of the Center[38]
Shangqing chuanban	Transmission Tablet of Highest Purity

Note: Those who receive these have the title PRECEPTORS OF PERFECTION CAVERN.

SHANGQING COVENANT SCRIPTURES [5.1A][39]

Dadong zhenjing	Perfect Scripture of Great Profundity (39 sections, 1 *juan*) [A 1, DZ 6, 7, 5, 103]

---

38. The last eight texts here are also listed in *Zhengyi xiuzhen lueyi* 17b–18a.

39. All texts listed in the next section begin with the classification *Shangqing* (Highest Purity). It has been left out throughout. The numbering (A . . . , B . . .) and some of the interpretations of the titles in this section follow Robinet 1984, vol. 1.

Taishang yinshu jinzhen yuguang	Highest Secret Writings on Golden Perfection and Jade Radiance (1 *juan*) [A 2, DZ 1378]
Basu zhenjing fu riyue huanghua	Nourishing on the Sovereign Efflorescences of the Sun and the Moon in the Perfect Scripture of the Eight Simplicities (1 *juan*) [A 3, DZ 426, 1323]
Fei tiangang shexing qiyuan	Flying through the Heavenly Net and Walking about the Seven Primes (1 *juan*) [A 4, DZ 1316]
Jiuzhen zhongjing huanglao biyan	Secret Words of the Yellow Elder in the Central Scripture of Ninefold Perfection (1 *juan*) [A 5, DZ 1376, 1377]
Shangqing bianhua qishisi fang	47 Techniques of Transformation from the Highest Scriptures of Highest Purity (1 *juan*) [A 6, lost]
Chu liutian wen santian zhengfa	Proper Methods of the Three Heavens to Abolish the Writ of the Six Heavens (1 *juan*) [A 7, lost]
Huangqi yangjing sandao xunxing	Correct Practice of the Three Ways to [Gather] Yellow *Qi* and Yang Essence (1 *juan*) [A 8, DZ 33]
Waiguo fangpin qingtong neiwen	Esoteric Text of the Green Lad on Objects from Foreign Lands (2 *juan*) [A 9, DZ 1373]
Jinque shangji lingshu ziwen	Numinous Book in Purple Characters in the Superior Record of [Lord] Goldtower (1 *juan*) [A 10, DZ 639, 255, 179, 442]
Zidu yanguang shenxuan bianjing	Divine and Mysterious Scripture of Transformations of Purple Transcendence and Fiery Radiance (1 *juan*) [A 11, HY 1332] [1b]
Qingyao zishu jin'gen shangjing	Superior Scripture of the Golden Root from the Purple Book of Green Essence (1 *juan*) [A 12, HY 1315]
Yuqing zhenjue sanjiu suyu	Simple Sayings of the Three and Nine from the Perfected Instructions of Jade Purity (1 *juan*) [A 13, DZ 1327][40]
Sanyuan yujian sanyuan bujing	The Unfolded [*Qi*] Scripture of the Three Primes and the Jade Envelope of the Three Primes (1 *juan*) [A 14, DZ 354]

---

40. The text here has *yujing* 玉精, "Jade Essence," but the title usually reads *yuqing* 玉清, "Jade Purity."

Shijing jinguang zangjing luxing	Purifying the Body by Storing the Luminosity of Mineral Essences and Golden Radiances (1 *juan*) [A 15, lost]
Danjing daojing yindi bashu	Eight Arts to Hide in the Earth [with the Help] of Cinnabar Essence and the Lumninosity of the Dao (2 *juan*) [A 16, DZ 1359]
Shenzhou qizhuan qibian wutian jing	Heavenly Dances through the Divine Continent in Seven Revolutions and Seven Transformations (1 *juan*) [A 17, DZ 1331]
Dayou basu taidan yinshu	Secret Writings of the Great Cinnabar [Palace] and the Eight Simplicities of Great Existence (1 *juan*) [A 18, DZ 1330]
Ttianguang santu qixing yidu	Going Beyond to the Seven Stars and Three Ways to Transcend the Heavenly Pass (1 *juan*) [A 19, DZ 1317, 1366]
Jiudan shanghua taijing zhongji	Central Record of Womb Essence and the Superb Transformations of the Nine Elixirs (1 *juan*) [A 20, DZ 1382]
Taishang liujia jiuchi banfu	Nine Red Classified Talismans of the Six Jia Gods (1 *juan*) [A 21, DZ 1329]
Senhu shangfu xiaomo zhihui	Superior Talisman of the Divine Tiger That Dissolves Evil and [Raises] Wisdom (1 *juan*) [A 22, DZ 1344]
Qusu juesi wuxing bifu	Secret Talismans of the Five Phases and Instructive Verses on the Spiral of Simplicity (1 *juan*) [A 23, DZ 1372]
Baiyu heige feixing yujing	Scripture on Flying with White Wings and Black Feathers (1 *juan*) [A 24, DZ 1351, 428, 1326, 876]
Suzou danfu lingfei liujia	Simple Memorials and Cinnabar Talismans of the Numinous Flying Six Jia Gods (1 *juan*) [A 25, DZ 84, 1391] [2a]
Yupei jindang taiji jinshu	Great Ultimate Golden Book of [the Gods] Jade Pendant and Ring of Gold (1 *juan*) [A 26, DZ 56]
Jiuling taimiao guishan yuanlu	Primordial Register of the Ninefold Numinous and Wondrous Turtle Mountain (3 *juan*) [A 27, DZ 1393]
Qisheng xuanji huitian jiuxiao	Mysterious Record of the Seven Sages about Flying off to Heaven and the

	Ninefold Empyrean (1 *juan*) [A 28, DZ 1379]
Taishang huangsu sishisi fang	44 Techniques of the Great Yellow Simplicity (1 *juan*) [A 29, DZ 1380]
Taixiao langshu qiongwen di zhang	Jade Book of the Great Empyrean, Jasper Text and Imperial Stanzas (1 *juan*) [A 30, DZ 55]

Note: These thirty-four juan [of texts], originating in Jade Purity, Purple Purity, and Great Purity and following the *Scripture of Great Pervasion*, were transmitted by Lord Wang to the Southern Perfected.

Gaoshang miemo dongjing jinxuan yuqing yinshu	The Eminent Hidden Book of Jade Purity, Golden and Mysterious, That Destroys Evil and Helps Pervade the Luminants (4 *juan*) [A 31, DZ 1356, 1357, 1358, 1339]
Taiwei tian dijun jinhu zhenfu	Perfect Talisman of the Golden Tiger [Issued] by the Imperial Lord of the Heaven of Great Tenuity (1 *juan*) [A 32, DZ 1336, 1337]
Taiwei tian dijun shenhu yujing zhenfu	Perfect Talisman and Jade Scripture of the Golden Tiger [Issued] by the Imperial Lord of the Heaven of Great Tenuity (1 *juan*) [A 33, DZ 1333, 1336]
Taishang huangting neijing yujing taidi neishu	Inner Book of the Great Emperor on the Highest Jade Scripture of the Interior Luminants of the Yellow Court (1 *juan*) [A 34]

Note: These seven *juan* [of texts] were transmitted to earth by Lady Wei, the Highest Perfected of the Southern Mountain and Goddess of Purple Emptiness.

Shangqing sanyuan zhaiyi	Highest Purity Purgation Observances for the Three Primes (2 *juan*)
Shangqing chuanshou yi	Highest Purity Transmission Observances (1 *juan*)
Shangqing gaomeng yi	Highest Purity Announcement Observances (1 *juan*)
Shangqing chaoyi	Highest Purity Audience Observances (1 *juan*)
Shangqing toujian wen	Highest Purity Text on Throwing the Tablet (1 *juan*)
Dengzhen yinjue	Secret Instructions on the Ascent to the Perfected (25 *juan*) [C 2, DZ 193]

Zhen'gao	Declarations of the Perfected (10 *juan*) [C 1, DZ 1016] [2b]
Bazhen qizhuan	Seven Biographies of the Eight Perfected (7 *juan*)[41]
Dngzhen guanshen sanbai dajie wen	Text of the 300 Great Precepts of Self-Observation, of Perfection Cavern (1 *juan*) [DZ 1364]

Note: Those who receive these have the title PRECEPTORS OF ALL-HIGHEST PERFECTION CAVERN.[42]

Collected scriptures of Highest Purity (150 *juan*)
Interlocking belt of Great Simplicity
Interlocking belt of Mystery Metropolis
Interlocking belt with white lines
Interlocking belt with green and purple lines
—Also called interlocking belt of the revolving carriage, contract of the ultimate path, or great contract of primordial beginning

Note: Those who receive these have the title DISCIPLES OF THE GREAT CAVERN'S THREE LUMINARIES AND THE MYSTERY METROPOLIS OF HIGHEST PURITY, PRECEPTORS OF THE ALL-HIGHEST THREE CAVERNS.

The *Rules* say: All Daoists, whether male or female, when they receive the scriptures, precepts, ritual methods, and registers, must follow this specific order in regard with the proper ranks and titles without favoritism or fakery. On the day of transmission, the preceptors must examine all section [candidates] in detail and give clear instructions about the proper ranks and their order. Failure to comply carries a subtraction of 3,600 [days of life].

The *Rules* say: All Daoists, whether male or female, after they have received the scriptural precepts, must recite the text of these precepts, [3a] so that they develop a keen enthusiasm for them. Then, on the first, fifteenth, and thirtieth of each month, they have to attend the comprehensive assembly in the Hall of the Divine Law to present themselves for inspection. Three violations of non-attendance will be punished with five pounds of incense. Failure to comply carries a subtraction of 1,200 [days of life].

The *Rules* say: All Daoists, whether male or female, after they have received the scriptures, precepts, ritual methods, and registers, must copy them in their proper order, wrap or mount them, and enter them into a repository. This should then be kept in the scripture hall, oratory, or a suitable pavilion, as prescribed by the divine law. It should be adorned with dragons, jade disks, banners, and flowers. The perfect texts should be presented offerings every morning and

41. This probably refers to the biographies of the major Shangqing sages, such as Lord Su, Lord Wang, Lord Pei, the Perfected of Purple Yang, Lord Mao, and Lady Wei. They are today contained mostly in the *Yunji qiqian*. See Robinet 1984, 1:C 6–11.

42. This section appears in Benn 1991 as level 11, with two subdivisions. He does not provide a complete list (96–7). Reiter provides a comparative list of these texts with materials described in the *Sandong zhunang* and *Shangqing daolei shixiang* (1998, 151–8).

evening and also be the center of obeisances and confessions. They must never be treated lightly or with contempt, be divulged or defiled, or transmitted to other people. Instead, they should be constantly recited and remembered, turned and read.[43]

After this body [has passed on], followers and fellow students examine his or her registers and present suitable offerings.[44] They make sure the texts are neither divulged nor treated with contempt. His or her talismans and registers of Orthodox Unity, as well as the various contracts and tallies, are collected in a case and buried next to the deceased master in the mountain valley or placed in a separate pit within the tomb. All other sacred materials must not be put immediately next to the body. The reason for this is that the perfect scriptures are precious and serious, and the numinous officials attend and worship them. [3b] In contrast the decaying corpse is full of foulness, so how could they [the gods] ever get close? Be most extremely careful about this! If you fail to comply, the spirit soul will be banished and the Three Bureaus will visit calamities on your descendants for seven generations! Always be clear and careful about it!

The *Rules* say: Whenever a Daoist, whether male or female, has comprehensively passed through the aforementioned rituals [of ordination] and prepares to cultivate or practice accordingly, he or she must first deliver a memorial of announcement. It runs:

"A disciple of the Great Cavern's Three Luminaries of the Mystery Metropolis of Highest Purity, I now worship and practice as a preceptor of Ascension to the Mystery and of the Spontaneity of Numinous Treasure. Here, on the sacred mountain so-and-so, I address the imperial perfected, the Three Sovereigns of the Spirit Cavern, the Divine Incantations of the Abyss Cavern, the absorption crowd of the great ancestors, and all the perfected of lesser omen. Their obedient servant, I, so-and-so, offer this announcement . . ."

While saying this, pay obeisance repeatedly.

In case of a ritual of Orthodox Unity, prepare to say:

"In the lineage of the *qi* of Orthodox Unity of Highest Mystery Metropolis, I address the Celestial Masters and the [masters] of Yangping as well as all those who order the highest *qi* of the center, govern the twenty-four energies of life, oversee the twenty-four parishes, [measure] the merit of the Three and Five in the Great Capital, to all the perfected of primordial life and the masters of the dignified covenant of Orthodox Unity. Their obedient servant, I, so-and-so, offer . . ."

Again, pay obeisance repeatedly while speaking these words.

Anyone assuming a rank without proper authorization will have his soul examined by the Three Bureaus, who will effect a comprehensive subtraction [of days of life]. Be careful, therefore, be very careful!

---

43. This injunction is also important in Buddhism. See Niida 1937, 638–48.
44. More details on the death of Daoists are found in *Zhengyi weiyi jing* 19ab; *Daoxue keyi* 2.16–19a; *Qianzhen ke* 20a; and *Yaoxiu keyi*, chaps. 15–16.

Section 14

Illustrations of Ritual Vestments

[5.4a] The *Rules* say: [Ritual] vestments serve as images of virtue and give physical shape to the observances. All Daoists, whether male or female, place them first in their dignified observances, and with them honor and give respect to the divine law and the scriptures. Each must prepare them carefully, entirely in accordance with the fundamental divine law and without any favoritism or fakery. Failure to comply carries a subtraction of 3,600 [days of life].[1]

A preceptor of Orthodox Unity wears a dark headdress, a yellow skirt, a scarlet gown, and a scarlet cape with twenty-four folds. For details see the enclosed illustration.[2]

[4b] A preceptor of Highest Mystery wears a dark headdress, a yellow skirt, a yellow gown, and a yellow cape with twenty-eight folds. For details see the enclosed illustration.

A preceptor of Cavern Spirit wears a dark headdress, a yellow skirt, a green gown, and a yellow cape with thirty-two folds. For details see the enclosed illustration.

[5a] A preceptor of Cavern Mystery wears a hibiscus [colored] headdress, a yellow gown, a yellow skirt, and a purple cape with thirty-two folds. For details see the enclosed illustration.

A preceptor of Cavern Perfection wears a headdress of primordial beginning, a green skirt, a purple gown, and a purple cape with green lining. It has twenty-four folds on the outside and fifteen folds on the inside. For details see the enclosed illustration.

[5b] A preceptor of Great Profundity wears a headdress of primordial beginning, a yellow skirt, and a purple gown, as prescribed by the divine law of Highest Purity. He also wears a five-colored cape of clouds and mist. For details see the enclosed illustration.

A lecturer and preceptor of the Three Caverns wears a headdress of primordial beginning, a yellow gown, a scarlet skirt, and a nine-colored cape of variegated gauze. For details see the enclosed illustration.

[6a] The *Rules* say: All Daoists, whether male or female, unless they are dressed in these ritual vestments, are not permitted to touch or move the precious scriptures.

All ritual vestments have their specific divine lads as attendant guardians: The vestments of Orthodox Unity have five generals and eight demigods as guardians. Those of Eminent Mystery have two spirit lads and spirit maidens as

---

1. Beginning with the following paragraph, this section is also found in *Miaomen youqi* 19b–20a. See Yoshioka 1976, 97.

2. The illustrations tend to look alike, since the print does not provide coloring. I enclose one as an example (see fig. 1).

FIG. I. A Daoist in full ceremonial regalia.
Source: *Fengdao kejie.*

guardians. Those of Spirit Cavern have three celestial lads and three celestial maidens as guardians.

Those of Mystery Cavern have eight jade lads and eight jade maidens as guardians.

Those of Perfection Cavern, Great Profundity, and the Three Caverns all have twelve jade lads and twelve jade maidens as guardians.

These garments are comprehensively called ritual vestments. Failure to comply [with their rules] causes the attending lads to remove themselves far from the [Daoist's] body. Then the four officers will judge the soul, and effect a subtraction of 2,400 [days of life].[3]

The *Rules* say: All Daoists, whether male or female, who wish to participate in rituals involving the scriptures, must wear ritual vestments. For purgation announcements, transmission ceremonies, and rank completions,[4] they must wear headdress, belt, and full ritual vestments. Holding their ritual tablets, they

3. The citation in the *Miaomen youqi* ends here.
4. This translates *weiqi* 位吃, a phrase that is rather unclear.

state their rank and position, bow to their original master, and perform audience rites to the Highest Lord.

[6b] Failure to comply [with these rules] causes the numinous officials to stay away, the soul to be judged by the five divine emperors, and a subtraction of 1,200 [days of life].

The *Rules* say: Female Daoists have ritual vestments that are basically the same as those of their male counterparts. Only the headdress is different in structure and pattern as it has parts of dark gauze in front and back as well as to the right and left. On three sides these leaves of gauze are not firmly attached but flap freely in the wind.

Female Daoists of Highest Purity and Great Profundity [ranks] wear a headdress of flying clouds and phoenix *qi*. For details see the enclosed illustration.

[7a] Mountain recluse preceptors have ritual vestments that include a headdress of the two forces and upper and lower yellow skirt, as well as a cape with thirty-six folds. For details see the enclosed illustration.

Ordinary male Daoists have ritual vestments that include a flat headdress, an upper and lower yellow skirt, and a cape with twenty-four folds. For details see the enclosed illustration.

[7b] Ordinary female Daoists have ritual vestments that include a dark headdress, an upper and lower yellow skirt, and a cape with eighteen folds. For details see the enclosed illustration.

The *Rules* say: All Daoists, whether male or female, wear shoes and slippers made from straw, wood, pure lacquer, cotton fabric, or coarse silk. While robes and capes can be ornamented with the two forces or representations of mountains, shoes should be kept plain and simple both inside and out, without colorful ornamentation or flowery embroidery. Failure to comply carries a subtraction of 1,400 [days of life].

The *Rules* say: On the soles of all shoes should be divine dragon and tiger talismans.[5] At night, they should be placed on top of a board, bedmat, bed, or bench. Never place them immediately on the ground or wear them when going to the outhouse. Failure to comply carries a subtraction of 280 [days of life].

[8a] The *Rules* say: Hairpins should be made from ivory, horn, bamboo, or jade, in accordance with the relevant present circumstances. They should be neither carved nor engraved to resemble strange shapes or images. Failure to comply carries a subtraction of 820 [days of life].[6]

The *Rules* say: All Daoists, whether male or female, when using ritual vestments must never falsely assume them, expose them to pollution, or lend them to others. Rather, they must always keep them carefully folded in their proper chests and containers. The same applies to the headdress and shoes. Failure to comply carries a subtraction of 1,200 [days of life].

---

5. Reading *fu* 符, "talisman," for *fu* 伏, "crouch."

6. A set of instructions regarding hair accessories is also found in *Yunji qiqian* 42. Further information on combing is contained in *Daoxue keyi* 1.12a–13b.

Section 15

Regular Audience Services

[6.1a] *Note:* The rites that should be performed regularly every morning and evening by the [members of the] four orders of the Three Caverns are called "regular audience services." Still, the same five-part audience ritual applies when one enters the oratory on a separate occasion to have an audience with the perfected.

Wash and rinse as prescribed by the divine law. Then, when you first enter the hall, offer incense and swing it [for fumigation]. Then recite the following hymn:

> To study the Dao, I work diligently and painstakingly,
> To develop faith, I stir up cinnabar sincerity.
> Burning incense, I surrender to the Highest Lord.
> As perfect *qi* mixes with the rising smoke,
> I only wish that he extend his great forgiveness,
> So my ancestors of seven generations may be released from the dark
>   underworld.

Offer incense three times.

Next, each participant should stand upright in proper order of rank and, holding his or her ritual tablet, pay obeisance to the ten directions, beginning with the east. To do so, first offer incense, then intone while bowing in respect:[1]

> With all my heart I surrender my life
> To the Heavenly Worthy of the East,
> Sovereign Highest [Lord] of Jade Treasure.
>
> With all my heart I surrender my life
> To the Heavenly Worthy of the South,
> The Mysterious Perfected Who Brings a Myriad Good Fortunes. [1b]
>
> With all my heart I surrender my life
> To the Heavenly Worthy of the West,
> The Utmost Ultimate of Great Wonder.
>
> With all my heart I surrender my life
> To the Heavenly Worthy of the North,
> The [Lord of] Jade Dawn Who Resides above the Mystery.

---

1. The same titles of the ten worthies are also found in *Huanglu zhai shi tianzun yi* 黃籙齋十天尊儀 (Observances for [Worshiping] the Ten Worthies During the Yellow Register Purgation, DZ 512), a text of the Song dynasty. For a discussion, see Yûsa 1989, 32; Ren and Zhong 1991, 375.

With all my heart I surrender my life
To the Heavenly Worthy of the Northeast,
The Highest Sage Who Saves All to Be Immortals.

With all my heart I surrender my life
To the Heavenly Worthy of the Southeast,
The Savior of Life Who Cherishes All Living Beings.

With all my heart I surrender my life
To the Heavenly Worthy of the Southwest,
The Sovereign of Emptiness and Great Numen.

With all my heart I surrender my life
To the Heavenly Worthy of the Northwest,
The [Lord of] Great Splendor without Measure.

With all my heart I surrender my life
To the Heavenly Worthy of the Above,
The Luminous Sovereign of Jade Emptiness.

With all my heart I surrender my life
To the Heavenly Worthy of the Below,
The All-Pervasive Spirit and Sovereign of Perfection.

Next, all kneel, with backs straight and holding their ritual tablets, and make a formal repentance of sins. For this, recite:

Before all ranks, with all my heart I surrender my body
To the Heavenly Worthies of the Nonultimate Great Dao.
I repent all the transgressions of personal and physical body
Vis-à-vis all beings and all ranks,
From the imperial family on down to my own,
the humble so-and-so's,
That I may have committed in an earlier or my present body,
I have raised and employed my four limbs [wrongly];
I have acted contrary to the precepts and statutes;
I have failed to rely on scriptures and manuals–
Thus with my body I have committed great sins,
without measure, without bounds. [2a]

Therefore I now pay obeisance in repentance,
Begging to be cleansed and purged
And devotedly praying before all ranks
That my body may enter utmost immortality,
Encounter the Dao and find perfection.
I knock my head to the ten directions
And to the Three Treasures of Right Perfection.

Before all ranks, with all my heart I surrender my spirit
To the Heavenly Worthies of the Nonultimate Great Dao.
I repent all the transgressions of spirit and consciousness

Vis-à-vis all beings and all ranks,
From the imperial family on down to my own,
the humble so-and-so's,
That I may have committed in an earlier or my present body.
I have been unfocused in my will and remembrance;
I have been fleeting in my emotions, agitated in my intention;
I have galloped about unceasingly [in my thoughts]–
Thus with my mind I have committed great sins,
without measure, without bounds.

Therefore I now pay obeisance in repentance,
Begging to be cleansed and purged
And devotedly praying before all ranks
That my spirit may merge with perfect serenity
And pervasively enter spontaneity.
I knock my head to the ten directions
And to the Three Treasures of Right Perfection.

Before all ranks, with all my heart I surrender my life
To the Heavenly Worthies of the Nonultimate Great Dao.
I repent all the transgressions of mouth and verbal action
Vis-à-vis all beings and all ranks,
From the imperial family on down to my own,
the humble so-and-so's,
That I may have committed in an earlier or my present form.
I have argued and debated good and evil;
I have used fancy words and glossed over being wrong;
I have deluded the masses with rhetorical flourishes–
Thus with my mouth I have accumulated great sin,
without measure, without bounds. [2b]

Therefore I now pay obeisance in repentance,
Begging to be cleansed and purged
And devotedly praying before all ranks
That my inner nature and life may merge with the Dao
And mysteriously join nonaction.
I knock my head to the ten directions
And to the Three Treasures of Right Perfection.

[Following this rite of repentance], each participant stands up again for further intonation. Give one bow facing north, stand up straight, and recite the "Hymn to the Scriptures":[2]

---

2. The first paragraph of this hymn is adapted from the early Lingbao corpus of the fifth century, where it appears in *Benyuan dajie* 本願大戒 (Great Precepts and Original Vows, DZ 344), 7b–8a. The latter text was known as the *Xiaomo dajie* 消魔大戒 (Great Precepts to Dissolve Evil) originally (Yamada 2000, 235). It was revealed by the Perfected of the Great Ultimate to Ge Xuan the legendary founder of the Lingbao school. It also occurs in the sixth-century collection of Louguan precepts *Taishang Laojun jiejing* 太上老君戒經 (Great Precepts of Lord Lao, DZ 784)

May I enjoy the divine law as if it were my dear wife,
Love the scriptures like a precious piece of jade,
Uphold the precepts and control all my six passions,
Be mindful of the Dao and eliminate desires!
In deep serenity, may my good *qi* be stable,
In calm reverence, may my spirit be silent and at peace!
Celestial demon kings respect me and protect me,
So for generations I find great happiness.

Thickly growing, may my family and state expand,
More and more, may scriptures and Dao flourish.
May all celestials and people join this prayer,
Whirl far away and enter the Great Vehicle!
May I follow my heart and set up fields of blessedness,
Slowly, slowly rise up through the divine law's wheel!
May my ancestors of seven generations be born in the heavenly halls,
And I myself ascend there in broad daylight. [3a]

As the Great Dao pervades mystery and emptiness,
May I be mindful, so none will not be matched,
Refine my material being and join immortals and perfected,
Then obtain a diamond body for myself!
May I go well beyond the hardships of the Three Worlds,
Be free forever from life in hell and the five bad rebirths!
Utterly surrendering to all the highest scriptures
In tranquil mindfulness I knock my head and pay obeisance.

With all my heart I knock my head
To the Great Dao of the Highest Nonultimate!
With all my heart I knock my head
To the Venerable Scriptures in Thirty-Six Sections!
With all my heart I knock my head
To the Great Preceptors of the Mysterious Center!

First Prayer:
  May the two forces be eternal,
  Covering and supporting all without end!
  With all my heart I knock my head
  To the Three Treasures of Right Perfection.

1ab. The latter is a document of the northern Celestial Masters, dated to the late sixth century (see Kohn 1994, 198–201).

The entire sequence of three stanzas reappears in the ritual collection *Jidu jinshu* 濟度金書 (Golden Book on Rescue and Salvation, DZ 466), compiled originally in 12 *juan* by Lin Lingzhen 林靈真 and dated to 1302, then expanded under the Yuan and Ming to the 321 *juan* it has today (Ren and Zhong 1991, 346–8). The stanzas are found twice, first in a chapter collecting ritual hymns (10.10a), then again in one on the performance of purgations (65.5–6a). It is still being sung today as part of the central rite of the *jiao* ritual, in a three-part ritual sequence of about 35 minutes, one stanza appearing in each part. See Ôfuchi 1983, 257a; Lagerwey 1987, 137, 139, 141–2. According to the *Benyuan dajie*, when the attendant immortal lads and jade maidens hear this hymn, they are very happy and come to bring help and support. It has to be chanted when activating any of the major scriptures, silently so before reciting the scripture mentally (8a).

Second Prayer:
>   May the sun and the moon revolve in their orbits,
>   And their bright light illuminate all!
>   With all my heart I knock my head
>   To the Three Treasures of Right Perfection.

Third Prayer:
>   May the imperial family's
>   Enshrined ancestors and numinous predecessors
>   In their spirits ascend to the nine heavens!
>   With all my heart I knock my head[3]
>   To the Three Treasures of Right Perfection.

Fourth Prayer:
>   May our sovereign emperor's
>   sage rule be never ending
>   And his virtue serve to harmonize the two forces!
>   With all my heart I knock my head
>   To the Three Treasures of Right Perfection.

Fifth Prayer:
>   May the heir apparent
>   Be benevolent and filial, pure and bright,
>   And continue the imperial line with eminence! [3b]
>   With all my heart I knock my head
>   To the Three Treasures of Right Perfection.

Sixth Prayer:
>   May the various princes, older and younger
>   And all the officials, civil and military
>   Serve [the empire] with exhaustive sincerity,
>   Pacify the people and make good use of the Dao!
>   With all my heart I knock my head
>   To the Three Treasures of Right Perfection.

Seventh Prayer:
>   May the empire attain great peace
>   And all weapons of war be laid to rest!
>   With all my heart I knock my head
>   To the Three Treasures of Right Perfection.

Eighth Prayer:
>   May the preceptors, fathers, and mothers
>   Who have passed on be reborn in heaven
>   Experience continued peace and happiness!
>   With all my heart I knock my head
>   To the Three Treasures of Right Perfection.

Ninth Prayer:
>   May the beings of all ranks
>   Find their karmic insight daily new

---

3. The text here contains a misprint, reading *zhi* 志, "will," for *zhi* 至, "all," "utmost."

And their lamp of wisdom inexhaustible!
With all my heart I knock my head
To the Three Treasures of Right Perfection.
  Tenth Prayer:
    May the donors of the ten directions
    And all those who have karmic concerns [for the Dao]
    Eliminate all causes of their suffering,
    And climb the shores of Dao!
    With all my heart I knock my head
    To the Three Treasures of Right Perfection.
  Eleventh Prayer:
    May the numinous powers in all worlds of the law
    And all the diamond kings and strong demigods
    Make good use of the Dao and attain supernatural powers
    To pacify evil and help all to surrender to the right path!
    With all my heart I knock my head
    To the Three Treasures of Right Perfection.
  Twelfth Prayer:
    May those in the three deepest hells and five bad rebirths
    And all living beings in all worlds of the divine law
    Come out of the fetters of desire
    And together ascend to the shores of blessedness! [4a]
    With all my heart I knock my head
    To the Three Treasures of Right Perfection.

[To close the daily service, all participants] chant "The Hymn to Studying Immortality":[4]

We study immortality and our practice is most urgent;
By honoring the precepts, we control the passionate mind.
As we grow empty and serene, good *qi* comes to reside,
And immortality and sagehood are found spontaneously.
Without faith in the words of the divine law,
How can we ever become recluses in the mountain groves?

The *Rules* say: All audience services must be performed according to these observances. Failure to comply carries a subtraction of 1,200 [days of life].

---

4. This also goes back to a Lingbao model, where it is found in the *Benyuan dajie*, 16b–17a, as the seventh of altogether eight stanzas. The complete text begins by lamenting the state of humanity as mired in sins, envy, and jealousy, then encourages everyone to recognize the fact that their fate is self-made and have faith in their potential to improve their karma. Once they start changing, the text claims, they will be able to transcend human life, but to do so the study of immortality is of utmost urgency. The stanza used here, without the other stanzas, also appears in the later collection *Jidu jinshu*, 10.10b, as the "Hymn to Studying the Dao."

Section 16

The Noon Purgation[1]

[6.4a] As the time [of the ceremony] approaches, wash and rinse, then prepare the presentation of offerings, all as prescribed by the divine law. Then intone, as each participant bows in respect:

> With all my heart I knock my head
> To the Great Dao of the Highest Nonultimate!
> With all my heart I knock my head
> To the Venerable Scriptures in Thirty-Six Sections!
> With all my heart I knock my head
> To the Great Preceptors of the Mysterious Center!

Next, begin the rites to the Dao by burning incense. While doing so, all stand together in a great host and recite the hymn on offering incense to the All-Highest Worthies: [4b][2]

> In the Dao, purgation comes first,
> Its diligent practice leading to the Golden Towers!
> Set up as a bridge to the great divine law,
> It saves people and beings everywhere.
> As a reward for kindness and virtue in previous lives,
> The pure mind of Dao transcendentally arises,
> The body flies up to Mystery Metropolis,
> And all ancestors of seven generations are fully liberated.
> With all my heart I knock my head
> To the Highest Three Worthies
> And the host of sages of the ten directions.

Next, the donor kneels reverently and proclaims the merit and virtue of the Dao. He says:

---

1. This section describes the daily ritual to be undertaken at the ceremonial noon-meal, when food is offered to the gods and shared by the monastics, ideally in the presence of one or several donors who use the occasion to gain particular merit for their families and/or a specific affair. The events are also described in *Zhengyi weiyi jing* (9b–10b, 15ab) and *Shishi weiyi* (9b–12a), with further details found in *Qianzhen ke* 5ab, 29ab. The latter specifies that the more elaborate memorials and chants performed by the donor only occur when he is actually present in person. In other words, often mealtime ceremonies would not include every item described here, while still containing the sharing of food with the gods and all beings and the gratitude and good wishes offered to the donor(s).
2. The same chant appears also in section 17. It is later found in the *Jidu jinshu* (10.7b–8a).

In the beginning, the form of no-form[3] displayed its wondrous form among humanity; the body of no-body manifested its perfect body beyond the multitude. Thus they could take shape and divide into hundreds and myriads, changing and transforming without end; they could merge and disperse into millions and billions, following and meeting each other without measure.

Then [the Dao in] compassion [began to] circulate through the words of the divine law, saving people kalpa after kalpa; [in] virtue [it began to] spread across the worlds of dust, teaching and converting [people] in region after region. It traveled through the eighty-one countries to convert the western barbarians; then again it remained in the world for over nine hundred years to give guidance to the people of Middle Xia [China]. [5a]

Everywhere [the Dao] caused people and celestials to awaken to the Dao and to undertake the long climb to the gates of liberation; it caused those in life-and-death to surrender to perfection and to come out of the waves of transmigration. After that, its spirit congealed in the Golden Towers [of heaven] and in complete aloneness it became the ancestor of the myriad sages. Its physical body turned wondrous in the Jasper Capital and in high eminence it strolled above the Nine Purities. Thus we know that above and below heaven, throughout the Three Worlds and in the ten directions, there is nothing but our great Dao—majestic, lofty, and most worthy.

Today, this donor so-and-so on behalf of such-and-such an affair, has carefully prepared these wondrous offerings for formal presentation. With humble sincerity I surrender my life to the ten directions and deliver my heart to the Three Treasures.

Now all pray:

> May the divine power [of the Dao] arise spontaneously
> And come down to care for all living beings!
> May it wondrously accord with all without bounds,
> Steeping all in compassion, whether up or down!
> May it cause the flying celestials
> To descend and proclaim the rules of suffering and good fortune!
> May it wondrously approach this rite of purgation
> To enter it into the ledgers of cause and retribution!
>
> May all the errors and entanglements of the world of dust,
> We beg, be eradicated and dissolved!
> May all the faults and transgressions of even the greatest kalpa,

---

3. The word for "form" here is *se* 色, literally "color" but used in Buddhist texts to translate *rūpa*, the first of the five skandhas of physical matter or form. Since it is paired here with *shen* 身, "body" or "self," the terms carries its more Buddhist-inspired than literal meaning.

We humbly pray, be destroyed and purged!
May the roots of goodness planted in the present
Increase and grow ever longer,
Join to form a soaring tree that lasts forever!

May the karma of bad deeds created in the past
Dissolve and vanish completely,
Transform into a fragrant forest that gives happiness!
May superior good fortune thus created
Spread everywhere without end! [5b]

May the nine underworlds stop
Housing souls in suffering and torment!
May the six realms of rebirth cease
To hold sentient [beings] in the wheel of transmigration!
May this benefit extend to all species and types,
To all that contains numinous power!
May all together cross the river of love and desires,
And jointly step on the shore of free and easy wandering.

Prayer:

May our [generous] donor's
Father and mother, and ancestors of seven generations
Be spiritually reborn in the pure land
And attain karmic rewards without end!
With all my heart I knock my head
To the Three Treasures of Right Perfection.

Prayer :

May our [generous] donor's
House and home be tranquil and at peace,
And his family live in harmony!
With all my heart I knock my head
To the Three Treasures of Right Perfection.

Prayer:

May our [generous] donor's
Descendants be numerous and prosperous,
And each generation bring forth the worthy and enlightened!
With all my heart I knock my head
To the Three Treasures of Right Perfection.

Prayer:

May our [generous] donor's
Accumulated sins be purged and eradicated,
And his good fortune and wisdom abound!

> With all my heart I knock my head
> To the Three Treasures of Right Perfection.

Prayer:

> May the empire attain great peace[4]
> And the myriad families be contented and happy!
> With all my heart I knock my head
> To the Three Treasures of Right Perfection.

Prayer:

> May all living beings
> Be forever liberated from all suffering
> And together enter Right Perfection!
> With all my heart I knock my head
> To the host of sages and those who have attained the Dao.

[6a] Next, all sit down as prescribed by the divine law. While the food is being brought out, all chant the following prayer incantation. *Note:* This is the incantation to receive food.[5]

> Among all the ways to establish fields of blessedness
> Donating food is by far the best.
> In this life it spreads pure happiness,
> After this life it gives rebirth in heaven
> And a future residence in the pure land
> Where all food and clothing arrive spontaneously.
> Therefore we present this offering today
> Spreading it equally to the various heavens.

Next, the food is passed around. All fold their hands over their chests and chant:

> This fragrant feast and wondrous offering
> Above we give to the Heavenly Worthies,
> In the middle to the perfected and sages,
> Below to the host of living beings.
> May all be equally full and satisfied,
> While good fortune flows to our [generous] donor
> Like rivers pouring into the sea.

After the meal, there is a formal memorial of repentance [for possible transgressions] during the donation of food. For this, make the following announcement:

> To the Highest Worthies of the ten directions!
> Respectfully see here before you

---

4. This section of the prayer sequence is also referred to in *Shishi weiyi* 10a, with the note that the more complete text is found in "Qizhen's Rules."

5. The same text is also found in *Shishi weiyi* 10a.

This great crowd of disciples.
Today, during the presentation of food,
We fear that
Our hands were smudgy and not clean,
Our garb was not properly purified,
Our utensils were not pure,
Our rice and millet was not sifted,
And all manner of things and acts
Were not as prescribed by the divine law.

Thus we pray:[6]

May the Three Treasures spread their mercy upon us
And widely give us joy and cheerfulness. [6b]

Any food left over from the offerings should be distributed among all beings with the following prayer on one's lips:

May all thus giving attain good fortune!
May all thus eating be free from sin!

With that, the donor takes a pinch of incense and presents it as an offering, as prescribed by the divine law. Doing so, he recites the following hymn of praise, again as prescribed by the divine law:

For all those born in future
I have done this good deed of karmic connection.
May it be like a sprout that grows to enlightenment
And receive the sages' grace.

Next, the donor holds up a purified offering and chants the incantation of donation:

To the Three Treasures and the ten directions!
To all the perfected and sages!
This donor so-and-so
on behalf of such-and-such an affair
Has now concluded the purgation.
Still I fear[7]
That the accumulated merit is not complete
And pledge to throw away more pure wealth
And give massively to the Three Treasures.
I pray:
May after this generous donation
All my ancestors of seven generations be reborn in heaven
And forever experience happiness and joy!
May I, generation after generation, life after life,
Attain good fortune without measure. [7a]

6. This part is again referred to in *Shishi weiyi* (11a), with a reference to the fuller text being in "Qizhen's Rules."
7. This section of the chant is apparent in *Shishi weiyi* 11b.

Next, all join in the chant of proper mindfulness. For this bow in respect and [mentally] with all your heart knock your head to the Highest Three Worthies and the host of the sages of the ten direction. Then pray:[8]

> May our [generous] donor
> Have a hundred kinds of good fortune, strong and vigorous,
> And ten thousand good deeds that assemble like clouds!
> With all my heart I knock my head
> To the Three Treasures of Right Perfection.
> Through establishing this purgation
> May merit and virtue protect and envelope all
> And the host of living beings be freed from suffering and find
>   liberation!
> With all my heart I knock my head
> To the host of sages and those who have attained the Dao!

The *Rules* say: All noontime purgations must be performed according to these observances. Failure to comply carries a subtraction of 1,600 [days of life].

Section 17

Major Assemblies[1]

[6.7a] The [head of the] household joining the Daoist community washes and rinses,[2] then offers a pinch of incense and claps his teeth, just as if he prepared to attend rites to the Dao.

Then, [with the donor] presenting the incense burner, [the officiating priest] chants the following incantation:[3]

---

8. This last prayer is identical to the one used at the end of lecturing on the scriptures in section 12, except that the very first line refers to the "sovereign emperor" instead of the donor and the beginning of the second stanza extends hope for the merit gained by the lecture on the scriptures rather than the noon purgation. A reference to the chant is also found in *Shishi weiyi* 11b.

1. This section describes *zhai* 齋 performed for the sake of the community and specific members. More details, including the titles and roles of the different officiants, are found in *Yaoxiu keyi* 8.7b–16b. Many chants recorded here are still actively used today.

2. Amending the reading of the text, which literally has "chants an incantation and rinses."

3. The text leaves it unclear whether the donor or the officiant presents the burner and chants the incantation. It becomes clear from modern sources, which describe a similar sequence of Lighting the Burner (as part of the *jiao*

Oh, Highest Lord Lao
Of the All-Highest Three Heavens,
The mysterious, primordial, and beginning *qi*:
Summon all the spirits residing in my—so-and-so's—body:
The meritorious officers of the Three and Five,[4]
The officials and messengers of the left and right,
The incense-attending jade lads,
The word-transmitting jade maidens,
[7b] And the upright talisman [bearers] of the Five Emperors,
All thirty-six personages—
May they emerge from my body to announce themselves
To the correct god and perfected officials
Of this village and community's soil.[5]
Here today I burn incense and pray:
May the wondrous *qi* of Right Perfection
Of the highest ten directions
Descend to pour into my—so-and-so's—body!
May this announcement of mine be delivered with all haste
And brought before the Utmost Perfect Dao of Nonultimate!

Now follows the first statement of name and rank:[6]

As preceptor of the Mystery Cavern
Of Highest Numinous Treasure,
Perfected on the sacred mountain so-and-so,
I, so-and-so, announce:
To the Great Dao of the Highest Nonultimate,
To the Venerable Scriptures in Thirty-Six Sections,
To the Great Preceptors of the Mysterious Center,
To the many officials of the Three Worlds,
To all the numinous powers!

Here today I burn incense and pray:
May you take this merit and virtue

---

ceremony), that the donor is present and holds an incense burner or other ritual implement, while the officiating priest engages in the chanting and visualization. See Lagerwey 1987, 122–3. A discussion of incense and its presentation is also found in *Zhengyi weiyi jing* 12ab.

4. This section of the incantation, with minor variants, also appears in *Jidu jinshu* 12.2a as part of a rite to announce the intention of the purgation. It evokes thirty-two gods instead of thirty-six. A modern version is also found in Lagerwey 1987, 123.

5. The modern version of the last several lines reads:

> May they emerge, each and all properly attired,
> In order to report to
> The correct god and perfect officer
> Of this district's soil. (Lagerwey 1987, 123)

6. On this practice as undertaken today, see Ōfuchi 1983, 300. The modern expression is *cheng fawei* 稱法位 instead of *cheng mingwei* 稱名位. Lagerwey translates it as "self introduction" (1987, 124). The same text is also found in *Jidu jinshu* 12.2a.

And return it flowingly to so-and-so's family,
Including all his nine mysterious forebears and seven ancestors,
All members of his clan, whether present or former!
I beg that you pardon completely
All violations committed by them,
Whether in former lives or present bodies,
All their acts of disobedience and ugly deeds of evil,
Their millions of sins and billions of transgressions, [8a]
Them all, I beg, eradicate and purge!

Also, I pray that the deceased [members of his clan]
May ascend to be reborn in the heavenly halls,
Have food and clothing come to them spontaneously,
Be forever free from disasters and bad fortune,
And live eternally in blissful delight,
Surrounded by good karmic rewards.
May his clan and household be pure and noble,
With sons and grandsons numerous and prosperous,
Generation after generation enjoying endless blessings!
Thus, I pray ten thousandfold with all my heart.
Here today I burn incense
To send this speedily and straight
Before the Nonultimate Dao.

[All chant]

With all my heart, I knock my head
To the Heavenly Worthy of the East,
[Lord of] Nonultimate Highest Numinous Treasure.

Repeat for all ten directions, in the following order: south, west, north, northeast, southeast, southwest, northwest, above, and below. Then [all] chant the three surrenders:

With all my heart I knock my head
To the Great Dao of the Highest Nonultimate!
With all my heart I knock my head
To the Venerable Scriptures in Thirty-Six Sections! [8b]
With all my heart I knock my head
To the Great Preceptors of the Mysterious Center!

Next comes the second statement of name and rank:

As preceptor of the Mystery Cavern
Of Highest Numinous Treasure,
Perfected of the sacred mountain so-and-so,
I, so-and-so, announce:

To the Great Dao of the Highest Nonultimate,
To the Venerable Scriptures in Thirty-Six Sections,

To the Great Preceptors of the Mysterious Center,
To the highest administrators and highest officials,
To the four commanders and five emperors,
To the many officials of the Three Worlds,
To all the numinous powers!

Here today I burn incense and pray
On behalf of so-and-so, ready to repent and confess
That for kalpas without measure
And even to the present day,
During life and death,
He has accumulated karmic sins and serious transgressions.
He has gone against heaven and violated earth,
Treated the Three Treasures with contempt,
Killed and harmed the host of living beings,
Scolded and railed, cursed and sworn.[7]

He has been full of jealousy and envy, stinginess and greed,
Engaged in licentiousness and given free rein to his passions,
Been stupid and obstinate, a robber and a thief,
Said "yea" with his mouth while thinking "nay" in his heart.
[Committed] with all three karmic conditions and six senses,
His sins and faults are without measure.
Therefore today he knocks his head and confesses all,
Begs that his sins may all be purged and eradicated.
I pray that
The deceased [members of his clan] may be reborn in heaven
And there experience eternal peace and happiness!
That his sons and grandsons be numerous and prosperous, [9a]
With good fortune and delight coming to them spontaneously.
Also, may all those beings
Under heaven and above the earth,
In the five sufferings and three bad rebirths
Come out of their dark prisons
And together find the benefit of wisdom!
May all sentient beings
Join to enter the sacred space of the Dao!

After the officiant has humbly presented this memorial, he offers incense twice and, again presenting the incense burner, intones:[8]

To the
Incense officials and messengers,
The dragon and tiger lords to the left and right,

---

7. For a translation of a full confession as used today, applying many of the same expressions and stereotypes, see Lagerwey 1987, 124.

8. The following is similar to a chant found in the *Shangqing lingbao dafa* 上清靈寶大法 (Great Ritual Methods of Highest Purity and Numinous Treasure, DZ 1223) by Jin Yunzhong 金允中 of the thirteenth century (11.7a).

And all the numinous officials in attendance of incense:
Make that
Today in this place of formal audience assembly,
Golden fluid and cinnabar turquoise [jade],
Immortal fungus and the hundred numinous [substances]
Sprout spontaneously!

May the [faithful] crowd and the perfected
Meet together and assemble
Before this incense fire!
May the immortal lads of the ten directions,
The jade maidens and attendant guardians,
Transmit my, so-and-so's, memorial through the incense smoke
So that it comes speedily and straight
Before the Nonultimate Dao.

[The officiants then] exit the hall as they chant the hymn to the practice of giving:[9]

In the Dao, purgation comes first,
Its diligent practice leading to the Golden Towers!
Set up as a bridge to the great divine law,
It saves people and beings everywhere.
As a reward for kindness and virtue in previous lives,
The pure mind of Dao transcendentally arises, [9b]
The body flies up to Mystery Metropolis,
And all ancestors of seven generations are fully liberated.

The *Rules* say: All major assemblies must be held according to these obser-vances. Failure to comply carries a subtraction of 1,600 [days of life].

---

9. The same chant is also recorded in section 16.

Section 18

Formal Ordinations[1]

[6.9b] As the time of the purgation ceremony approaches, the ordinands line up at the bottom of the [altar] stairs. Facing west, they bid farewell to their fathers and mothers and give thanks to their nine mysterious [forebears], bowing altogether twelve times. Then they turn to face north and bow to the emperor four times. The reason for this is that, once they have donned the ritual vestments of the Heavenly Worthies, they will never again bow to parents or worldly rulers. Therefore, when anyone joins the Daoist community, he or she must first bid farewell and give thanks.

Following this, the ordinands stand erect with their palms joined at chest level.[2] Still facing north, they surrender themselves three times to the Three Treasures, bowing three times. They say:

> With all my heart I surrender my body
> To the Great Dao of the Highest Nonultimate.
> With all my heart I surrender my spirit
> To the Venerable Scriptures in Thirty-Six Sections.
> With all my heart I surrender my life
> To the Great Preceptors of the Mysterious Center. [10a]

Then they turn to face west and pay obeisance to the three ordination masters, giving three bows to each. This done, they kneel formally. First the Master of Elevation Protection presents them with the ritual skirt; next, the Master of Ordinand Supervision presents them with the [gown of] cloudy sleeves; third, the Master of Ordination presents them with the ritual cape.

Thereafter the ordinands are crowned with the ritual headdress. Once this is done, they step back to pay obeisance again to the three masters, bowing three times to each. Turning to face north, they then hold their ritual tablets and stand erect, with the masters, who are still facing east, standing on the same level. The ordinands then recite the three stanzas on wisdom. Their text goes:[3]

> Wisdom arises from original nonbeing,
> Brightly it goes beyond the ten directions.[4]

---

1. For laws on ordinations and rules regarding certificates, see Twitchett 1956, 134; Ch'en 1973, 95–103. More on ordination is also found in *Zhengyi weiyi jing* 1a–5a. Pledges are described in *Yinyuan jing* 4.5b.

2. This gesture, Jap. *gasshô* 合掌, means that the hands are folded vertically, palm against palm, on the level of the chest. See Saunders 1960, 76.

3. The following chant is also found in the sixth-century Lingbao text *Guanshen jing* 觀身經 (Scripture on Observing the Body, DZ 350), 1b–2a, with minor character variations. It later appears, exactly as in the *Fengdao kejie*, in the ritual collection *Jidu jinshu* 10.6b.

4. The *Guanshen jing* here has *zhao* 照, "illuminates," for *chao* 超, "go beyond."

Combined in the void, formed in the mysterious empyrean—
It pours from the various heavens as flowing fragrance.
Its wonders are beyond belief,
Its empty impulse truly beyond the real.
It is right there, yet ultimately it is not—
It is not there, yet nothing appears without it.[5]

In wisdom to steadily observe the body,[6]
Is foremost in studying the Dao.
As I thereby imperceptibly enter the mysterious ford,
So spontaneously my spirit is registered above.
The Heavenly Worthies always give me protection,
The demon kings cast supportive words for me.[7]
Brilliantly shining in my diamond body,
I go beyond ever father to Highest Purity.[8] [10b]

Wisdom arises from the root of the precepts,[9]
The Dao of perfection has the precepts as its key.
The Three Treasures all begin through them,
And they are honored and received even by lofty sages.
Floating in this boat of no-death,
I suddenly am saved in the [heaven of] Great Existence.
When I then recount the precepts,
Celestials the line up to knock their heads to me.[10]

Whenever the ordinands come to the end of a stanza in their joint intonation, they pay skillful obeisance with one bow. When all is concluded, they turn their bodies to pay obeisance to the ten directions, beginning with the north. They say:

With all my heart I surrender my life
To the Heavenly Worthy of the North,
[Lord of] Nonultimate Highest Numinous Treasure.

They repeat this for all ten directions, in the following order: east, south, west, southeast, northeast, southwest, northwest, above, and below.

Next, they step back and stand to the east, facing west, while the masters stand east, facing west. The latter then transmit the ten precepts. Each in turn, the newly ordained Daoists state their names and receive the holy words of the Heavenly Worthy.[11]

---

5. The *Guanshen jing* here has *you* 有, "it is," for *jing* 境, "ultimately;" and *wu* 無, "is not," for *rong* 容, "appears."

6. The *Guanshen jing* uses *chang* 常 instead of *heng* 恒 for "steadily."

7. The *Guanshen jing* here reads: "guard me with precious words."

8. The *Guanshen jing* here has *xian* 仙, "immortality," instead of *qing* 清, "Purity."

9. This stanza is also found, with no character variants, in Du Guangting's *Jinlu dazhai shuojie yi*, 3a. On the text, see Ren and Zhong 1991, 358.

10. The *Guanshen jing* here has *lai* 來, "come," for *bing* 并, "line up."

11. The following speech and precepts are adapted from the *Shijie jing* (DZ 459), also found in Dunhuang manuscripts S. 645, P. 2347, P. 2350, P. 3770 (Ōfuchi 1979b, 108), and cited in *Taishang jiejing* 太上戒經 (DZ 787), 13b. The role of the ten precepts in medieval ordination is discussed in Schipper 1985, 135. For its use today, see Ōfuchi 1983, 191–201.

Oh good men and good women [of the Dao]! You were able to develop an intention for the Dao of spontaneity and have come to enter the river[12] of the divine law. Now receive my ten precepts and thus become Disciples of Pure Faith in the great Dao,[13] gaining courage and strength to fly to the heavens and increase your merit! [11a]

From here onward you will never slide back again but most certainly attain transcendence and go beyond the Three Worlds to become perfected of Highest Purity. For this, now bow down and receive [the precepts], listening to them with truth in your hearts:

1. Do not kill, but be always mindful of the host of living beings!
2. Do not commit immoral deeds or think depraved thoughts![14]
3. Do not steal or receive unrighteous wealth!
4. Do not cheat or misrepresent good and evil!
5. Do not get intoxicated, but always think of pure conduct!
6. I will maintain harmony with my ancestors and family and never do anything that harms my kin!
7. When I see someone do good, I will support him in with joy and cheerfulness in my heart!
8. When I see someone unfortunate, I will support him to recover good fortune!
9. When someone comes to do me harm, I will not harbor thoughts of revenge!
10. As long as all beings have not attained the Dao, I will not expect to do so myself!

As the Heavenly Worthy said: Cultivate and uphold these pure precepts, and you will always be in harmony with the mind of heaven and always act with great compassion. Take a strong resolution now that you will serve and spread the worthy teaching everywhere, never daring to be lazy. Rather stick to the good and die than do anything bad and live! [11b]

From here onward you will never slide back again but most certainly attain liberation from the five realms and will never again walk in the three bad rebirths. Practice long purgations and uphold the precepts, and you will spontaneously go beyond the world.[15]

At this point the newly ordained Daoists pay obeisance to the masters again by bowing three times. Then, facing north, they pay obeisance to the Three Worthies with three further bows.

---

12. Reading *he* 河, "river," for *he* 何, "what."

13. This title is *qingxin dizi* 清信弟子, an adaptation from Buddhism, used for first-level ordinands who have taken the ten precepts. See Kusuyama 1982.

14. This precept reads "Do not be lascivious or debauch another's wife!" in all other versions of the list.

15. A description of the power of the precepts is also found in *Qianzhen ke* 2b, 7b, 10a.

Then all chant the "Hymn to Honoring the Precepts." Its text goes:[16]
The Dao is the ancestor of no-mind,
Everywhere creating fields of blessedness.
Establishing merit is the key to being without constraint,
So the original vow must come from each of us.
Emptying the self and going along with all beings,
Pouring the mind into everything with perfect evenness,
The great sages spread the utmost teaching
Like rain descending from the sky.

The high hill [of the Dao] encompasses all,
Yet it is also always low and forms a deep abyss–
Like the ocean is the king of the hundred rivers,
And therefore can contain even dragons and scaly creatures.
For many kalpas we maintain wisdom in all applications,
How could we use it only in specific years?
Honoring the precepts without a moment's relapse,
Generation after generation we create nothing but good karma.
With keen concentration we are mindful of the Great Vehicle,
And soon come to embody the perfection of the Dao.

[12a] The *Rules* say: All formal ordinations must be performed according to these observances. Failure to comply carries a subtraction of 1,200 [days of life].

The *Rules* say: These eight observances[17] describe the essential points of the [ritual] affairs undertaken by all Daoists, whether male or female. At all times Daoists should collect and consult these scrolls to perform [the rites] in accordance with their instruction. Failure to comply will cause the four marshals to judge the soul and prevent one's name from ever again being entered into Daoist ledgers. It carries a subtraction of 2,400 [days of life].

---

16. This chant is first found in the *Lingbao shoudu yi* 靈寶授度儀 (DZ 528), 49b–50a. It later appears in Du Guangting's *Jinlu dazhai shuojie yi* 5b–6a and in *Jidu jinshu* 10.7a.

17. This refers to the items in chapters 4–6 that have *yi* in their titles, i.e., sections 11–18.

Fragments and Citations

Translator's Note

The following renders passages from the *Fengdao kejie* found in Dunhuang manuscripts or as citations in contemporaneous works. Section numbers have been supplied to make access easier, but they are largely conjecture. Section 24, complete with heading and number, appears in P. 3682. The manuscript also contains the end of the previous section, which was accordingly numbered 23. The last sentence of this section, in turn, appears in a citation in the *Miaomen youqi*, thus allowing me to give the Section number 22 to this citation. Numbers 20 and 21 were assigned arbitrarily. Headings, too, were supplied by the translator.

Section 20

Transmission Details[1]

[1] [. . .] throughout the year at all [purgations held] use the hymns in the fundamental scriptures to create a unified intention and joint mind that matches master and disciples. [. . .][2] Otherwise the right impulse is not achieved, and one violates the dignified observances on the outside and becomes remiss and lax in one's mind on the inside. Therefore every time they ascend the altar, enter the oratory, perform rites to the Dao, or hold a purgation, all disciples must prostrate themselves with elbows on the ground, while the chimes sound a sincere rhythm, never dropping off or slowing down. Failure to comply carries a subtraction of 1,200 [days of life].

[7] The *Rules* say: All holding of purgations must follow the fundamental observances. When transmitting the ritual methods of Orthodox Unity, use an Orthodox Unity purgation. For the ritual methods of the Rite of Instruction[3] or of the "Scripture in Five Thousand Words" [*Daode jing*], use the methods of Numinous Treasure. For the Spirit Cavern of the Three Sovereigns, the Mystery Cavern [of Numinous Treasure], and the Perfection Cavern of Highest Purity, in each case use the purgation that matches their original ritual methods. Announce them properly, never allowing a deviation. If there are disciples participating who are not of the same status—that is, some are higher and some are lower [in rank]—use the ritual methods of Numinous Treasure. The reason for this is that Numinous Treasure ways can equally apply to higher and lower Caverns.

[11] Once the purgation announcement is over, the masters and disciples involved in it must all receive admonitions and precepts, and their numinous power must correspond to auspicious omens. Only then may they ascend the altar, announce their pledges, and receive the scriptures, ritual methods, precepts, and registers. Even if the wind does not blow and the stars and chronograms are shining bright,[4] yet there is no appropriate response to the impulse [of a certain person], this participant must in all cases withdraw from the purgation and cannot join.

The masters, moreover, should prepare everything in close compliance with the rules and statutes, setting up the proper observances and formalities without coveting personal fame and gain or violating the luminous prohibitions. These

---

1. This text is found in the Dunhuang manuscript S. 809, reproduced in Ôfuchi 1979b, 222. A reprint is found in Tonkô kôza 1983, 176. The text begins in the middle and has no heading; the title was supplied by the translator. Numbers in brackets at the beginning of paragraphs indicate the line numbers as found in Ôfuchi 1979b.

2. Three characters are illegible here.

3. This refers to the *zhijiao zhai* 指教齋 or "Purgation of Instruction," one of the original Lingbao rites. It served to achieve purification and mental clarity. See Yamada 2000, 249.

4. The following sentence and the next paragraph are left out in the transcription in Tonkô kôza 1983, 176.

are avoidances of utmost import! They must be followed with great care. Failure to comply carries a subtraction of 1,200 [days of life].

[18] The *Rules* say: The transmission of the great scriptures of the Three Caverns happens only in limited years. The highest sages transmit only once in forty thousand kalpas; the highest perfected, in four kalpas; the highest immortals in four thousand, one thousand, or seven hundred years. Each generation [on earth] has one transmission in forty years.

The luminous scriptures cannot be easily attained, and their excellent wisdom is hard to encounter. For this reason one must make sure that all disciples pour their whole heart [into the effort] and wait for the one encounter when, once in ten thousand kalpas, a master or perfected transmits the Dao to them.

[22] If during a certain generation there is indeed the right person, one can have him join the Dao either in the morning or the evening. If at the time there is no such person, then one cannot [ordain him] even in ten thousand kalpas.

An inestimable person of this kind, when transmitted the scriptures and receiving the precepts, will keep them deep in his heart and in his essence will join the luminous spirits. Such a one must give his pledge and receive transmission. If he does not wish to be selected, he is most perfect; if he is eager for selection, he is still acceptable but only for the practice of minor ritual methods, which do not reach all the way to the great Dao.

[26] At the time when the ordinand is ready for transmission, he should first receive only the scriptures and ritual methods that have been prepared [for his particular rank]. To receive them, he must undergo the proper purgation to its very limit. Only when this is concluded, can he receive also the precepts and registers. Never must this process be cut short or abbreviated.

Also, if the chosen month and day arrive and the time comes close but the scriptures and ritual methods are not all ready, some people have their ordinands receive blank sheets of paper or a roll of plain silk. This is an insult to the scriptures and a major fraud! It constitutes a fake ascent to the altar that is deeply in violation of the instructions of the sages. How can one, before the very eyes of one's disciples, commit such a falsehood? Indeed, even if one is the chief preceptor, the underworld authorities will punish severely. Thus, failure to comply carries a subtraction of 2,400 [days of life].

[31] The *Rules* say: Three days after receiving the divine law, the disciples must all choose an appropriate time and prepare an offering purgation as a present to the great sages, masters, and worthies of the various heavens. This is to thank them for their enfolding grace without which the transmission could not have taken place. Failure to comply carries a subtraction of 2,800 [days of life].

[34] The *Rules* say: After the master has transmitted the scriptures and precepts, he must prepare a detailed record and clear instructions on how the disciples are to follow the rules and precepts and how they must, in all activities, remain within the proper order of the ritual ranks. Failure to comply carries a subtraction of 1,200 [days of life].

Section 21

Annual Purgations[1]

[9a] The "Rules for Worshiping the Dao according to the Three Caverns" says:

The first day of the first month is the purgation of devotion to longevity.
The seventh day of the first month is the purgation to extend spirit.
The eighth day of the second month is the purgation for a plentiful spring.[2]
[9b] The eighth day of the fourth month is the purgation to announce summer.
The fifth day of the fifth month is the purgation for continued life.
The sixth day of the sixth month is the purgation for clear heat.
The seventh day of the seventh month is the purgation to welcome fall.
The first day of the eighth month is the purgation to drive out evil.
The ninth day of the ninth month is the purgation to extend the reckoning.
The first day of the tenth month is the purgation to create good fortune.
The fifteenth day of the eleventh month is the purgation to announce good fortune.
The La festival [fifth] day of the twelfth month is the purgation of hundredfold good fortune.
The twenty-eighth day of the twelfth month is the purgation to welcome the new year.
The beginning of spring is the purgation to establish goodness.
The spring equinox is the purgation to extend good fortune.
The beginning of summer is the purgation to lengthen goodness.
The summer solstice is the purgation of vermilion brightness.
The beginning of fall is the purgation of advancing old age.
The fall equinox is the purgation to repent sins.
The beginning of winter is the purgation to venerate goodness.
The winter solstice is the purgation of wide blessings.

All these purgations must be performed according to the observances and orders contained in the fundamental scriptures. [They are essential], thus all students of the Dao unless they cultivate these purgations and their accompanying precepts will labor in vain in the mountains and forests.

---

1. This section is passage found as a citation in the *Zhaijie lu* 齋戒録 (Record of Purgations and Precepts, DZ 464), 9a–10a. This eighth-century ritual collection is studied and partially translated in Malek 1985. The same text, verbatim, is also found in *Yunji qiqian* 37.10ab; and with minor variants, in the *Zhiyan zong* 至言總 (Comprehensive Perfect Words, DZ 1033) of the early ninth (1.4b–5b). The first part only, with some variation, appears also in the *Yinyuan jing*, a precursor of the *Fengdao kejie* (4.11a). For a punctuated reprint of the passage and a discussion of its variants, see Yoshioka 1976, 97–9. The section heading was supplied by the translator.

2. The *Yinyuan jing* here has "purgation to welcome auspiciousness." It then adds one item: "The third day of the third month is the purgation to destroy evil."

Now, to perform purgations properly, you must be pure and empty, serene and tranquil, withdrawing and humble, respectful and devout. [10a] You should be terrified and trembling with fear as if you were walking over a frozen abyss. As if facing a stern lord, you should exhibit cinnabar sincerity and a humble demeanor; as if urgently praying for a numinous response, you should be restrained and controlled both inside and out. Never be boisterous or behave in an irregular manner.

Anyone participating in a purgation ceremony must observe the avoidance of filial sons in deep mourning and of women after parturition or during menstruation. Also, anyone afflicted by[3] fevers and boils or otherwise maimed and disabled must not be allowed to ascend to the purgation hall or the altar area. None should rush about in order to present a prayer or in a state of suffering pursue the purgation.[4]

Those who wish to beg for exoneration from their transgressions should bring forth their statements in the proper way of the ritual for the confession of sins. Under no circumstances must they climb to the sacred hall[5] in an irregular manner. In addition, anyone actively involved in the rites should be moved aside and seated separately, always also avoiding [contact with] the six domestic animals.

Note: People like these defile and despoil the perfected numinous powers, so that the sages and wise ones do not descend and the purgation ceremony remains without merit.

Section 22

Levels of Daoists[1]

[18a] The "Rules and Precepts for Worshiping the Dao According to the Three Caverns" says:

There are six levels of Daoists beyond the bounds [of ordinary society]:

---

3. The word "afflicted" is supplied in the *Zhiyan zong*.
4. The emphasis that only proper participants should join the purgation is also found in *Qianzhen ke* 4b–5a.
5. The *Zhiyan zong* has "altar" for "hall."

1. This section is a citation from the *Miaomen youqi* 妙門由起 (Entrance to the Gate of all Wonders, DZ 1123), the postface of a lost collection of scriptural commentaries sponsored by Emperor Xuanzong in 713, 17b–18b. For a punctuated reprint of this passage, see Yoshioka 1976, 96. A discussion of its import for ordained, nonlay Daoists under the Tang is found in Ōzaki 1984, 100–103.

1. celestial perfected
2. spirit immortals
3. mountain recluses
4. ordained monastics [18b]
5. devout householders
6. libationers

The meaning of these appellations is as follows.

(1) Celestial perfected freely transform their bodies, matching the changes in chaos and spontaneity. Their way of being rests with the Three Purities, their wisdom enfolds the myriad beings. They are followers of the Sovereign of Lofty Mystery.

(2) Spirit immortals have merit accumulated over a succession of kalpas, their virtue that covers the entire world of dust and grime. They transform in their spirits without bounds and fly soaringly about in natural so-being. They are the equals of Du Chong and Yin Gui.[2]

(3) Mountain recluses rest in nonaction and no-desire, guarding the Dao and preserving their essence. Their *qi* is crowned by the hazy empyrean, while their minds are concentrated in utter serenity. They are comparable to Xu You and Chaofu.[3]

(4) Ordained monastics reject and stand apart from all confusion and filth, forget and abandon all strength and greed. As their minds let go of the myriad beings, their spirits become kings in the nine empty [heavens]. Subtly they come out of the bars and cages [of worldly life], forever leaving behind their wives and offspring. They are companions of Song Lun and Peng Chen.[4]

(5) Devout householders dissolve their voices to the point of complete engulfment and harmonize their radiance in going along with the world. Their minds set on the ultimate of the Dao, their bodies are yet submerged in human affairs. They practice breathing in [the new] and out [the old] to rest themselves, and wander about free and easy in singular attainment. They are the equals of Huang Qiong and Jian Jian.[5]

(6) Libationers [jijiu] in their activities leave traces in empty and far-off [regions], in their wills go into the void and harmonious [spaces]. With compassion they come to rescue the people; with inner harmony they support all creatures. Free from greed, free from desires, they abandon sight and give up sound. Alone they evolve a mind of rectitude, surrender with sincerity completely to the Dao. Their activity of making offerings [ji] shows their control; their work of pouring libations [jiu] shows their harmony. They control the hard and strong

---

2. Du Chong 杜沖 and Yin Gui 尹軌 are legendary Louguan masters dated to the Zhou dynasty. See Kohn 1997b. A definition of immortals as being pure and empty is also found in *Qianzhen ke* 1b.

3. Xu You 許由 and Chaofu 巢父 are Confucian heroes who lived as morally unsullied hermits. They are both mentioned in the *Zhuangzi*.

4. Song Lun 宋倫 and Peng Chen 彭諶 are two further legendary Louguan patriarchs. See Kohn 1997b. On Song Lun, see also Ôzaki 1983, 103.

5. Huang Qiong 黃瓊 and Jian Jian 鑑鑒 are medieval householders of some renown. See Ôzaki 1984, 103.

and harmonize themselves and others. They are the kinds of Li Dong and Gan Shi.[6]

The reason why all these are called Daoists is that they are not actively involved in worldly affairs but strive to serve the permanent Dao. Also, they each receive specific sets of dignified observances of the Dao, so that in their minds and behavior they are significantly different from ordinary people. As they unfold their mysterious transformation here, moreover, they also extend prosperity for the imperial rule there.

For this reason, they do not bow to princes and nobles, nor perform prostrations to the Son of Heaven. Daoists today are by and large ordained monks. As such, they should relate to the ruler of the country with a maximum of loyalty and highest obeisance,[7] to the prime minister, great ministers, public administrators, and various lords, with deepest respect. Under no circumstances must they wantonly seek them out to gain personal power or advantage. Failure to comply carries a subtraction of 360 [days of life].

Section 23

Interaction with Ordinary People[1]

[1] . . . to the prime minister, great ministers, public administrators, and various lords, with deepest respect. Under no circumstances must they wantonly seek them out to gain personal power or advantage. Failure to comply carries a subtraction of 360 [days of life].[2]

[3] The *Rules* say: All Daoists, whether male or female, whenever they meet ordinary people should join their palms [at chest level] and behave properly in guestlike manner. As the occasion affords, they may guide and attract [the ordinary folk], causing them to surrender to the orthodox Dao. Under no circum-

---

6. Li Dong 李東 and Gan Shi 干室 are Han dynasty followers of Lord Lao and founders of Daoist groups. Gan Shi, in particular, is better known as Gan Ji 干吉, the alleged recipient of the *Taiping jing* 太平經 (Scripture of Great Peace). See Ōzaki 1984, 103; Maeda 1985; Petersen 1989.

7. With this part of the sentence begins the manuscript P. 3682, translated in section 23.

1. This and the following section are contained in the Dunhuang manuscript P. 3682, reproduced in Ōfuchi 1979b, 219–20, and reprinted in Tonkō kōza 1983, 174–5. Only the last few items of this section remain in the manuscript. The section number was obvious from the following section, which is numbered 24; the section heading was supplied by the translator. The manuscript continues directly the passage cited in the *Miaomen youqi* and translated in the previous section. Numbers in brackets refer to the line count as found in Ofuchi 1979b.

2. This first part is identical with the last sentences of the citation in the *Miaomen youqi*.

stances must they get upset or angry. Failure to comply carries a subtraction of 120 [days of life].[3]

[5] The *Rules* say: All Daoists, whether male or female, whenever they have ordinary people coming to pay respect and obeisances to them, should join their palms [at chest level] and return the bow with respect, invoking the Three Treasures that they dissolve all [the ordinary folk's] immeasurable sins and give them good fortune without measure. Under no circumstances must they be arrogant or boastful. Failure to comply carries a subtraction of 120 [days of life].

[8] The *Rules* say: Whenever Daoists joined by fellow monastics encounter a worthy on the road, they must step off the road and bow in salute. If the parties happen to be of the same rank, a mere salute is sufficient. If a female meets a male Daoist, regardless of who is older or younger, she must step aside to let him pass, but there is no need to acknowledge or salute him. Under no circumstances must they simply pass each other straight by. Failure to comply carries a subtraction of 120 [days of life].

[12] The *Rules* say: All Daoists, whether male or female, whenever they receive a donation should join their palms [at chest level] and intone: "May the generous donor in all his/her future lives receive good fortune without measure." Failure to comply carries a subtraction of 130 [days of life].

[14] The *Rules* say: Daoists who have been ordained at the same time but have not yet received the scriptural precepts should calculate their age in order to establish seniority. Once they have received the scriptural precepts, they should calculate their superior or inferior rank in order to establish seniority. There are seven ranks:

1. Great Profundity
2. Perfection Cavern
3. Mystery Cavern
4. Spirit Cavern
5. Eminent Mystery
6. Register Pupil
7. Pure Faith

A Pure Faith must not sit together with a Register Pupil. A Register Pupil must not sit together with an Eminent Mystery, and so on, up to a Mystery Cavern never sitting with a Perfection Cavern.[4]

Now, if someone has been ordained earlier but received the scriptures and his ritual rank later, or again if someone is advanced in age but low in rank, he or she must still follow the above system in sitting down. Failure to comply will cause the Three Bureaus to judge the soul to a subtraction of 1,600 [days of life].

3. On behavior among ordinary people, see also *Zhengyi weiyi jing* 17b; *Qianzhen ke* 1b. See also Zürcher 1980, 130 n. 83.

4. The same passage is also found in the *Zhengyi weiyi jing* 5a, with minor differences. First, this text adds that "an ordinary person must not sit with a Disciple of Pure Faith; a Disciple of Pure Faith must not sit with a Daoist of Pure Faith," thus adding two lower levels to the list of ranks. Also, it replaces "Register Pupil" with "Orthodox Unity." Otherwise both the diction and the sentiment are the same. See also Yoshioka 1976, 144.

[21] The *Rules* say: All Daoists, whether male or female, whenever they have a ritual implement on their persons, or even if they are without a ritual implement but wear the ritual vestments of the Heavenly Worthies, must always stand or sit in a completely separate place, even if with important kin or dignitaries, such as their father and mother, emperor and prince. They must not sit together with them but must strictly remain in the isolated position of the ordained.[5] Failure to comply will cause the Five Emperors to punish the soul with a subtraction of 1,200 [days of life].

Section 24

Compassionate Assistance[1]

Note: 19 entries.

[26] The *Rules* say: After becoming an ordained monk [or nun], always make compassion foremost. In each affair, serve with your whole heart and always bring forth loving mindfulness. Whether walking, sitting, lying down, or resting, constantly think of being of assistance in the salvation [of all]. Among all the myriad activities, this is the most urgent. If you fail to comply with this behavioral [attitude], you cannot attain the Dao. Failure to comply carries a subtraction of 1,600 [days of life].

[30] The *Rules* say: All Daoists, whether male or female, whenever they are in uninhabited mountains or on winding roads, should always be mindful and develop the good intention that they should build and set up free lodging halls to allow all travelers, past and future, who [suffer from] wind and cold, heat and humidity, mud and rain, labor and hardships, to gain rest from their exhaustion and fatigue and forever avoid storms and exposure. May they all attain good fortune without measure! This [attitude] carries an addition of 360 [days of life].

[33] The *Rules* say: All Daoists, whether male or female, whenever [encountering] fords and stream crossings, roads and ways that are blocked and impassable, or bridges and overpasses under construction or repair, should always be

---

5. A similar injunction is also found in *Qianzhen ke* 11b.

1. This continues the translation of the Dunhuang manuscript P. 3682, reproduced in Ôfuchi 1979b, 220–1, and reprinted in Tonkô kôza 1983, 175–6. The section heading literally reads "Dao Rules for Compassionate Assistance." A section of the same title but with more anecdotal rather than regulatory contents is also found in section 14 of the Sui dynasty work *Yinyuan jing* (6.1a–3a).

mindful and develop the good intention that all living beings, past, future, and present, should be free from all obstacles and obstructions May they all attain good fortune without measure! This [attitude] carries an addition of 420 [days of life].

[36] The *Rules* say: All Daoists, whether male or female, whenever they are in endless mountains and on far roads, should always be mindful and develop the good intention that they should set up free wells everywhere to allow all living beings, past, future, and present, to be liberated from burning and thirst and find moisture and shade without obstruction. May they all attain good fortune without measure! This [attitude] carries an addition of 360 [days of life].

[39] The *Rules* say: All Daoists, whether male or female, wherever they may be, should always be mindful and develop the good intention that they should widely plant fruit trees to allow all living beings, past, future, and present, to attain the [fruits'] sweetness and avoid the pains of hunger. May they all attain good fortune without measure! This [attitude] carries an addition of 360 [days of life].

[42] The *Rules* say: All Daoists, whether male or female, whenever in conditions of severe heat, should always be mindful and develop the good intention that they should set up free juice [stands] everywhere to give freely to all [beings], allowing them to avoid the disaster of [dying from] thirst. May they all attain good fortune without measure! This [attitude] carries an addition of 220 [days of life].

[45] The *Rules* say: All Daoists, whether male or female, wherever they may be, should develop the good intention that they should constantly create fields of compassion and universally pray that those among all living beings who are hungry, cold, old, sick, or otherwise not hale, may find satiation and warmth. May they all attain good fortune without measure! This [attitude] carries an addition of 520 [days of life].

[48] The *Rules* say: All Daoists, whether male or female, should always be mindful and develop good intention on behalf of all those imprisoned and banished, old and sick, or facing all kinds of dangers and difficulties. For all of them equally they should pray that they may be freed and find salvation from their afflictions to forever be free from all danger and disaster. May they all attain good fortune without measure! This [attitude] carries an addition of 320 [days of life].

[51] The *Rules* say: All Daoists, whether male or female, should always be mindful and develop good intention on behalf of all those among living beings who are anxious and ready to jump [to death]. For all them they should pray that they be rescued and saved and forever be free from all sorrow and pain. May they all attain good fortune without measure! This [attitude] carries an addition of 360 [days of life].

[54] The *Rules* say: All Daoists, whether male or female, should always be mindful and develop good intention on behalf of themselves, their parents, siblings, other relatives, lords of the country, princes, emperors, and all living beings. For all them they should pray that they redeem all life and avoid all death,

pain, and sickness. May they attain exemption from death, freedom from prison, emergence from danger, and complete salvation. May they attain good fortune without measure! This [attitude] carries an addition of 620 [days of life].

[58] The *Rules* say: All Daoists, whether male or female, should always be mindful and develop good intention on behalf of all living beings that are in cages and dungeons, shackles and fetters. For all of them equally they should pray that they may be set free and gain their liberty. May they all attain good fortune without measure! This [attitude] carries an addition of 620 [days of life].

[61] The *Rules* say: All Daoists, whether male or female, should always be mindful and develop good intention on behalf of all slaves, lowly born, and unfree people. For all of them they should pray that they may be released to follow wisdom and goodness and forever be in happiness and good cheer. May they all attain good fortune without measure! This [attitude] carries an addition of 720 [days of life].

[64] The *Rules* say: All Daoists, whether male or female, should always be mindful and develop good intention on behalf of all poor and indigent people. They should constantly pray that they be rescued and supported and forever live in plenitude and contentment. May they all attain good fortune without measure! This [attitude] carries an addition of 720 [days of life].

[66] The *Rules* say: All Daoists, whether male or female, should always be mindful and develop the good intention that they may always distribute charity, so that their merit and virtue finds successful completion and their fields of blessedness are strong and full, allowing all those hungry and cold to be satiated and content, all those poor and destitute to be benefited and well. May they all attain good fortune without measure! This [attitude] carries an addition of 820 [days of life].

[69] The *Rules* say: All Daoists, whether male or female, should always be mindful and develop the good intention that they may always spread divine water to wash and purify all living beings, taking out their karmic roots of sins and afflictions and their serious diseases of long standing, making them all clean and pure. May they all attain good fortune without measure! This [attitude] carries an addition of 520 [days of life].

[72] The *Rules* say: All Daoists, whether male or female, should always be mindful and develop the good intention to distribute all kinds of beneficent medicines to heal the pain and diseases of all beings, allowing them to be free and healed and fully restored to their former haleness. May they all attain good fortune without measure! This [attitude] carries an addition of 520 [days of life].

[75] The *Rules* say: All Daoists, whether male or female, should always be mindful and develop good intention, praying that with the help of divine talismans they may destroy all demons and bringers of evil, allowing all people to be at peace and happy. May they all attain good fortune without measure! This [attitude] carries an addition of 520 [days of life].

[78] The *Rules* say: All Daoists, whether male or female, should always be mindful and develop the good intention to distribute food of blessedness to all

living beings, allowing them to be satiated and full. May they all attain good fortune without measure! This [attitude] carries an addition of 620 [days of life].

[80] The *Rules* say: All Daoists, whether male or female, should always be mindful and develop the good intention to create goodness and merit, compassion and sympathy to encourage and induce all living beings to awaken to the Dao. May they all attain good fortune and benefits forever! This [attitude] carries an addition of 1,200 [days of life].

Glossary

These are the most commonly used technical terms in the *Fengdao kejie* and other texts on medieval Daoist institutions.

bai 拜, bow
ban 版, tablet
biao 表, memorial
bu 步, step = 1.50 meters
chang 唱, intone
changchao 常朝, regular audience services
changnian faxin 常念發心, always be mindful and develop the [good] intention
changshi 長世, numerous and prosperous (descendants)
changzhu 常住, permanent residents/staff, permanent residences
chanhui 懺悔, repentance of sins
chao 朝, audience service
chengjiu 成就, successful completion
che'niu fang 車牛坊, carriage house
chi 尺, foot = about 30 cm
chuanshou 傳授, transmission
chujia 出家, ordained monk or nun
chujia fashen 出家法身, the holy body of an ordained monk or nun
chumen 初門, beginners
cun 寸, inch = about 3 cm
dade 大德, (master of) great virtue
dan 石, picul = 72 kilos (120 *jin*)
dancheng 丹誠, cinnabar sincerity
danfang 丹房, elixir chamber
daochang 道場, sacred space of the Dao, Daoist ritual center
daomen 道門, Daoist followers
daomin 道民, people of the Dao
daoshi nüguan 道士女冠, all Daoists, whether male or female

daoxing 道行, Daoist practice
dazao jingxiang 大造經象, widely produced scriptures and sacred images
dengzhai 登齋, enter the refectory
dian 殿, sanctuary
diao 雕, carve
dizi 弟子, disciples
dong 洞, cavern
dongshen 洞神, Spirit Cavern
dongxuan 洞玄, Mystery Cavern
dongzhen 洞真, Perfection Cavern
dou 斗, peck = about 7 liters
du 讀, read
duizhai 對齋, hold a purgation rite
dujiang 都講, cantor
dujing an 讀經案, lectern
duren 度人, ordination, salvation
dushi 度世, leave the world
fa 法, divine law, ritual methods
faci 法次, ritual order
fajiao 法教, teaching of the divine law
faju 法具, ritual implements
famen 法門, followers of the divine law
fan 反, violate
fang 房, chamber
fanxian 飯賢, rice for the wise (ritual banquet)
fashen 法身, holy body, dharma body (Dao), holy person (Daoists)
fashi 法士, preceptor
fatu 法徒, followers of the divine law
fawei 法位, ritual ranks
feifa 非法, religious misconduct, nonritual (utensils)
feng 奉, worship (Dao), honor (precepts)
fengdao chijie 奉道持戒, worship the Dao and uphold the precepts
fudi 福地, auspicious places
futian 福田, fields of bliss
gao 告, report
ge 閣, pavilion
gong 宮, palace
gong 拱, fold hands on chest
gongjing 恭敬, bow in respect
gongyang 供養, presentation of offerings
guan¹ 館, abode, rest house, center
guan³ 觀, monastery
guan 觀, observe
guan 冠, headdress, cap, crown
guangjian futian 廣建福田, widely establish fields of blessedness
guanyu 觀宇, monastic residences
guanzhu 觀住, abbot
gui 軌, organization (pattern)
gui 歸皈, refuge, surrender
guiming 皈命, surrender one's life

guishen 皈身, surrender one's self
guishen 皈神, surrender one's spirit
guixin 皈心, surrender one's heart
guoqu 過去, having passed through this, once the present is past
guoyuan 果園, orchard
he 褐, gown
hezhang 合掌, join palms
huchang 戶長, household elder
hui 會, assembly
ji 紀, period (of 100 days)
ji 集, gathering
ji 忌, taboo, avoidance
jian 簡, bay = about 5 meters
jian 減, subtraction (from the lifespan)
jiangjing tang 講經堂, scriptural lecture hall
jianshi 見世, in this life, self over several lives
jianzhai 監齋, purgation overseer
jiao 醮, offering
jiashi 家世, families for generations
jidu 濟度, help and save (lit., carry across)
jie 戒, precepts
jikai 稽開, open the hands and place the head between them on the floor
jin 斤, catty = 597 grams (16 liang)
jin 錦, brocade
jin 禁, prohibition
jing 敬, respect, devotion
jing 精, essential, keen
jingang 金鋼, diamond gods or vajras
jingfa 經法, divine law of the scriptures, scriptures and ritual methods
jingjiao 經教, teaching of the scriptures
jingjie 經戒, scriptural precepts, scriptures and precepts
jinglou 經樓, scripture tower
jingren 淨人, monastic servants
jingren fang 淨人坊, servants' quarters
jingshi 靜室, oratory, chamber of tranquility
jingsi yuan 靜思院, meditation building
jishen 己身, self in this life
jishou 稽首, prostration, kowtow
kaidu 開度, attain final salvation
ke 科, rules
kefang 客坊, guest quarters
kejie 科戒, rules and precepts
kemu 科目, standardized rules
ketou 磕頭, knock head to the ground
ku 苦, suffering (liberate from), painstakingly (practice Dao)
leima fang 騾馬坊, stable
li 里, mile = about 500 meters
li 禮, bow
liang 兩, ounce = 37 grams
libai 禮拜, pay obeisance to

ling 令, ordinance
lingguan xuantan 靈觀玄壇, sacred altar in a numinous monastery
lishi 力士, demigods or viras
lishi 禮師, pay obeisance to the master
liuqu 六區, six realms of rebirth
liushi 六時, six daily times (of worship)
liutong 流通, smooth flow
lou 樓, tower
lou 鏤, engraved
lü 律, statutes
luo 羅, gauze
lusheng 錄生, register disciple
man 慢, rudeness, contempt
men 門, gate, school, followers
menlou 門樓, gate house
mentu 門徒, new disciples (postulants)
mingshi 明示, give clear instructions
mingsuan 命筭, life expectancy
mu 畝, acre = 450–600 square meters
nian 念, chant, remember, continuous prayer
niandao 念道, be mindful of the Dao
nianjing 念經, recite the scriptures
nianwei 碾磑, water mill
nie 捻, take a pinch
pei 帔, cape, cloak
pindao 貧道, poor Daoists
pingli 平立, stand upright
pingzuo 平坐, kneel with straight back
qi 啓, invocation
qi 契, tally
qibai 啓白, invocation, communication
qing 請, prayer, request
qinshu 親疏, kin and stranger (related and distant)
qingxin dizi 清信弟子, disciples of pure faith
quan 卷, contract
que 缺, leave aside
qun 裙, skirt, inner robe
rao 繞, circumambulate
renshi suoyou 任時所有, what is available in accordance with the time, the relevant present circumstances
rudao 入道, join the Daoist community
ru diyu 入地獄, fall into hell
sandong 三洞, Three Caverns
sandong dizi 三洞弟子, Disciple of the Three Caverns
sangui 三皈, three surrenders
sanyuan 三元, Three Primes
shangren 上人, elders
shangxiang 上香, offer incense
shan nanren 善男人, good men
shan nüzi 善女子, good women

shaoxiang yuan 燒香院, incense building
sheng 升, pint = about 0.7 liters
shengshi 生世, on this earth
shengxia yuan 昇遐院, ascension building
shenwang 神王, divine kings or râjâs
shi 式, formalities
shi 施, bestow, grant, charity
shibu 施布, give in charity (dâna)
shideng 侍燈, lamp attendant
shifang 師房, masters' chambers, cells
shifang ke 十方客, ordained visitors
shixiang 侍香, incense attendant
shizhi 十直, ten days of uprightness
shizhu 施主, benefactor
shoudao yuan 授道院, transmission building
shouyan 首言, confession
shuofa yuan 説法院, law explanation building
sibei 四輩, four ranks = monks, nuns, lay men, lay women
siyi 四宜, four orders
song 誦, recite
song 頌, hymn
suan 箕, reckoning
suke 俗客, lay guests
sun 損, inconvenience (lessen the comfort of), neglect (rules)
suren 俗人, ordinary people
tai 臺, terrace
tan 貪, addiction, craving
tan 壇, altar
tang 堂, hall
tao 濤, cast
Tianzun 天尊, Heavenly Worthy
tianzun dian 天尊殿, sanctuary to the Heavenly Worthies
ting 亭, community hall
tingzhuan 亭傳, traveling halls
wei 違, go against, failure to comply
weiyi 威儀, dignified observances
wuyu 屋宇, rooms
xiang 象, sacred images
xieguo 謝過, repentance
xiejing fang 寫經坊, scriptorium
xing 行, observe (rules)
xingdao 行道, perform rites to the Dao, offer prayers
xinli 心禮, mental obeisance
xinshi 信士, believers
xuantan 玄壇, sacred altar
yaopu 藥圃, garden
ye 業, affairs, business, karma, devotion to (scriptures, practice)
yi 儀, observances
yibian 宜便, suitability and convenience
yinyuan 因緣, karmic retribution

yong 詠, chant
yuan 緣, karmic effects, necessities
yuan 院, building, subtemple, cloister
yuan 願, resolution, vow, prayer
yutang 浴堂, bath house
zaishi 在事, relevant present circumstances
zaitian 菜田, vegetable plot
zan 贊, verse of praise, encomium
ze 側, regulations
zhai 齋, purification, ceremonial meal, temporary renunciation, purgation, festival
zhaichu 齋廚, kitchen
zhaifu 齋服, consecrated food
zhaiguan 齋官, donor, purgation rite leader
zhaijie 齋戒, precepts and purgations
zhaiqi 齊器, ceremonial dishes
zhairen 齋人, purgation participant
zhaishi 齋食, ceremonial meal, consecrated food
zhaitang 齋堂, refectory
zhaizhu 齋主, donor
zhanfawei 站法位, occupy a position in the divine law
zhang 章, petition
zhang 丈, ten feet = about 30 meters
zhendao 真道, Dao of perfection
zheng 正, right path
zhengdao 正道, orthodox Dao
zhengfa 正法, right divine law
zhengzhen 正真, right perfection
zhi 治, parish center, communal hall
zhixin 至心, with all one's heart
zhongge 鍾閣, bell pavilion
zhou 咒, incantation, spell, mantra
zhuan 轉, turn (scripture), recite repeatedly
zhuang 狀, bed platform
zhuangtian 莊田, agricultural estates
zhuansong cijing 轉誦此經, turn and recite this scripture
zougao 奏告, memorial and report (to the gods)
zui 罪, sin, crime, wrong, guilt, suffering, retribution, punishment
zuifu 罪福, suffering and good fortune
zunke 遵科, rules and regulations
zunshi 尊師, venerated masters
zuo 座, seat, throne
zuoju 坐具, seat cloth
zuoli 作禮, bow
zuotan 坐壇, seat platform

Bibliography

Akizuki Kan'ei 秋月觀英. 1960. "Tonkô hakken Shinjin setsu sangen igi kangôkyô tanken to Dai bikuni sansen igi" 敦煌發見神人説三元威儀觀行經斷簡と大比丘三千威儀. *Jimbun shakai* 人文社會 19: 1–26.

Akizuki Kan'ei. 1964. "Rikuchô dôkyô ni okeru ôhôsetsu no hatten" 六朝道教における應報説の發展. *Hirosaki daigaku jimbun shakai* 弘前大學人文社會 33: 25–60.

Akizuki Kan'ei. 1965. "Sairon sangen shisô no keisei" 再論三元思想の形成. *Hirosaki daigaku bunkyô ronsô* 弘前大學文經論叢 1: 437–56.

Andersen, Poul. 1980. *The Method of Holding the Three Ones*. London: Curzon Press.

Barnhart, Richard. 1990. *Chinese Calligraphy: The Inner World of the Brush*. New Haven: Yale University Press.

Barrett, T. H. 1996. *Taoism under the T'ang: Religion and Empire during the Golden Age of Chinese History*. London: Wellsweep Press.

Barrett, T. H. 1997. "The *Feng-dao k'o* and Printing on Paper in Seventh-Century China." *Bulletin of the School of African and Oriental Studies* 60.3: 538–40.

Benn, Charles D. 1977. "Taoism as Ideology in the Reign of Emperor Hsüan-tsung." Ph.D. diss., University of Michigan, Ann Arbor.

Benn, Charles D. 1991. *The Cavern Mystery Transmission: A Taoist Ordination Rite of A.D. 711*. Honolulu: University of Hawaii Press.

Benn, Charles. 2000. "Daoist Ordination and *Zhai* Rituals." In *Daoism Handbook*, edited by Livia Kohn, 309–38. Leiden: Brill.

Bingham, Woodridge. 1970. *The Founding of the T'ang Dynasty: The Fall of Sui and the Rise of T'ang*. Baltimore: Waverly Press.

Bokenkamp, Stephen. 1986. "The Peach Flower Font and the Grotto Passage." *Journal of the American Oriental Society* 106: 65–79.

Bokenkamp, Stephen. 1989. "Death and Ascent in Ling-pao Taoism." *Taoist Resources* 1.2: 1–20.

Bokenkamp, Stephen. 1991. "Taoism and Literature: The *Pi-lo* Question." *Taoist Resources* 3.1: 57–72.

Bokenkamp, Stephen R. 1983. "Sources of the Ling-pao Scriptures." In *Tantric and Taoist Studies*, edited by Michel Strickmann, 2: 434–86. Brussels: Institut Belge des Hautes Etudes Chinoises.

Bokenkamp, Stephen R. 1994. "Time after Time: Taoist Apocalyptic History and the Founding of the T'ang Dynasty." *Asia Major* 7.1: 59–88.

Bokenkamp, Stephen R. 1997. *Early Daoist Scriptures*. With a contribution by Peter Nickerson. Berkeley: University of California Press.

Bumbacher, Stephan Peter. 2000a. *The Fragments of the Daoxue zhuan*. Frankfurt: Lang.

Bumbacher, Stephan Peter. 2000b. "On Pre-Tang Monastic Establishments at Mao Shan, According to *Daoxue zhuan*." *Journal of Chinese Religions* 28: 145–60.

Chan, Wing-tsit. 1963. *A Source Book in Chinese Philosophy*. Princeton: Princeton University Press.

Ch'en, Kenneth. 1973. *The Chinese Transformation of Buddhism*. Princeton: Princeton University Press.

Chen Guofu 陳國符. 1975. *Daozang yuanliu kao* 道藏源流考. Taipei: Guting.

Cleary, Thomas. 1984. *The Flower Ornament Scripture*. Boston: Shambhala.

Cole, Alan. 1998. *Mothers and Sons in Chinese Buddhism*. Stanford: Stanford University Press.

Davis, Winston. 1980. *Dojo: Magic and Exorcism in Modern Japan*. Stanford: Stanford University Press.

Doub, William C. 1971. "A Taoist Adept's Quest for Immortality: A Preliminary Study of the *Chou-shih Ming-t'ung chi* by T'ao Hung-ching." Ph.D. diss., University of Washington, Seattle.

Dudley, Martin. 1991. "The Monastic Priest." In *Monastic Studies, II*, edited by Judith Loades, 183–92. Bangor, Me.: Headstart History.

Eberhard, Wolfram. 1967. *Guilt and Sin in Traditional China*. Berkeley: University of California Press.

Foulk, T. Griffith. 1991. "The Sinification of Buddhist Monasticism." Paper presented at the 44th Annual South Asia Seminar, Philadelphia.

Foulk, T. Griffith. 1993. "Myth, Ritual, and Monastic Practice in Sung Ch'an Buddhism." In *Religion and Society in T'ang and Sung China*, edited by P. B. Ebrey and P. N. Gregory, 147–208. Honolulu: University of Hawaii Press.

Fukui Kôjun 福井康順. 1952. *Dôkyô no kisoteki kenkyû* 道教の基礎的研究. Tokyo: Risosha.

Fukui Kôjun. 1960. "Jôseikyô ni tsuite" 上清經について. *Mikkyô bunka* 密教文化 48–50: 5–18.

Funayama Tôru 船山徹. 1998. "Tô Hôkei to bukkyô no kairitsu" 陶弘景と佛教の戒律. In *Rikuchô dôkyô no kenkyû* 六朝道教の研究, edited by Yoshikawa Tadao 吉川忠夫, 353–76. Kyoto: Shunjusha.

Gernet, Jacques. 1995 [1956]. *Buddhism in Chinese Society: An Economic History from the Fifth to the Tenth Centuries*. Translated by Franciscus Verellen. New York: Columbia University Press.

Goodrich, Charles. 1942. "The Revolving Book Case in China." *Harvard Journal of Asiatic Studies* 13: 130–61.

Groner, Paul. 1990. "The *Fan-wang ching* and Monastic Discipline in Japanese Tendai: A Study of Annen's *Futsu jubosatsukai koshaku*." In *Chinese Buddhist Apocrypha*, edited by Robert E. Buswell, Jr., 251–90. Honolulu: University of Hawaii Press.

Hahn, Thomas H. 2000. "Daoist Sacred Sites." In *Daoism Handbook*, edited by Livia Kohn, 683–707. Leiden: Brill.

Hansen, Valerie L. 1990. *Changing Gods in Medieval China, 1127–1276*. Princeton: Princeton University Press.

Hansen, Valerie. 1995. "Why Bury Contracts in Tombs?" *Cahiers d'Extrême-Asie* 8: 59–66.

Hendrischke, Barbara. 1993. "Der Taoismus in der Tang-Zeit." *Minima sinica* 1993/1: 110–43.

Hendrischke, Barbara. 2000. "Early Daoist Movements." In *Daoism Handbook*, edited by Livia Kohn, 134–64. Leiden: Brill.

Hendrischke, Barbara, and Benjamin Penny. 1996. "*The 180 Precepts Spoken by Lord Lao*: A Translation and Textual Study." *Taoist Resources* 6.2: 17–29.

Hirakawa Akira 平川明. 1960. *Ritsuzô no kenkyû* 律藏の研究. Tokyo: Sankibô Busshôin.

Inoue Yutaka 井上豐. 1992. "Rokutei, rokka jin no henyû" 六丁六甲神の變容. *Tôhôshûkyô* 東方宗教 80: 15–32.

Ishii Masako 石井昌子. 1983. "Dôkyô no kamigami" 道教の神神. In *Dôkyô* 道教, edited by Fukui Kôjun 福井康順, Yamazaki Hiroshi 山崎宏, Kimura Eiichi 木村英一, Sakai Tadao 酒井忠夫, 1: 121–88. Tokyo: Hirakawa.

Jan, Yün-hua. 1986. "Cultural Borrowing and Religious Identity: A Case Study of the Taoist Religious Codes." *Hanxue yanjiu* 漢學研究 4.1: 281–95.

Kamitsuka Yoshiko 神塚淑子. 1993. "Nanbokuchô jidai no dôkyô zôzô" 南北朝時代の道教造像. In *Chûgoku chûsei no bunbutsu* 中國中世の文物, edited by Tonami Mamoru 礪波護, 225–89. Kyoto: Kyoto University, Jimbun kagaku kenkyûjo.

Kamitsuka, Yoshiko. 1998. "Lao-tzu in Six Dynasties Sculpture." In *Lao-tzu and the Tao-te-ching*, edited by Livia Kohn and Michael LaFargue, 63–85. Albany: State University of New York Press.

Kamitsuka, Yoshiko. 1996. "The Concept of Mara and the Idea of Expelling Demons." *Taoist Resources* 6.2: 30–50.

Kiyota, Minoru, ed. 1978. *Mayahana Buddhist Meditation: Theory and Practice*. Honolulu: University of Hawaii Press.

Kobayashi Masayoshi 小林正美. 1990. *Rikuchô dôkyôshi kenkyû* 六朝道教史研究. Tokyo: Sôbunsha.

Kobayashi, Masayoshi. 1992. "The Celestial Masters under the Eastern Jin and Liu-Song Dynasties." *Taoist Resources* 3.2: 17–45.

Kohn, Livia. 1989. "Guarding the One: Concentrative Meditation in Taoism." In *Taoist Meditation and Longevity Techniques*, edited by Livia Kohn, 123–56. Ann Arbor: University of Michigan, Center for Chinese Studies Publications.

Kohn, Livia. 1993. *The Taoist Experience: An Anthology*. Albany: State University of New York Press.

Kohn, Livia. 1994. "The Five Precepts of the Venerable Lord." *Monumenta Serica* 42: 171–215.

Kohn, Livia. 1995. *Laughing at the Tao: Debates among Buddhists and Taoists in Medieval China*. Princeton: Princeton University Press.

Kohn, Livia. 1996. "The Looks of Laozi." *Asian Folklore Studies* 55.2: 193–236.

Kohn, Livia. 1997a. "The Date and Compilation of the *Fengdao kejie*: The First Handbook of Monastic Daoism." *East Asian History* 13: 91–118.

Kohn, Livia. 1997b. "Yin Xi: The Master at the Beginning of the Scripture." *Journal of Chinese Religions* 25: 83–139.

Kohn, Livia. 1998a. "Counting Good Deeds and Days of Life: The Quantification of Fate in Medieval China." *Asiatische Studien/Etudes Asiatiques* 52: 833–70.

Kohn, Livia. 1998b. *God of the Dao: Lord Lao in History and Myth*. Ann Arbor: University of Michigan, Center for Chinese Studies.

Kohn, Livia. 1998c. "Steal Holy Food and Come Back as a Viper: Conceptions of Karma and Rebirth in Medieval Daoism." *Early Medieval China* 4: 1–48.

Kohn, Livia. 2000. "A Home for the Immortals: The Layout and Development of Medieval Daoist Monasteries." *Acta Orientalia* 53: 79–106.

Kohn, Livia. 2001. "Daoist Monastic Discipline:Hygiene, Meals, and Etiquette." *T'oung Pao* 87: 153–93.

Kohn, Livia. 2003. *Monastic Life in Medieval Daoism: A Cross-Cultural Perspective.* Honolulu: University of Hawai'i Press.

Kohn, Livia. Forthcoming. *How to Be a Daoist: Behavioral Guidelines through the Ages.* Cambridge, Mass.: Three Pines Press.

Kohn, Livia, and J. Russell Kirkland. 2000. "Daoism in the Tang (618–907)." In *Daoism Handbook*, edited by Livia Kohn, 339–83. Leiden: Brill.

Komjathy, Louis. 2002. *Title Index to Daoist Collections.* Cambridge, Mass.: Three Pines Press.

Kusuyama Haruki 楠山春樹. 1982. "Dôkyô ni okeru jûkai" 道教における十戒. *Bungaku kenkyûkai kiyô* 文化研究會紀要 28: 55–72.

Kusuyama Haruki. 1983. "Dôkyô to jukyô" 道教と儒教. In *Dôkyô* 道教, edited by Fukui Kôjun 福井康順, Yamazaki Hiroshi 山崎宏, Kimura Eiichi 木村英一, Sakai Tadao 酒井忠夫, 2: 49–94. Tokyo: Hirakawa.

Lagerwey, John. 1981. *Wu-shang pi-yao:Somme taoïste du VIe siècle.* Paris: Publications de l'Ecole Française d'Extrême-Orient.

Lagerwey, John. 1987. *Taoist Ritual in Chinese Society and History.* New York: Macmillan.

Liu Tsun-yan 柳存仁. 1986. "Sandong fengdao kejie yifan juan diwu: P. 2337 zhong Jin Ming Qizhen yici zhi tuice" 三洞奉道科戒儀範卷第五 P. 2337 中金明七真遺冊之推測. *Hanxue yanjiu* 漢學研究 4.2: 509–31.

Loon, Piet van der. 1984. *Taoist Books in the Libraries of the Sung Period.* London: Oxford Oriental Institute.

Maeda Ryôichi 前田良一. 1989. "Kyu kyu nyo ritsurei o saguru" 急急如律令をさくる. In *Dôkyô to higashi Ajia* 道教と東アジア, edited by Fukunaga Mitsuji 福永光司, 101–25. Kyoto: Jimbun shoin.

Maeda Shigeki 前田繁樹. 1985. "Rôkun setsu ippyaku hachiju kaijo no seiritsu ni tsuite" 老君説一百八十戒序の成立について. *Tôyô no shisô to shûkyô* 東洋思想と宗教 2: 81–94.

Maeda Shigeki. 1994. "Tonkôhon to Dôzôhon no sabetsu ni tsuite" 敦煌本と道藏本の作別 について. *Tôhôshûkyô* 東方宗教 84: 1–19.

Major, John S. 1986. "New Light on the Dark Warrior." *Journal of Chinese Religions* 13/14: 65–87.

Malek, Roman. 1985. *Das Chai-chieh-lu.* Würzburger Sino-Japonica 14. Frankfurt: Lang.

Mather, Richard. 1979. "K'ou Ch'ien-chih and the Taoist Theocracy at the Northern Wei Court 425–451." In *Facets of Taoism*, edited by Holmes Welch and Anna Seidel, 103–22. New Haven, Conn.: Yale University Press.

Mather, Richard B. 1981. "The Bonze's Begging Bowl: Eating Practices in Buddhist Monasteries of Medieval India and China." *Journal of the American Oriental Society* 101: 417–23.

Matsumura Takumi 松樹巧. 1992. "Tenmon jiko kô" 天門地戶考. In *Chûgoku ko dôkyô shi kenkyû* 中國古道教史研究, edited by Yoshikawa Tadao 吉川忠夫, 145–74. Kyoto: Dôhôsha.

Mitamura, Keiko. 2002. "Daoist Hand Signs and Buddhist Mudras." In *Daoist Identity: History, Lineage, and Ritual*, edited by Livia Kohn and Harold D. Roth, 235–55. Honolulu: University of Hawai'i Press.

Miura Kunio 三蒲國雄. 1983. "Dôten fukuchi koron" 洞天福地小論. *Tôhôshûkyô* 東方宗教 61: 1–23.

Miyakawa Hisayuki 宮川尚志. 1991. "Tenchisui sankan to dôten" 天地水三官と洞天. *Tôhôshûkyô* 東方宗教 78: 1–22.

Miyazawa Masayori 宮澤正順. 1994. "Kyu kyu nyo ritsurei ni tsuite" 急急如律令 について. *Girei bunka* 儀禮文化 20: 14–35.

Mochizuki Shinkô 望月信享. 1936. *Bukkyô daijiten* 佛教大辭典. 7 vols. Tokyo: Sekai seiten kankô kyôkai.

Mollier, Christine. 1990. *Une apocalypse taoïste: Le livre des grottes abyssales.* Paris: Ecole Française d'Extrême-Orient.

Mollier, Christine. 2000. "Les cuisines de Laozi et du Buddha." *Cahiers d'Extrême-Asie* 11: 45–90.

Nakajima Ryûzô 中島隆藏. 1984. "Taijô gyôhô ingenkyô ni okeru ôhôron" 太上業報因緣經 における應報論. In *Makio Ryokai hakase shoju kinen ronshû Chûgoku no shûkyô shisô to kagaku* 牧尾良海博士頌壽記念論集中國の宗教思想と科學, 335–54. Tokyo: Kokusho kankôkai.

Nakamura Hajime 中村元. 1975. *Bukkyôgo daijiten* 佛教語大辭典. Tokyo: Tôkyô shoshiki.

Nickerson, Peter. 1996. "Abridged Codes of Master Lu for the Daoist Community." In *Religions of China in Practice*, edited by Donald S. Lopez, Jr., 347–59. Princeton: Princeton University Press.

Nickerson, Peter. 2000. "The Southern Celestial Masters." In *Daoism Handbook*, edited by Livia Kohn, 256–82. Leiden: Brill.

Niida Noboru 仁井田陞. 1937. *Tô-Sô hôritsu bunsho no kenkyû* 唐宋法律文書の研究. Tokyo.

Noguchi Tetsurô 野口鐵郎, Sakade Yoshinobu 阪出祥伸, Fukui Fumimasa 福井文雅, and Yamada Toshiaki 山田利明, eds. 1994. *Dôkyô jiten* 道教事典. Tokyo: Hirakawa.

Ôfuchi Ninji 大淵忍爾. 1959. "Sankôbun yori dôshinbu" 三皇文より洞神部. *Shigaku zasshi* 史學雜誌 68.2: 119–58.

Ôfuchi Ninji. 1964. *Dôkyôshi no kenkyû* 道教史の研究. Okayama: Chûgoku insatsu.

Ôfuchi Ninji. 1974. "On *Ku Ling-pao ching*." *Acta Asiatica* 27: 33–56.

Ôfuchi Ninji. 1979a. "The Formation of the Taoist Canon." In *Facets of Taoism*, edited by Holmes Welch and Anna Seidel, 253–68. New Haven: Yale University Press.

Ôfuchi Ninji, ed. 1983. *Chûgokujin no shukyô girei* 中國人の宗教儀禮. Tokyo: Shukubu.

Ôfuchi Ninji. 1979b. *Tonkô dokei: Zuroku hen* 敦煌道經-圖錄篇. Tokyo: Kokubu shoten.

Ôfuchi Ninji. 1997. *Dôkyô to sono kyôten* 道教とその經典. Tokyo: Sôbunsha.

Ôfuchi Ninji and Ishii Masako 石井昌子. 1988. *Dôkyô tenseki mokuroku, sakuin* 道教典籍目錄, 索引. Tokyo: Kokusho kankôkai.

Ôno Genmyô 大野現明, ed. 1980. *Bussho kaisetsu daijiten* 佛書戒説大辭典. 13 vols. Tokyo: Daitô.

Ôzaki Masaharu 尾岐正治. 1983. "Dôkyô kyôten" 道教經典. In *Dôkyô* 道教, edited by Fukui Kôjun 福井康順, Yamazaki Hiroshi 山崎宥, Kimura Eiichi 木樹英一, Sakai Tadao 酒井忠夫, 1: 73–120. Tokyo: Hirakawa.

Ôzaki Masaharu. 1984. "The Taoist Priesthood." In *Religion and Family in East Asia*, edited by G. DeVos and T. Sofue, 97–109. Osaka: National Museum of Ethnology.

Ôzaki Masaharu. 1996. "Rekishi shinsen taidô tôken no tekisto ni tsuite" 歷世真仙體道通鑒のテキストについて. *Tôhôshûkyô* 東方宗教 88: 37–54.

Pas, Julian F. 1987. "Six Daily Periods of Worship: Symbolic Meaning in Buddhist Liturgy and Eschatology." *Monumenta Serica* 37: 49–82.

Penny, Benjamin. 1996. "Buddhism and Daoism in *The 180 Precepts Spoken by Lord Lao*." *Taoist Resources* 6.2: 1–16.

Petersen, Jens O. 1989. "The Early Traditions Relating to the Han-Dynasty Transmission of the *Taiping jing*." *Acta Orientalia* 50: 133–71 and 51: 165–216.

Pontynen, Arthur J. 1983. "The Early Development of Taoist Art." Ph.D. dissertation, University of Iowa, Iowa City.

Porter, Bill. 1993. *The Road to Heaven: Encounters with Chinese Hermits*. San Francisco: Mercury House.

Read, Bernard E. 1982. *Chinese Medical Plants from the Pen Ts'ao Kang Mu, A.D. 1596 of a Botanical, Chemical, and Pharmacological Reference List*. Taipei: Southern Materials Center.

Reiter, Florian C. 1983. "Some Observations Concerning Taoist Foundations in Traditional China." *Zeitschrift der deutschen morgenländischen Gesellschaft* 133: 363–76.

Reiter, Florian C. 1988. "The Visible Divinity: The Sacred Image in Religious Taoism." *Nachrichten der deutschen Gesellschaft für Natur- und Völkerkunde Ostasiens* 144: 51–70.

Reiter, Florian C. 1990. *Der Perlenbeutel aus den drei Höhlen: Arbeitsmaterialien zum Taoismus der frühen T'ang-Zeit*. Asiatische Forschungen, vol. 12. Wiesbaden: Harrassowitz.

Reiter, Florian C. 1998. *The Aspirations and Standards of Taoist Priests in the Early T'ang Period*. Wiesbaden: Harrassowitz.

Ren Jiyu 任繼愈. 1990. *Zhongguo daojiao shi* 中國道教史. Shanghai: Renmin.

Ren Jiyu and Zhong Zhaopeng 鍾肇鵬, eds. 1991. *Daozang tiyao* 道藏提要. Beijing: Zhongguo shehui kexue chubanshe.

Robinet, Isabelle. 1984. *La révélation du Shangqing dans l'histoire du taoïsme*. 2 vols. Paris: Publications de l'Ecole Française d'Extrême-Orient.

Robinet, Isabelle. 2000. "Shangqing—Highest Clarity." In *Daoism Handbook*, edited by Livia Kohn, 196–224. Leiden: Brill.

Sargent, Galen E. 1957. "T'an-yao and His Time." *Monumenta Serica* 16: 363–96.

Saunders, E. Dale. 1960. *Mudra: A Study of Symbolic Gestures in Japanese Buddhist Sculpture*. Princeton: Princeton University Press.

Sawada Mizuhô 澤田瑞穗. 1968. *Jigoku hen* 地獄篇. Kyoto: Hôzôkan.

Schafer, Edward H. 1963. *The Golden Peaches of Samarkand: A Study of T'ang Exotics*. Berkeley: University of California Press.

Schafer, Edward H. 1978. "The Capeline Cantos: Verses on the Divine Loves of Taoist Priestesses." *Asiatische Studien/Etudes Asiatiques* 32: 5–65.

Schipper, Kristofer. 1975. *Concordance du Tao Tsang: Titres des ouvrages*. Paris: Publications de l'Ecole Française d'Extrême-Orient.

Schipper, Kristofer. 1984. "Le monachisme taoïste." In *Incontro di religioni in Asia tra il terzo e il decimo secolo d. C.*, edited by Lionello Lanciotti, pp 199–215. Firenze: Olschki.

Schipper, Kristofer. 1985. "Taoist Ordination Ranks in the Tunhuang Manuscripts." In *Religion und Philosophie in Ostasien: Festschrift für Hans Steininger*, edited by G. Naundorf, K. H. Pohl, and H. H. Schmidt, 127–48. Würzburg: Königshausen and Neumann.

Schipper, Kristofer. 2001. "Daoist Ecology: The Inner Transformation. A Study of the Precepts of the Early Daoist Ecclesia." In *Daoism and Ecology: Ways within a Cosmic Landscape*, edited by Norman Girardot, James Miller, and Liu Xiaogan, 79–94. Cambridge, Mass.: Harvard University Press.

Schmidt, Hans-Hermann. 1985. "Die hundertachtzig Vorschriften von Lao-chün." In *Religion und Philosophie in Ostasien: Festschrift für Hans Steininger*, edited by G. Naundorf, K. H. Pohl, and H. H. Schmidt, 151–59. Würzburg: Königshausen and Neumann.

Seidel, Anna. 1984. "Taoist Messianism." *Numen* 31: 161–74.

Seidel, Anna. 1987. "Traces of Han Religion in Funeral Texts Found in Tombs." In *Dôkyô to shûkyô bunka*, 21–57. Festschrift für Akizuki Kan'ei. Tokyo: Hirakawa.

Smith, Thomas E. 1990. "The Record of the Ten Continents." *Taoist Resources* 2.2: 87–119.

Soothill, William E., and Lewis Hudous. 1937. *A Dictionary of Chinese Buddhist Terms.* London: Kegan Paul.

Soymié, Michel. 1977. "Les dix jours du jeune taoiste." In *Yoshioka Yoshitoyo hakase kanri kinen Dôkyô kenkyû ronshû* 吉岡義豐博士還歷記念道教研究論集, 1–21. Tokyo: Kokusho kankôkai.

Staal, Julius. 1984. *Stars of Jade: Calendar Lore, Mythology, Legends and Star Stories of Ancient China.* Decatur, Ga.: Writ Press.

Stein, Rolf A. 1963. "Remarques sur les mouvements du taoïsme politico-religieux au IIe siècle ap. J.-C." *T'oung Pao* 50: 1–78.

Stein, Rolf A. 1971. "Les fêtes de cuisine du taoïsme religieux." *Annuaire du Collège de France* 71: 431–40.

Steinhardt, Nancy S. 1990. *Chinese Imperial City Planning.* Honolulu: University of Hawaii Press.

Strickmann, Michel. 1978. "A Taoist Confirmation of Liang Wu-ti's Suppression of Taoism." *Journal of the American Oriental Society* 98: 467–74.

Strickmann, Michel. 1979. "On the Alchemy of T'ao Hung-ching." In *Facets of Taoism,* edited by Holmes Welch and Anna Seidel, 123–92. New Haven: Yale University Press.

Strickmann, Michel. 1981. *Le taoïsme du Mao chan; chronique d'une révélation.* Paris: Collège du France, Institut des Hautes Etudes Chinoises.

Strickmann, Michel. 1996. *Mantras et mandarins: Le bouddhisme tantrique en Chine.* Paris: Gallimard.

Teiser, Stephen F. 1988. *The Yü-lan-p'en Festival in Medieval Chinese Religion.* Princeton: Princeton University Press.

Tonkô kôza 敦煌講座, ed. 1983. *Tonkô to Chûgoku dôkyô* 敦煌と中國道教. Tokyo: Daitô.

Tso, Sze-bong. 1991. "The Conflict between *Vinaya* and the Chinese Monastic Rule: The Dilemma of Disciplinarian Venerable Hung-i." In *Buddhist Ethics and Modern Society: An International Symposium,* edited by Charles W. H. Fu and Sandra A. Wawrytko, 69–80. New York: Greenwood Press.

Tsuchiya, Masaaki. 2002. "Confession of Sins and Awareness of Self in the *Taiping jing.*" In *Daoist Identity: History, Lineage, and Ritual,* edited by Livia Kohn and Harold D. Roth, 39–57. Honolulu: University of Hawaii Press.

Tsukamoto, Zenryû, and Leon Hurvitz. 1985. *A History of Early Chinese Buddhism.* 2 vols. Tokyo: Kodansha.

Turner, Victor W. 1969. *The Ritual Process: Structure and Anti-Structure.* Chicago: Aldine.

Twitchett, Denis W. 1956. "Monastic Estates in T'ang China." *Asia Major,* new series, 5: 123–46.

Twitchett, Denis W. 1957. "The Monasteries and China's Economy in Mediaeval China." *Bulletin of the School of Oriental and African Studies* 19: 526–49.

Wechsler, Howard. 1985. *Offerings of Jade and Silk.* New Haven: Yale University Press.

Weng, Dujian. 1935. *Combined Indices to the Authors and Titles of Books in Two Collections of Taoist Literature.* Beijing: Harvard-Yenching Sinological Index Series no. 25.

Wu, Chi-yu. 1960. *Pen-tsi king, Livre du terme originel: Ouvrage taoiste inédit du VII siècle.* Paris: Centre National des Recherches Scientifiques.

Xiong, Victor. 2000. *Sui Tang Chang'an: A Study in the Urban History of Medieval China.* Ann Arbor: University of Michigan, Center for Chinese Studies.

Yamada Takashi 山田俊. 1992. *Kohon Shôgenkyô* 槁本昇玄經. Sendai: Tôhoku daigaku.

Yamada Takashi. 1995. "Michi wa hito o sukuhazu, hito mizukara michi o motomu: Taijô myôhô honsôkyô no shisô" 道は人を度はず人自ら道を求お: 太上妙法本相經の思想. *Kumamoto kenritsu daigaku bungakubu kiyô* 熊本縣立大學文學部紀要 1: 227–50.

Yamada Toshiaki. 1989. "Longevity Techniques and the Compilation of the *Lingbao wufuxu*." In *Taoist Meditation and Longevity Techniques*, edited by L. Kohn, 97–122. Ann Arbor: University of Michigan, Center for Chinese Studies.

Yamada Toshiaki 山田利明. 1999. *Rikuchô dôkyô girei no kenkyû* 六朝道教儀禮の研究. Tokyo: Tôhô shoten.

Yamada Toshiaki. 2000. "The Lingbao School." In *Daoism Handbook*, edited by Livia Kohn, 225–55. Leiden: Brill.

Yan Shanzhao 嚴善炤. 2001. "Shoki dôkyô to kôshi konki hôchûjutsu" 初期道教の黄赤混氣房中術. *Tôhôshûkyô* 東方宗教 97: 1–19.

Yang Liansheng. 1956. "Laojun yinsong jiejing jiaoshi" 老君音誦誡經校釋. *Zhongyang yanjiu yuan lishi yuyen yanjiusuo jikan* 中央研究院歷史言語研究所集刊 28: 17–54.

Yoshikawa Tadao 吉川忠夫. 1987. "Seishitsu kô" 靜室考. *Tôhô gakuhô* 東方學報 59: 125–62.

Yoshikawa Tadao. 1990. "Ô Genshi kô 王遠知考". *Tôhô gakuhô* 東方學報 62: 69–98.

Yoshioka Yoshitoyo 吉岡義豐. 1955. *Dôkyô kyôten shiron* 道教經典史論. Tokyo: Dôkyô kankôkai.

Yoshioka Yoshitoyo. 1960. "Chisôshi chûkaikyô to kôka shisô" 赤松子中戒經と功過思想. In *Fukui hakase sôshu kinen Tôyôshisô ronshû* 福井博士頌壽記念東洋思想論集, 722–37. Tokyo: Waseda University. Reprinted in Yoshioka 1970, 212–27.

Yoshioka Yoshitoyo. 1961. "Bukkyô jûkai shisô no Chûgoku teki shûyô" 佛教十戒思想の中國的受容. *Shûkyô kenkyû* 宗教研究 35.1: 1–72.

Yoshioka Yoshitoyo. 1963. "Dôkyôgaku seiritsu no ichi kôsatsu" 道教學成立の一考察. *Taishô daigaku kenkyûjo kiyô* 大正大學研究所紀要 48: 81–128.

Yoshioka Yoshitoyo. 1964. "Shichigatsu jûgo nichi chûgensetsu ni tsuite" 七月十五日中元節について. In *Iwai hakase koseki kinen Tenseki ronshû* 岩井博士古稀記念典籍論集, 793–99. Tokyo: Dai'an.

Yoshioka Yoshitoyo. 1967. "Zaikairoku to Chigonsô" 齋戒錄と至言總. *Taishô daigaku kenkyûjo kiyô* 大正大學研究所紀要 52: 283–302.

Yoshioka Yoshitoyo. 1970. *Dôkyô to bukkyô* 道教と佛教. Vol. 2. Tokyo: Kokusho kankôkai.

Yoshioka Yoshitoyo. 1976. *Dôkyô to bukkyô* 道教と佛教. Vol. 3. Tokyo: Kokusho kankôkai.

Yûsa Noboru 遊左昇. 1981. "Tonkô bunseki yori mita Tô, Godai ni okeru minkan shinkô no ichisokumen" 敦煌文籍より見た唐五代における民間信仰の一側面. *Tôhôshûkyô* 東方宗教 57: 55–70.

Yûsa Noboru. 1989. "Tôdai ni mirareru kyukutenson shinkô ni tsuite" 唐代に見られる救苦天尊信仰について. *Tôhô shûkyô* 東方宗教 73: 19–40.

Zhang Zhizhe 張智轍. 1994. *Daojiao wenhua cidian* 道教文化辭典. Jiangsu: Guji chubanshe.

Zhu Yueli 朱越利. 1992. *Daojiao yaoji gailun* 道教要籍概論. Daojiao wenhua congshu, vol. 2. Beijing: Yenshan chubanshe.

Zürcher, Erik. 1959. *The Buddhist Conquest of China: The Spread and Adaptation of Buddhism in Early Medieval China*. 2 vols. Leiden: Brill.

Zürcher, Erik. 1980. "Buddhist Influence on Early Taoism." *T'oung Pao* 66: 84–147.

Index